The Christian Church

The Christian Church

An Introduction to the Major Traditions

Edited by Paul Avis

First published in Great Britain in 2002 by
Society for Promoting Christian Knowledge
Holy Trinity Church
Marylebone Road
London NW1 4DU

British Library Cataloguing-in-Publication Data
A catalogue record for this book is available from the British Library

ISBN 0-281-05246-8

Typeset by David Gregson Associates, Beccles, Suffolk
Printed in Great Britain by
Antony Rowe Ltd, Chippenham, Wiltshire

Contents

Contributors

Sr Dr M. Cecily Boulding OP, formerly on the staff of Ushaw College, University of Durham (The Roman Catholic Church).

David Carter MA, theologian and writer (The Methodist Churches).

The Revd Professor David Fergusson, University of Edinburgh (The Reformed Churches).

The Revd Dr Brian Haymes, formerly Principal of Bristol Baptist College (The Baptist and Pentecostal Churches).

Professor Nicolas Lossky, Orthodox Theological Institute of St Sergius, Paris and Emeritus Professor at the University of Paris-Nanterre and the Catholic Institute, Paris (The Orthodox Church).

Professor Michael Root, Trinity Lutheran Seminary, Columbus, Ohio and formerly Director of the Institute for Ecumenical Research, Strasbourg (The Lutheran Churches).

The Revd Professor Urs von Arx, University of Bern, Switzerland (The Old Catholic Churches of the Union of Utrecht).

The Revd Prebendary Dr Paul Avis, General Secretary of the Council for Christian Unity of the Church of England, Sub-Dean of Exeter Cathedral, Director of the Centre for the Study of the Christian Church, Research Fellow in the Department of Theology at the University of Exeter (The Churches of the Anglican Communion and Editor).

Editor's Foreword

This book provides an introduction to the major traditions of the Christian Church. It explains how they understand themselves as 'church', how they relate to other churches, and how they approach issues of unity and diversity within the orbit of ecumenism. It sets out their structures of ministry, authority and oversight. It expounds the fundamental theological commitments that, at one and the same time, keep the churches apart in organizational and structural terms, and link them together in an extensive common life and mission. Above all, perhaps, it tries to show what 'makes them tick'.

The approach adopted here is not a purely descriptive, phenomenological approach. That could lead to a relativistic assumption that the differences between the various expressions of the Christian Church are merely superficial – a matter of semantics or of cultural diversity. It does not pretend that there are not real and important differences between them. Rather, it aims to bring out the distinctiveness of the churches and to exhibit the living traditions in their strength and integrity. It allows them to speak for themselves through interpreters who are deeply and passionately committed to them. Needless to say, they are even more deeply and passionately committed to the one, holy, catholic and apostolic Church, the Mystical Body of Christ, that transcends all actual churches and before which they are all very imperfect.

All too often it is assumed that the demands of unity (whatever form it is envisaged unity may take) involves glossing over the differences between the churches, closing our eyes to what makes them distinctive. Difficult questions are sidelined. From this angle, the unforgivable sin is to upset one's ecumenical partners. The common ground becomes the whole landscape.

The result is actually a travesty of the true vision of unity. Ecumenism is regarded as a soft option, permeated by sentiment and pragmatism. The lowest common denominator approach results in ecumenical entropy – lack of energy, lack of direction, lack of movement, lack of life.

Some 35 years ago, as a sixth former, I read an article by Malcolm Muggeridge about the ecumenical movement. (I think that, at that time, he had not yet had his rather public, heart-on-sleeve conversion to Christianity.) The ecumenical movement was something of which I then knew virtually nothing. The piece may have been triggered by the developing Anglican–Methodist conversations. The title – glib though it now seems – stuck in my mind: 'Backward Christian Soldiers'. I am not sure now where I read it: it may have been in the *New Statesman* or *The Listener*, though the reactionary tone is more suited to *The Spectator*. But I think I can recall the essence of Muggeridge's argument.

The churches, he claimed, were declining in an increasingly secular culture. They were looking to one another for the support that they were failing to find in society. The ecumenical movement stood for a retreat from the Church's militant engagement with the world to a cosy, vapid Christianity. Ironic though it may be for me as a professional ecumenist and ecumenical theologian to say so, I am afraid that the old cynic had a point. I thought so then and I think so now.

Those of us who are continuously drawn into ecumenical activity recognize the signs. Amid much that retains its vitality and challenge, we are also familiar with the ethos of ecumenical mish-mash, where everything that stands out as different, as contestable, as exciting – as worth living and dying for – has been ironed out in deference to supposed ecumenical courtesy. The result is both boring and sterile. Where traditions are not encouraged to flourish in their distinctiveness and vitality, ecumenism – ecumenical worship, in particular – degenerates into an ecumenical soup that has lost its savour. It is also far from nourishing. The glory, that resides in the lived experience, the historic identity of the traditions, and motivates their adherents, has departed.

In the Council for Christian Unity of the Church of England, my colleagues and I are saddened when we encounter, within our own church or elsewhere, a resigned and weary approach to ecumenism, one lacking in vision and dynamism. We are disturbed by the tacit assumption that unity is about declining churches propping up one another by sharing dwindling resources and growing old gracefully together. It is not surprising that there are some who view the whole ecumenical enterprise with scepticism and disillusionment. That is not the way to do ecumenism and it is not how we see our task.

The cause of Church unity cannot be promoted by Christians, locally or nationally, desperately trying to invent extra activities that provide a pretext for them to come together with ecumenical partners. Piling additional meetings on to already overworked people is a recipe for burn-out as well as turn-off. That well-meant but unimaginative approach is now thoroughly discredited. We need to liven up the ecumenical movement, to recapture the momentum in all its vigour and rigour. We can do this, I believe, if we take our bearings in the unity quest from two quarters: the imperative of mission and the reality of diversity. Energy comes from authenticity, not from pretending. And authenticity – reality – is found where people practise a hard-won way of life together, one that has been honed by centuries of work, conflict and steadfastness. The most exciting moment in the ecumenical quest is when we touch the heart of ecclesial identity in another tradition, and know that this is how our brothers and sisters experience God in his Church.

True ecumenism is about engaging together, across the divided churches so far as possible, in the core tasks of the Christian Church, the things (all of them) that we are called to do anyway: prayer and worship, preaching and teaching, mission and evangelism, fellowship and service. Churches that work together in mission in the locality and in community projects linked to evangelism tend to find that unity issues come alive. A passionate concern to break down the remaining barriers (of theological disagreement, eucharistic hospitality, integrated ministries, common oversight) springs up when Christians pull together in mission that is undergirded by prayer, Bible study and fellowship.

This book consists of a series of commissioned essays from an international team of distinguished scholars who represent each of the major Christian traditions. Each contributor describes the *ecclesial identity* of their own Church and explains its standpoint in relation to other Churches. The traditions covered are global in their scope. The panel of contributors is cosmopolitan in its make-up. It includes a Roman Catholic religious and a Methodist layman; an American Lutheran who, until recently, was directing research in Strasbourg; a Scottish Reformed scholar who recently gave the Bampton Lectures in Oxford; an Old Catholic scholar from Switzerland; and a Russian Orthodox scholar, based in Paris, but noted for a study of seventeenth-century Anglican spirituality.

The major traditions are identified here (in alphabetical order) as: Anglican, Baptist (and Pentecostal), Lutheran, Methodist, Old Catholic, Orthodox, Reformed and Roman Catholic.

The contributors have been fairly free to treat the material as they feel best, but each has been asked to cover the following issues:

- How, as churches, do we see ourselves and other churches? What claims do we make for ourselves and how do we view the claims of others?
- What are the authoritative sources for our ecclesiology (Scripture, tradition, reason, councils, historic formularies, etc.)?
- How do we understand the essential nature of the Church of Christ, its mission and purpose?
- What do we believe about the four dimensions of the Church that are affirmed in the Niceno-Constantinopolitan Creed: its unity, holiness, catholicity and apostolicity?
- What are our distinctive structures of ministry? What is the place of deacons, presbyters, bishops and other recognized ministers?
- How is leadership practised in our church and what are our structures of church government?
- What does the fundamental New Testament reality of *koinonia* (communion, fellowship) means to us?
- What scope do we have for diversity of belief and practice within our communion?
- What is our vision, as a church or family of churches, for the ecumenical future for the churches? In what ways are we committed to the quest for visible unity?

I cannot promise that every chapter explicitly covers every one of these items. But, taken as a whole, these topics describe the ground covered in this book.

In addition to explanatory notes and references for each chapter, each contributor provides a short bibliography of key sources and further reading.

This work is intended as an essential resource for the study of the Church in departments of theology and religious studies, in ordination training in seminaries and theological colleges and courses and in training programmes for lay ministry. I hope that it will prove to be a useful resource for ecumenical dialogue and discussion at all levels, including the more high-powered ecumenical local study groups.

1

The Orthodox Churches

Nicolas Lossky

In 1936, in his book on *The Orthodox Church*,[1] Father Sergius Bulgakov wrote that 'the Church of Christ is not an institution but a new life in Christ moved by the Holy Spirit' – and, we might add, to the glory of God the Father. It is certainly important to begin by recalling that the Church is the Church of Christ in which the Spirit blows where it wills (John 3.8). The Church is *creatura Christi and creatura Spiritus*, created by the redemptive work of Christ the Son of the Father, instituted at Pentecost by the sending of the Holy Spirit who proceeds from the Father and rests in the Son. The Church is thus that dimension of creation in which human beings are enabled to 'partake of the divine nature' (2 Peter 1.4; biblical quotations are from the Authorized [King James] Version), which means to be made partakers of trinitarian life. This is undoubtedly the most essential foundation for any approach to ecclesiology in an Orthodox, or in any other truly Christian, perspective.

However, if the Church is in its essence not 'of this world', it is nevertheless called to live in the world and to offer the Eucharist 'for the life of the world' (eucharistic prayers of the Byzantine tradition in the Orthodox Church[2]). It follows that although essentially the Church is not an institution, at the same time it has of necessity an institutional dimension. This is also an important aspect of ecclesiology.

It must immediately be added that, in a truly Orthodox perspective (that is in the perspective of Orthodoxy faithful to itself), any institutional aspect must be true to the deep, essential nature of the Church and not be contaminated by the categories of this world. 'The kings of the Gentiles exercise lordship over them; and they that exercise authority upon them are called benefactors. But ye shall not be so: but he that is greatest among you, let him be as the younger; and he that is chief, as he that doth serve. For whether is greater, he that sitteth at meat, or he that serveth? is not he that sitteth at meat? But I am among you as he that serveth' (Luke 22.25–7). And elsewhere: 'Ye call me Master and Lord: and ye say well; for so I am. If I then, your Lord and Master, have washed your feet; ye also ought to wash one another's feet. For I have given you an example, that ye should do as I have done to you' (John 13.13–15). All in the Church should be organized and lived in the light of these words of Jesus, particularly the exercise of hierarchy.

If the exercise of hierarchy should, as has just been said, tend as much as possible towards the ideal pastoral figure offered by Christ himself, the practical organization of this hierarchy in the Orthodox Church is the traditional ministry: the 'major' orders of bishop, priest and deacon, and the 'minor' orders of sub-deacon and reader which have been preserved. It should be added that the terminology of 'major' and 'minor' levels of ministry does not correspond to Orthodox tradition; it has crept into the Orthodox world under Latin influence (Peter Moghila of Kiev, Dositheus of Jerusalem and the Western type of teaching in Orthodox seminaries and academies from the seventeenth century onwards). Naturally, in authentic Orthodoxy, the ministry of all believers is strongly affirmed, especially by all the best ecclesiologists of the twentieth century. The iconostasis, built as a wall separating the sanctuary from the nave, is a late development (fourteenth– fifteenth centuries). This has given rise with some people to wrong ideas about the clergy and the 'simple' faithful, the laity.

The Orthodox conception of the organization of the Church on earth is rooted in St Paul's manner of addressing communities in various places: 'the Church of God which is at Corinth' for example (1 Corinthians 1.2; 2 Corinthians 1.1). The phrase 'Church of God' is to be understood as conveying mainly two notions. One level of meaning is that all the Christians of a given place are gathered in one eucharistic community, whatever the ethnic group they belong to, whatever their social status, whatever their gender. The Church of God is the reality of Galatians 3.28 in which 'there is neither Jew nor Greek, there is neither bond nor free, there is neither male nor female: for ye are all one in Christ Jesus'. Yet it would be a mistake, it seems to me, to understand Galatians 3.28 as a suppression of identities. In Corinth, as in other places, there were obviously Greeks, but also

Jews, passing merchants, bond and free, men, women and children. They did not cease to be what they were. But through unity in Christ Jesus, in one eucharistic community, their relations tended to cease to be those of this world, that is relations of domination-submission. They are relations of the members of one body (cf. 1 Corinthians 12), 'submitting [themselves] one to another in the fear of God' (Ephesians 5.21).

One community in one place: this first level of meaning of the phrase, 'the Church of God which is at' one place or another, provides the basic principle of the Orthodox *territorial* approach to ecclesiology. The local eucharistic community, the prototype of which consists in the people gathered around their bishop, is still today the same as what St Ignatius of Antioch described in the early second century: 'There is the catholic Church'.[3] (When a priest presides, he still does it by delegation from his bishop who remains the prototypical presiding minister.) The territorial principle in Orthodox ecclesiology is implicit in the Orthodox preference for the term 'local Church' (rather than 'particular Churches').

This naturally brings us to the second level of meaning of St Paul's address to 'the Church of God which is at' a given place. This time, the emphasis is on 'the *Church of God*'. The phrase 'Church of God' clearly indicates the Church in its fullness. In other words, in a given place, the Church is fully present. And if this is so, it will not be surprising that the adjective 'catholic' used by St Ignatius, however much it may be discussed by scholars, should be understood by the Orthodox in the true etymological sense of '*kath'olou*' = 'according to the whole', according to the fullness of the divine revelation and therefore the fullness of the Church. 'Catholic' in the sense of 'universal' is only a consequence of the true meaning: the local reception and therefore confession of the fullness of the divine revelation.

It is clear from the context that what St Ignatius meant by the presence of Jesus Christ, where the people are gathered around their bishop, is the eucharistic gathering. The Church of God in a given place is best expressed in the eucharistic gathering which, here on earth, is the climax of the experience of God, for it is a fore-taste of the Kingdom. If the fullness of the Church of God is present where the Eucharist is celebrated, the Orthodox conception of ecclesiology is clearly a eucharistic one. Eucharistic ecclesiology is therefore no discovery of the twentieth century. It may be a rediscovery, for even for the Orthodox, as well as for other Christians, the notion has sometimes been dimmed, forgotten or misunderstood. However, in a perspective faithful to true Orthodoxy, wherever and whenever the Eucharist is celebrated, there is the Church of God, fully.

If the Church is fully present in a local eucharistic gathering, the implication is that the local Church is the Church universal, an identification which, in the present context, may seem somewhat paradoxical if not totally absurd to some, especially to those for whom the Church universal is the sum total of local or 'particular' churches or something like a central 'super-Church' through which a local or 'particular' church is Church. If some Orthodox 'simple souls' are not far from holding one of these views, more or less consciously, ecclesiology in the true Orthodox perspective is quite different: the fullness of ecclesial reality is indeed present in the local eucharistic community, in other words in the local Church.

However, the affirmation that the universal Church is in the local Church or in the local eucharistic community may lead to some serious misunderstandings if it is not properly qualified. It might indeed be understood by some as suggesting that Orthodox ecclesiology is in fact something like extreme Congregationalism or Independency. Indeed, we must be grateful to the outstanding Orthodox theologian Fr Nicolas Afanassieff (1893–1966), for his rediscovery of the fullness of ecclesiality of the local Church expressed in the celebration of the sacrament of the Eucharist (*The Church of the Holy Spirit*, 1971).[4] Yet, several other Orthodox theologians of the so-called Parisian school – Fr Georges Florovsky, Fr Alexander Schmemann, Fr John Meyendorff, Fr Boris Bobrinskoy – and also a Greek, Metropolitan John of Pergamon (Zizioulas), have found it necessary to complement Fr Nicolas Afanassieff's ecclesiology. To these Orthodox names we must add one Roman Catholic who must be counted among the best ecclesiologists of the twentieth century, the late Fr J. M. R. Tillard.

All of them have emphasized that the Eucharist celebrated in a given place is indeed the Church of God in the full sense of the word on one essential condition: provided that this local Church is in full communion with all the churches that confess the faith and celebrate the Eucharist which is *one*. It is this very important condition which has led some of the theologians named above to suggest that instead of speaking of a eucharistic ecclesiology, it would be more appropriate to speak of an 'ecclesiology of communion', thus emphasizing the unity that must needs exist among local Churches that they might truly be recognized as 'the Church of God' in each place. This has led to the adoption in ecumenical dialogue of the original Greek word *koinonia*, diversely understood by various Christians in the world, but very clearly centred for the Orthodox on the core meaning: eucharistic communion, which implies all the other levels of communion.

The two levels of meaning of 'the Church of God which is at' a given place are very clearly summed up by Metropolitan John of Pergamon (Zizioulas): 'Just as a Eucharist which is not a transcendence of divisions within a certain locality is a false Eucharist, equally a Eucharist which takes place in conscious and intentional isolation and separation from other local communities in the world is not a true Eucharist. From that it follows inevitably that a local Church, in order to be not just local but also Church, must be in full communion with the rest of the local Churches in the world.'[5] This very firm statement, to which any truly conscious Orthodox must necessarily subscribe, is a reminder for the Orthodox world of the obligation to be active in the ecumenical movement as part of Orthodox ecclesiology: it is impossible to rest content with the state of Christian divisions, simply waiting for the 'others' to convert from 'their mistakes'. It is of the essence of the Church (in the sense of being members of the Church) to pray with all those who seek unity in Christ and gather together in His Name, and in this gathering, to endeavour to witness to authentic Orthodoxy. Ecclesiology implies taking an active part in the Orthodox Church's prayer 'For the union of all' (the 'Great Litany' prayed at the beginning of every major service or sacrament).

One final word on the term 'local'. Everyone knows how the one local community gathered around its bishop developed historically with the multiplication of places of worship (cathedral, parishes, monasteries, etc.) and how the development followed the administrative organization of the Empire. Everyone remembers that the word 'diocese' used to belong to imperial administrative terminology and only gradually acquired its ecclesiastical meaning of a territory representing the jurisdiction of one bishop. Several dioceses gathered together into a 'metropolis' (hence 'Metropolitan') or a province (with a primate, or presiding bishop). It is only later, with the development of sovereign states, that churches tended to be territorially identified with those states, and it is even later, with the development of modern nationalisms in the nineteenth century, that churches tended to become 'national'.

In this connection, it is useful to remember two things concerning Orthodox ecclesiology. One is the fact that an identification of Orthodox Christianity with one ethnic group (or tribe, *phyle* in Greek) was condemned as a heresy named Phyletism (or ethnophyletism) at the local Council of Constantinople held in 1872 and this decision was accepted by all the Orthodox. The other is the use by the Orthodox of the phrase 'local Church', not only for a parish or a diocese, but for any group of dioceses with a presiding bishop elected by his peers. Patriarch, Archbishop, Metropolitan: the titles vary but the situations are similar. An 'autocephalous' Church is one that elects its own primate; an 'autonomous' Church elects its primate with the participation of the primate of an autocephalous Church). The use of the term 'local' is a manner of remembering that the basic ecclesiological principle is territorial and not national (thus, the Church of Antioch, a very ancient Church, covers two sovereign states: Syria and Lebanon). These local Churches, in full communion with one another, call each other 'sister Churches'. This explains why the Orthodox have difficulties with using the same phrase in connection with Churches with which communion is still 'imperfect'.

The full communion among Orthodox sister Churches is expressed in several ways. One is the faithful adherence to the ancient tradition of co-consecrators for a new bishop. The presence and concelebration of several bishops of the province or from other sister Churches is an attestation of the faithful confession of the apostolic faith by the local Church in the person of its new bishop. When the presiding consecrator asks the bishop-elect to confess his faith, it is no formality. It aims at establishing this recognition by the sister Churches of one and the same apostolic faith, confessed in full communion with the 'cloud of witnesses' of all times (cf. Hebrews 12.1).

It is perhaps regrettable that this confession of faith by the bishop-elect has in the last nine or ten centuries become a fixed text. It is clear that this used to be a personal confession in the name of the local Church. This is to be seen in relation with the ancient tradition of a new bishop sending a confession of faith to his brothers in the episcopate. Unfortunately, this very meaningful tradition is no longer very much used. Indeed, its restoration could be very useful in the context of the ecumenical movement: the practice of exchanging confessions of faith could help to promote what the Commission on Faith and Order of the World Council of Churches has called 'ecumenical hermeneutics', that is developing the means to recognize the one faith confessed by partners in dialogue.

Another way of expressing full communion with all the sister Churches is the use of diptychs in the celebration of the Eucharist in particular. In this context, diptychs mean prayers for the local bishop (many mention the primate first), the link with all the other bishops (in the Cyprianic sense of episcopacy being one), for all the bishops of the province (when the bishop presides), for all the primates of all the sister Churches (when a primate presides). This is no mere politeness but an ecclesiological affirmation of unity in one faith and one Eucharist. When a Church is omitted in the diptychs, it has an ecclesiological meaning: this Church is no longer a sister Church for a doctrinal, or canonical, reason.

This brings us to another essential element of Orthodox ecclesiology: conciliarity. One might say that in a certain sense, in the light of what has been said about diptychs, whenever the Eucharist is celebrated, the Church is in Council. And even more than that: not only is communion with all the sister Churches throughout the world affirmed, but also communion throughout time, the offering being made 'for' (in the eucharistic prayer of St John Chrysostom) or 'with' (in that of St Basil the Great) the Communion of Saints, all the living, all the dead. This is what might be termed the supreme form of conciliarity since it is beyond the conciliarity lived in time; it is a foretaste of the Kingdom, the *eschata*.

In the concrete, every day life of the Church, conciliarity should prevail at every level. It concerns all the relations that exist, or should exist, among people who are all members of the one Body (cf. 1 Corinthians 12). At the Fifth World Conference on Faith and Order, held at Santiago de Compostella in August 1993, Metropolitan John of Pergamon (Zizioulas) clearly and firmly reminded us all of the fact that in the Church there is no place for individualism, that all relations should be in the image of the

Holy Trinity. The communion of the Three is the supreme model towards which we are all to tend, whatever the function we are entrusted with. There can be no room for domination-submission relations but only for mutual service (cf. the words of Christ quoted at the beginning of this essay). This is the very essence of an ecclesiology of communion.

Thus, a bishop is not somewhere above his community but within the community of the people of God. He does not cease to be a member the *laos*, the word which after all is the root from which the English 'lay' (or the French 'laic') are derived. In other words, the laity is by no means a kind of second-rate membership of the Church, as was mentioned above concerning the development of the iconostasis in Orthodox churches: it is the People of God in the noblest sense.[6] Paul Meyendorff very rightly pointed out at the Eighth Assembly of the World Council of Churches in December 1998 at Harare (Zimbabwe) that the only true ordination is baptism which makes us priests. The other ordinations are for specific functions. It is in this light that hierarchy (mentioned above), the structures of ministry, leadership and Church government, should be understood in an authentic Orthodox perspective. Needless to say, unfortunately, concrete reality seldom reflects this ideal approach.

To become priests through baptism-chrismation/confirmation (cf. 1 Peter 2.9) is also to become 'lively stones' for the edification of the Church (cf. 1 Peter 2.5). This means to become responsible members of the Church. Everyone is called to be responsible for the whole Body. The Church being *creatura Christi* and *creatura Spiritus*, there is no fusion of all the baptized in a kind of depersonalized super-individual. There is a communion of persons, at once all one and all diverse after the model of the Holy Trinity. In other words, diversity is as important as unity, and of course vice versa. There are no passive members of the Church. All are co-responsible, each one with unique gifts for the edification of all.

Vladimir Lossky insisted on the full responsibility of every member for the whole Church. This he expressed in speaking of everyone's vocation to become a 'catholic consciousness of the Church'. To achieve this, everyone is called to renounce the seeking of 'mine own, and to replace my self-consciousness by an *ecclesial* consciousness'. This is what he meant by a *catholic* consciousness. Let me add that for him catholic (and catholicity) meant unity in diversity, or diversity in unity.[7] This leads to

understanding conciliarity as a consensus of catholic conscious-
nesses, each one being responsible for the whole and therefore, in
a spirit of service, seeking this consensus, or what Fr Georges
Florovsky called the mind of the Church. This search for the
emergence of a consensus naturally is to be conducted under the
guidance of the Holy Spirit, who 'will guide you into all truth'
(John 16.13) and the whole Truth is Christ himself (John 14.6).

This constant attention paid to the guidance of the Holy Spirit,
who with Jesus Christ is the only criterion of truth for the
Orthodox, explains why, in ecumenical gatherings, the Orthodox
are so uneasy about any decision of importance being taken
through a vote. The majority is not necessarily, and in fact not
very often, right. And yet, as is well known, the Orthodox are
deeply attached to conciliarity, to Councils, to conciliar decisions.
The Orthodox Church is often described as the Church of the
Seven Ecumenical Councils. Many, including some Orthodox,
think in rather simplistic terms such as: 'Roman Catholics have
the Pope; the Orthodox have Councils.' In both cases, the
decision, be it the Pope's or that of a Council, is considered to be
automatically correct and therefore binding.

In fact, nothing could be further from the truth, in the realm of
authoritative teaching or the magisterium, so far as Orthodox
ecclesiology is concerned. In the Orthodox perspective properly
understood, a Council (or Synod; there is no difference for the
Orthodox) does indeed represent the supreme authority in
matters of faith and discipline. However, it will be clear to
everyone that a council may present all the characteristics
formally required and yet be rejected as a Council. The most
obvious example is of course the 'Robber Council' of Ephesus
(449). In other words, paradoxical or unconvincing as it may
sound, a Council expresses the truth of the Church only in so far
as it actually does express the truth of the Church, the Church
today, in unanimity with the Church of all times, in unity of the
one Spirit. The truth is its own criterion.

This naturally brings us to the other commonplace statement:
'the Orthodox Church is the Church of the Seven Ecumenical
Councils'. This is true provided it is not understood as a form of reactionary conservatism consisting in living in the past and merely
repeating what others have said before. The true meaning of the
faithfulness to the Seven Ecumenical Councils consists in a permanent reception *today* and *for today* of the faith of Nicaea, the apostolic

faith, the faith of our Fathers, the catholic faith (to quote the
confession proclaimed every year on the first Sunday in Lent,
dedicated to the 'Triumph of Orthodoxy', meaning the triumph
of purified christology). This reception is necessary for every
generation, and in the last analysis for every baptized Christian.
This is where we discover that, in addition to Scripture, which is
clearly one of its main sources as it appears in what has been described so far, Orthodox ecclesiology may be said to be based on
reason. However, the Orthodox would not spontaneously speak in
this way. Reason would be understood as reason enlightened by
the guidance of the Holy Spirit. And this is what the Orthodox
would quite naturally call Tradition (with a capital 'T'). Tradition
is precisely this perpetual reception by the Church of the fullness
of revelation, a reception in the Holy Spirit who is one, and it is
therefore a reception in unanimity with the witnesses of all times,
for the same Spirit inspires all. Thus, the sources of Orthodox ecclesiology are obviously Scriptures, councils (worthy of the name of
course), and reason but understood as Tradition which is
probably the most important as it is described by some as the very
breath of the Holy Spirit.[8] V. Lossky speaks of Tradition as the
breath of the Holy Spirit in the Church in terms of the critical
spirit of the Church, called upon to distinguish permanently
between what is fundamental and what is secondary (what
Richard Hooker described as the *adiaphora*).

Now, if a genuine Council is the supreme authority in matters of
faith and discipline, this does not mean that in Orthodox ecclesiology the famous question raised at the time of the Great Schism in
the West: 'The Pope above the Council; the Council above the
Pope', is answered with the second proposition. In fact, from an
Orthodox point of view, the problematic of the 'conciliarism' of
the fourteenth and fifteenth centuries has very little, if anything
at all, to do with conciliarity. To take but one example, the 'democratic' theories of Marsilius of Padua, which inspired some of the
'conciliarists', have no place in Orthodoxy. The priesthood of all
baptized believers has, in the Orthodox perspective, nothing in
common with political categories, as we have seen above in describing the Church as the communion of co-responsible persons
(not *individuals*).

Orthodox conciliarity, however (with regard to the other proposition: 'The Pope above the Council'), is closely linked with the
question of primacy. Indeed, for some Orthodox today, it is a

question. Some would state that there is no such thing in the Orthodox communion and would defend the idea of the independence of each local Church, thus introducing an element of individualism at the ecclesiological level in the relations among sister Churches. If, for some, this is due to insufficient knowledge of Church history or of Canon Law, it is strange to find such a learned theologian as Fr Nicolas Afanassieff stating in an otherwise very interesting essay that 'primacy' is a purely Western, legalistic notion, derived from St Cyprian's conception of the unity of the episcopate.[9] He distinguishes 'primacy' which is power, and what he calls 'priority' which is not power but grace and love. Consequently, in his view, although each local Church is autonomous and independent (the phrase is used several times) because it is the Church of God, one of them has priority among them. Since priority is not power, identified with primacy, this Church 'presides in love' (St Ignatius, 'To the Romans': Salutation).

It is not very clear why 'priority' should have a monopoly of grace and love and why 'primacy' should necessarily be deprived of either and be identified with legalistic power. This sounds particularly strange today, when the Pope himself speaks of primacy as presidency in love and over love and explicitly refuses the identification with power.[10] Although this opposition of the terms is not very clear, it is necessary to express gratitude and give credit to Fr Nicolas Afanassieff for strongly emphasizing that conciliarity and priority (which is clearly a form of primacy) not only do not represent a polarization between two forms of ecclesiology, but are inseparably linked together. The one implies the other. Unfortunately, some Orthodox retain only the notion of independence from Fr Nicolas' teaching and altogether forget the 'presidency in love'. Others speak of a presidency in terms of a primacy of honour, insisting so much on *primus inter pares* ('first among equals'), that in the end this primacy has no meaning whatever.

Probably the best expression of a truly Orthodox view of primacy in connection with communion is to be found in another essay in the book already referred to above: *The Primacy of Peter in the Orthodox Church*. It is an interesting contrast to read Fr Alexander Schmemann's essay, 'The Idea of Primacy in Orthodox Ecclesiology', after being slightly disconcerted by Fr Nicolas Afanassieff's negation of an Orthodox primacy. With his usual clarity of mind, intellectual honesty and an outstanding gift for striking right home, Father Alexander does not hesitate to use and clarify the notion of primacy (not 'priority'). He examines the different levels of this notion, culminating with 'the highest and ultimate form of primacy: *the universal primacy*' (Fr A. Schmemann's own italics). It is also of great interest to quote his reference to the probable reason for the denial or minimization by some Orthodox (as well as some theologians in Reformation Churches) of the necessity for a universal form of primacy. He refers to 'an age-long anti-Roman prejudice' which 'has led some Orthodox canonists simply to deny the existence of such primacy in the past or the need for it in the present'. He then adds something of paramount importance for the Orthodox in doubt: 'But an objective study of the canonical tradition cannot fail to establish beyond any doubt that, along with local centres of agreement or primacies, the Church had also known a universal primacy.'

It is also interesting to emphasize points in Fr Alexander's essay concerning the nature of this primacy, the manner in which it should be exercised, as though Fr Alexander were giving an anticipated response to Pope John Paul II's invitation to theologians in *Ut unum sint*. First of all, he defines primacy at all levels, including the universal one, as a 'centre of communion' which excludes any notion of 'supreme power', a notion that is 'incompatible with the nature of the Church as Body of Christ'. Secondly, Fr Alexander speaks with characteristic directness to some Orthodox when he says that primacy is not to be understood as 'a mere "chairmanship" if one understands this term in its modern, parliamentary and democratic connotations'. Then, implicitly complementing Fr Nicolas Afanassieff's eucharistic ecclesiology, Fr Alexander goes right to the heart of the nature of the relation between conciliarity and primacy by stating that no local Church can live in isolation: 'A local Church cut from this universal *koinonia* is indeed a *contradictio in adjecto*, for this *koinonia* is the very essence of the Church. And it has, therefore, its *form* and *expression*: primacy. Primacy is the necessary expression of the unity in faith and life of all local Churches, of their living and efficient *koinonia*.'

For the manner in which primacy (at all levels) should be exercised, all of us now quote the famous Canon 34 of the so-called *Apostolic Canons*. Fr Alexander Schmemann already quoted it in 1960:

> The bishops of each nation (*ethnous*, *regions*) must know who is the first (*proton*, primate) among them and acknowledge him as their head (*kephalen*; *caput*); they are to do nothing of

weight without his opinion and let everyone of them look after the affairs of his diocese and the regions depending thereon. But neither let him (the primate) do anything without the advice of all and thus, concord (*homonia; unanimitas*) will prevail to the glory of the Father, the Son and the Holy Spirit.[11]

As I always say when I quote this canon, in my opinion, the final doxology is certainly not some form of perfunctory formula. It is there to stress the fact that all relations within the Church, as well as among Churches, are to be lived after the model of the Persons of the Holy Trinity. It concerns all, in spite of the fact that it speaks only of bishops. We must never lose sight of the fact that, in faithful Orthodox ecclesiology, a bishop does not exist outside or above his Church. He is necessarily within the community of the people of God. He is the head but the head implies a body, just as a living body implies a head. A bishop severed from his community is no head but a skull; and a community without the bishop is no body but a skeleton.

It must be said in all fairness that Orthodox ecclesiology at all levels is full of beauty. The vision of Church unity devised at the Salamanca Faith and Order consultation in 1973 (a conciliar fellowship of local Churches in full communion in one faith and one Eucharist) and received at the Nairobi General Assembly of the World Council of Churches in 1975, is very much what the Orthodox teach. But today, in our historical existence, we have a long way to go to live up to our teaching. May the Lord and the prayers of our brothers and sisters throughout the world help us to correspond to our own model.

Two more difficult questions have to be examined. One is how the Orthodox see themselves; the other is how they see other Christians. The difficulty lies in the absence of unanimity on either of these subjects among the Orthodox, individually or as Churches.

All Orthodox agree in saying that the Orthodox Church is the One, Holy, Catholic and Apostolic Church, confessing belief in the article on the Church in the Nicene-Constantinopolitan creed. However, there is no unanimous interpretation of the verb 'to be' in the statement. Very conservative, or even fanatical, Orthodox would simply understand the statement in an exclusive manner, close to the well-known Roman Catholic attitude still professed in the early twentieth century: 'No salvation outside the

Church' – only in this case, not the Church of Rome but the Orthodox Church which is the only one in which all grace and all the means of salvation are to be found.

At the other end of the spectrum, other Orthodox would interpret the same statement in a manner much closer to what we find in the Vatican II Decree on Ecumenism: the *Una Sancta subsistit in* (subsists in) the Roman Catholic Church, in this case the Orthodox Church, thus leaving open the difficult question of the determination of the frontiers of the Church. Such people would refer to the Gospel statement which they interpret to mean that the Holy Spirit 'bloweth where it listeth' (John 3.8). As a result, they say: 'We know where the Church is; but we do not know where it ends.' They will also support this view by remembering the eucharistic prayer of the Liturgy of Saint Basil in which all people, the whole of creation, are prayed for. Between the two extremes there are many different shades of opinion. There is no official statement on the part of the Orthodox Church as a whole.

The latter is even more true concerning the second question: how do the Orthodox see other Christians? The spectrum in this case is very difficult to present, let alone analyse in any coherent way. Conservative, exclusive attitudes exist in practically all local Churches. The same is true of more open attitudes. In other words, it is not a matter of ecclesiastical geography. One element can serve as something of an indication: the manner of reception of non-Orthodox into the Orthodox Church. Thus the Church of Russia officially receives those whose baptism is uncertain (i.e. not really in the name of the Holy Trinity) through baptism; Protestants, through chrismation; Roman Catholics, through penitence (confession) with full recognition of holy orders. The case of Anglicans is at the moment not so clear, especially with the question of the ordination of women to the presidency of the Eucharist. However, even in the same Church of Russia, there are people who think that all should be rebaptized. This is also an opinion found in other parts of the Orthodox world and the current practice on Mount Athos. Some Orthodox (the Church of Romania for example, but others as well) used to recognize fully the validity of Anglican orders. Today, things are perhaps not so clear. Some Orthodox would recognize the ecclesial status of certain Churches and more or less unchurch others. Unfortunately, they would not necessarily be the same Churches! Hence the enormous difficulty in dealing with this subject. As a conclusion, one might say that most cultured Orthodox would agree that there are at least elements of Church in all communities that confess Jesus Christ as God and Saviour and the Holy Trinity.

This naturally brings us to the last point to be touched upon, once again, a complicated one. It is the attitude of the Orthodox towards the ecumenical future. Everyone knows that at the moment, there is something of a crisis in this area. It is due first of all to the existence of contradictory trends (to say the least) in most Orthodox local Churches. Practically every one has its fundamentalist minorities which persecute those who are open-minded and who are therefore accused of being liberal modernists who betray Orthodoxy. It is also due, this must be admitted, to certain forms of proselytism on the part of some groups (related to Churches which disown these actions) in areas which have suffered from a lack of proper education, especially of the clergy, owing to persecutions.

Curiously enough, practically every Orthodox Church is pursuing bilateral dialogues with most Christians and at the same time suffers from the pressure of those who regard ecumenism as 'the heresy of the twentieth century'. The present difficulty concerns the multilateral level as lived in the World Council of Churches. It is no secret that two Orthodox Churches, the Church of Georgia and the Church of Bulgaria, have withdrawn from the Council. However, within those very Churches there is no unanimity, let alone among all the Orthodox. Thank God, the Special Commission between the WCC and the Orthodox to examine the future of the Council has begun its work. May the Lord bless this undertaking and inspire all its members with his Holy Spirit so that all might move towards the visible unity in the confession of the one apostolic faith and the sharing of one Eucharist, with full respect for all legitimate diversities, which to me is the true vision of the future of the ecumenical movement. It will be clear to all that in my own conception of Orthodoxy, the ecumenical movement is part and parcel of Orthodox ecclesiology. It is an essential part of being Church.

FURTHER READING

Colosimo, J., 'L'invention de la double économie' in *La vie spirituelle* 730 (Mars 1999).

Florovsky, G., *The Collected Works*. 14 volumes. Belmont MA, Büchervertriebsanstalt, 1989.

Lossky, V., 'Ecueils ecclésiologiques' in *Messager de l'Exarchat du Patriarche Russe en Europe Occidentale* 1. Paris 1950. (In Russian and in French.)

Meyendorff, J., *L'Eglise Orthodoxe Hier et Aujourd'hui*. Nouvelle édition, revue et augmentée par Jean Meyendorff et Nicolas Lossky, Paris, Seuil, 1995 (E.T. *The Orthodox Church: Its Past and Its Role in the World Today*. Crestwood NY, SVS Press, 1996).

Podmore, C., ed., *Community-Unity-Communion: Essays in Honour of Mary Tanner*. Church House Publishing 1998.

Together on the Way: Official Report of the Eighth Assembly of the World Council of Churches, ed. Diane Kessler (and *Faisons Route Ensemble*, ed. N. Lossky). Geneva, WCC Publications, 1999.

Ware, T. (Bishop Kallistos of Diokleia), *The Orthodox Church*. Revised edn, Penguin 1993.

NOTES

1. Bulgakov, S., *Pravoslavie* (Paris, YMCA Press, 1935), p. 1 (in Russian).
2. Liturgy of St John Chrysostom and liturgy of St Basil the Great.
3. Ignatius, *Ad Smyrn.* 8, 2, *Sources Chrétiennes* 10, pp. 162–3.
4. Afanassieff, N., *The Church of the Holy Spirit*. Paris, YMCA Press, 1971 (in Russian); French translation, Paris, 1975.
5. Metropolitan John of Pergamon (Zizioulas), *Being as Communion* (New York, SVS Press, 1985), p. 257.
6. On the community of the baptized, the *Christifideles*, see Tillard, J. M. R., *L'Eglise locale; ecclésiologie de communion et catholicité*. Paris, Le Cerf, 1995, in particular chapter III, 'L'Eglise locale, Eglise des baptisés'.
7. Lossky, V., 'Catholic Consciousness: Anthropological Implications of the Dogma of the Church', *In the Image and Likeness of God*. E.T. Crestwood NY, SVS Press, 1974. See also the chapter preceding the one just quoted: 'Of the Third Attribute of the Church'.
8. Lossky, V. and Ouspensky, L., *The Meaning of Icons*. Olten, Switzerland, Urs Graf-Verlag, 1952. Ware, K., 'Tradition and traditions' in Lossky, N. et al., ed., *Dictionary of the*

Ecumenical Movement. Geneva, WCC Publications; Grand Rapids, Eerdmans, 1991.

9. 'The Church which Presides in Love' in Meyendorff, J., Schmemann, A., Afanassieff, N. and Koulomzine, N., *The Primacy of Peter in the Orthodox Church*. 2nd edn, Faith Press 1973. The original of this book was published in French in 1960 (Neuchâtel, Delachaux et Niestlé).

10. *Ut unum sint*, Nos 88, 94.

11. Cf. Ioannou, P. P., *Fonti; discipline générale antique* (Rome, Grottaferrata, 1962), t.I, 2, pp.162–5.

2

The Reformed Churches

David Fergusson

THE LUTHERAN BACKGROUND

As with other topics in Reformed doctrine, ecclesiology must be understood with reference to the historical context of the sixteenth century. Luther's doctrine of the Church is worked out initially in opposition to his Roman Catholic opponents, yet also in distinction from radical voices on the left wing of the Reformation. The Church is marked not by forms of historical continuity but by its constant return to the gospel of God's free grace for sinners in Jesus Christ. Luther thus emphasized the centrality of the Word of God which the congregation hears, receives and proclaims. The vital characteristic of the Church is the preaching of the gospel which precedes and constitutes the faithful as the Church of Christ. The Church is the communion of saints gathered in faith by the Holy Spirit under the Word. This creates the problem of how such a community receives outward institutional expression. Against those who criticized him for a 'Platonizing' of the church, Luther presented an account of the visible church. This became a pressing concern also in face of the anabaptist tendency to spiritualize the Church and set it apart from the mass of society. The individualism and anarchic trends of the radicals troubled Luther and were to shape his ecclesiology.[1]

In this situation, a more adequate account of the visible church in relation to the invisible was required.[2] Only God knows the identity of true believers. The composition of the true church remains invisible and hidden. Nonetheless, the outward institution containing both the faithful and the unfaithful is also the true church by virtue of its preaching of the gospel, the mark of baptism and the sharing of the Lord's Supper. In this visible church, the corrupt are to be found amongst the true people of

God just as tares remain amidst wheat and mouse droppings are found among peppercorns. While the church embraces a diversity of members not all of whom can be reckoned true believers, it remains the true church by virtue of its preaching of the gospel and administration of the sacraments. Here Luther tends to assign priority to the former over the latter as the primary mark or note of the church. His account of the visible church is Augustinian in an important respect. As Augustine had rejected the elitism of the Donatist view of the church, so also Luther rejects the radical attempt to purify the church through dissociation from society and the state. The visible church remains a mass movement supported by the civil authorities. But so long as the gospel is there preached, it remains the true church. Only the proclamation of false doctrine justifies secession for the sake of maintaining ecclesiastical purity.

This is set out in the *Augsburg Confession* (1530) and the *Augsburg Apology* (1531). The preaching of the Word and the proper administration of the sacraments are the defining marks of the visible church. The charge of postulating a 'Platonic republic' is firmly rejected. Hypocrites and unrepentant sinners are intermingled with the godly in the church. This does not in itself undermine the church's evangelical identity. The sacraments remain efficacious even though they are administered by wicked persons.[3] In his treatise *On the Councils and the Church* (1539),[4] Luther sets out seven signs by which the Christian people of God can be recognized. These include the Word of God, baptism, the Lord's Supper, the office of the keys whereby sinners are absolved or condemned, the ordained ministry, public worship, and the suffering that accompanies true discipleship. None of these makes mention of a historical episcopate, seven sacraments, the papacy, liturgical form or ecclesiastical tradition.

When dealing with the order of the church, Luther typically insists upon the priesthood of all believers. All who believe in Christ can offer themselves to his service through praise, intercession and acts of self-giving. Within the church, constituted by the preaching of the Word of God, all are priests. Yet not all are ministers. Only some are called and appointed to the office of preaching. Attention to the correct order of the church was to become a preoccupation of the Reformed church in its differing social context.

CALVIN'S ECCLESIOLOGY

Although Reformed theology is not synonymous with Calvinism, the writings of John Calvin – especially the *Institutes* – provide the clearest index to the theological characteristics of the Reformed movement. His discussion of the doctrine of the church builds upon much that can be found in Luther. He repeats the stress upon the marks of the preaching of the Word and the proper administration of the sacraments. But his more measured consideration of ecclesiology came subsequent to his time in Strasbourg where he was influenced by Bucer. A growing concern with church order and discipline reflects both the general consolidation of the Reformed movement and Calvin's own role in Genevan church and society.

Calvin's mature deliberations on the nature of the church are found in Book IV of the final edition of the *Institutes* (1559). The extensive treatment of ecclesiology has not always been recognized in discussions of his theology, yet the sheer space devoted by Calvin to the nature of the church both here and in other occasional writings indicates its importance for his life and work. He begins by employing the notion of accommodation which recurs throughout his theology. This is a decisive aspect of divine sovereignty which ought not to be understood in Calvin's thought merely in terms of sheer power and will. On account of our weakness, the church, together with its ordinances and offices, is given to increase faith within us. It is a gift from God which accommodates our frailty. Calvin uses similar language in relation to the incarnation, Scripture and the sacraments. This in itself indicates the centrality of the church in his thinking. Recalling Cyprian's dictum, Calvin argues that to those for whom God is Father, the Church is mother.[5]

Much of Calvin's discussion assumes Luther's coordination of the invisible and the visible church, albeit with greater stress upon divine election. The invisible church is the church 'catholic' or 'universal'. It comprises the elect of all ages. Yet since these are often hidden within large multitudes – a few grains of wheat covered by a pile of chaff – only God can know their names.[6] This distinction between invisible and visible church also informs Zwingli's ecclesiology and was shaped by the controversies with Roman Catholic and anabaptist opponents in Zurich.[7] Several Reformed confessions describe the church as the community of the elect through all ages beginning with Adam. This community though sometimes hidden will be preserved and maintained by God to the end of the world.[8] The church is catholic insofar as all the elect are united in Christ. They are members of his body and are dependent upon his headship. The stress on the oneness of the community of Israel and the Gentiles reflects the Reformed emphasis upon the unity of the two testaments and their dispensations. Bullinger's *Second Helvetic Confession* argues that although there is a diversity of signs and ceremonies there is one fellowship in the one Messiah of those who have been gathered into the church from among Jews and Gentiles.[9]

A consequence of equating the church with the company of the elect from all ages is that there is no salvation outside the invisible church. Thus the Reformers can affirm the ancient dictum, *extra ecclesiam nulla salus est*, outside the church there is no salvation. As Rohls points out, this is analytically true.[10] If the invisible church is simply the elect community, then only those who will be saved are included. Furthermore, given that the members of the invisible church have generally been found at one time or another in the visible church, it can also be assumed that outside it there is no ordinary possibility of salvation. Here the term 'ordinary' is crucial. The sovereignty of God is such that persons outwith the institutional church may nonetheless be redeemed, although God for the most part has chosen to mediate the divine decree by the preaching of the Word and the administration of the sacraments. This distinction between the ordinary and extraordinary possibilities of salvation became a contested matter within Reformed theology. Zwingli employed it to argue that the virtuous pagans were saved and he explicitly named Hercules, Theseus, Socrates, Aristides, Cato and others. This was criticized elsewhere on the grounds that it revived mediaeval notions of merit by which salvation was earned. Calvin argues that salvation comes only through the Christ who is present in Word and sacrament. On the basis of John 4.22, he claims that Christ 'both condemns all pagan religions as false and gives the reason that under the law the Redeemer was promised to the chosen people alone. From this it follows that no worship has ever pleased God except that which looked to Christ.'[11] In similar vein, the *Westminster Confession* holds that while those dying in infancy and the mentally handicapped may be numbered among the elect, this cannot be said of 'those not professing the Christian religion' however diligently they order their lives by the light of nature. To maintain such a position is 'very pernicious, and to be detested'.[12]

While affirming the invisible church, there is a concentration in Calvin's writings on the visible institution. He returns to the maternal image. 'For there is no other way to enter into life unless this mother conceive us in her womb, give us birth, nourish us at her breast, and lastly, unless she keep us under her care and guidance until, putting off mortal flesh, we become like the angels'.[13] The emphatic insistence that 'there is no other way' illustrates the necessity and importance of the church in Calvin's theology. Yet the dependence of the church upon the Word of God is revealed by the way in which Calvin exalts the preaching of true doctrine. This is argued by reference to a range of Scriptural examples. It is primarily through the preaching and teaching office of the church that believers are brought to faith and nourished therein. In this way the church's dependence upon and constant return to the gospel of Christ are shown. The visible church, though everywhere mixed and impure, is identified by the preaching and hearing of the Word and the sacraments administered according to Christ's institution. Where these marks are apparent, the visible church is to be respected. This is the standard by which every congregation is to be measured and accorded the title 'church'.[14] This guards against unnecessary separation and unlawful schism. Agreement on every point of doctrine and in all matters of practice is not required. Appealing to Paul, Calvin advocates the 'charitable judgement whereby we recognize as members of the church those who, by confession of faith, by example of life, and by partaking of the sacraments, profess the same God and Christ with us'.[15] This does not require the purity of the church's members or even its ministers. 'Nor are the sacraments less pure and salutary for a holy and upright man because they are handled by unclean persons.'[16] Calvin's claims for both the invisible and the visible church point to the christological determination of his ecclesiology. The marks of evangelical preaching and sacramental administration according to the command of Christ point to the unity of the church under its Lord. Similarly, the claim that the elect belong to the one church by virtue of the headship of Christ betokens the christological essence of the faith. 'The fundamental doctrine, on which it is never allowable to compromise, is that we should learn Christ, for Christ is the one single foundation of the Church.'[17]

In stressing this christological constitution of the Church, Calvin argues for the indivisibility of Word and Spirit. Christ is known to us through the Word of God, and it is to this Word that he directs us. This linkage of the second and the third articles is crucial in his polemics against both anabaptist and Roman Catholic opponents. He charges each side with abstracting the Spirit from the Word. In the former case, this amounts to a cult of individual licence. In the latter, it yields an account of the institutional church in which ideas, ceremonies, offices and practices are spawned without adequate reference to the Word. During his debate with Cardinal Sadoleto, Calvin claims that Christ has annexed his Spirit to the Word. This is what Paul intends when he speaks of the church as built upon the foundation of the prophets and apostles.[18] The Reformed movement is thus refashioning the church in accordance with Scripture and the practice of the ancient church. It reflects a desire for a constant assessment of the church by the standard of the Word of God. This gives rise to the famous slogan, *ecclesia reformata sed semper reformanda*, the church reformed but always having to be reformed.

Calvin's strict warnings against unnecessary separation may have been designed to counteract the centrifugal tendencies of the Reformation churches. Its fragmentation and repeated subdivisions were weaknesses by contrast with the more unitary nature of the Roman Catholic church. This created a burden on Calvin and other Reformers to justify secession. He labours at this task in distinguishing unnecessary from necessary separation. Here again Lutheran themes are recalled. The foundation of the church is the teaching of the apostles that salvation is by Christ alone. Remove that teaching and there is no church.[19] This Calvin argues has happened within the Roman Catholic church. Here doctrine has been corrupted, the Lord's Supper has become a blasphemy against the once for all sacrifice of Christ, and numerous superstitions have polluted the worship of God's people.[20] This is reinforced by the standard Reformed argument that apostolicity is not defined by the historical sequence of the holders of an episcopal office, but by faithfulness to the truth of Christ in the apostolic witness.

Apostolic fidelity to the Word of God rather than apostolic succession is what constitutes the true church. Calvin cites the Fathers in support of this conclusion, thus claiming that the Reformed are the true heirs of the ancient church. Appealing again to Cyprian, he asserts that the unity and peace of the church derive from Christ's episcopate alone. It is by virtue of the relationship that the members of the body have to their head that they belong to the church. The Roman Catholic church is likened to the synagogues from which the early Christians were cast (John 16.2). Here the vituperative rhetoric of the Reformation is both anti-Roman and anti-Semitic. This is displayed in lurid terms by the *Westminster Confession* (1647) with its references to the 'synagogues of Satan' and to the Pope as 'that antichrist, that man of sin, and son of perdition'.[21] Nonetheless, Calvin acknowledges that with the Roman Catholic church there remains the sign of baptism and other vestiges of true religion. '[W]hen we categorically deny to the papists the title of the church, we do not for this reason impugn the existence of churches among them.'[22]

CHURCH GOVERNMENT AND DISCIPLINE

The Reformed stress on sanctification and the preoccupation with the Christian life inevitably led to a greater concentration upon church order than was found in the Lutheran tradition. The church is gathered by the preaching of the gospel. This gospel is not only about the forgiveness of sins, however. It is about the regeneration of the sinner who by the Holy Spirit is united with Christ. The church, therefore, is the arena of the sanctified life. It is the locus of the Spirit's activity in the lives of the faithful who are bound together as the body of Christ. This Reformed emphasis brought with it a serious concern for the order, discipline and well-being of the church and of its host society. Furthermore, political threats to Reformed congregations in France and elsewhere entailed the need for organized, disciplined and homogeneous communities. Organization and order were thus crucial for survival in the face of hostile forces.[23] This was apparent in the Reformation in Strasbourg under the leadership of Martin Bucer, both a distinguished theologian and church administrator. Bucer includes the maintenance of pastoral discipline within the distinguishing marks of the church. 'The corruption of discipline ruins the entire ministry of teaching and sacraments, and the devil fills their place with fearful superstition.'[24] Other Reformed communities also exalted pastoral discipline as a mark of the church alongside the preaching of the Word and the administration of the sacraments.[25]

From 1538 to 1541, Calvin worked in Strasbourg as a teacher and pastor. There he came under the influence of Bucer, an influence that was to enrich his subsequent ministry in Geneva upon return there. Discipline was necessary for any church that was to remain faithful to Christ and to practice holiness in service to him. This, however, belonged to the organization and good order of the church rather than to its essence. Hence Calvin did not depart from Luther in stressing just two notes of the true church. Nonetheless, unlike Luther, both Bucer and Calvin sought to find in Scripture a model authorized by the Holy Spirit for the form of the church.[26] Four specialized ministries were identified: pastors, doctors, elders and deacons. In some places, this becomes a three-fold model through conflating the offices of pastor and doctor on account of their common tasks of proclamation and teaching. The pastor is charged with the tasks of preaching, teaching, administering the sacraments and participating in church government, the elder is a lay functionary who shares in the task of government, while the deacon is concerned with the care of the poor.[27]

In many respects, Calvin's account of the ordained ministry is a high doctrine.[28] That human instruments should be used to communicate God's Word is a sign of God's grace and an accommodation to our creaturely state. By the word of the minister, the gospel is communicated in the church. Calvin describes the ministry as the 'chief sinew' by which believers are held together in the body of Christ.[29] It is clear that the ministry for Calvin is permanent to the life and well-being of Christ's church and is not merely an occasional office which may at times be useful and appropriate to its needs. Nonetheless, it is not an office which creates or precedes the church. It is situated within the church and is appointed to serve it. The location of the pastor within the life of the congregation is stressed. Both an outward public call and the inward call of God are to be recognized. Appointment is not to be made without the consent of the people, although another pastor should preside at such an election 'in order that the multitude may not go wrong either though fickleness, through evil intentions, or through disorder'.[30] Ordination is an act involving the laying on of hands by other pastors in accordance with the Word of God. The ministry is an office of vital importance to the congregation. '[W]hen a puny man risen from the dust speaks in God's name, at this point we best evidence our piety and obedience toward God if we show ourselves teachable towards his minister, although he excels us in nothing.'[31]

It is worth recalling that this doctrine of ministry was held in conjunction with the priesthood of all believers. This latter doctrine did not entail that there was no ordained ministry or that the tasks of the minister could be devolved to any member of the congregation. The priesthood of all believers was in Luther a polemical criticism of the notion that there was some special and superior spiritual estate to which ministers were called, a priestly character which ordination conferred and which gave the holder a closer relationship to God. This notion was rejected. Christ alone is our high priest, yet all members of the church can participate in his priestly office. In this respect, this is no higher calling than baptism into the body of Christ. The priesthood of all believers implies that we each offer ourselves as living sacrifices in response to the work of Christ and are called upon to intercede for one another. There is no special priestly act at the altar which continues or contributes to the once for all priestly work of Christ.

The priesthood of all believers, however, does not prevent either Luther, Bucer or Calvin from recognizing that there is an office of ministry which Christ gives to his church and which is essential for its order, maintenance and well-being. This is the ordained ministry of Word and sacrament. This had significant practical consequences at the time of the Reformation. The principal task of the minister was no longer the sacrificial act at the altar. It was the preaching and teaching of the Word of God, the verbal declaration of the gospel, confirmed and sealed in the sacraments. The *Second Helvetic Confession* gives its own job description of the minister.

> The duties of ministers are various; yet for the most part they are restricted to two, in which all the rest are comprehended: to the teaching of the Gospel of Christ, and to the proper administration of the sacraments. For it is the duty of the ministers to gather together an assembly for worship in which to expound God's Word and to apply the whole doctrine to the care and use of the Church, so that what is taught may benefit the hearers and edify the faithful.[32]

This understanding of the office gave rise to other features of ministerial practice after the Reformation. Vestments once worn at the altar became more sober and modest for the task of preaching. Ministers were required to live in and to serve their parishes. They were not permitted to hold more than one living. There were no ranks or hierarchies within the order. The description of the office led to a levelling out of distinctions between the clergy and brought about the principle of the parity of ministers.[33] The normative significance of the parish ministry in the life of the church was stressed.

In dealing with the episcopal office, Calvin notes the way in which the New Testament often uses terms like pastor, bishop and presbyter interchangeably. The bishop is to be understood as a presbyter who exercises a ministry of preaching. In this respect, he belongs to the same rank as other ministers. When the category of 'bishop' denotes the exercise of a specific function it is where presbyters elect one of their number to preside, report, admonish, exhort and to carry out what has been resolved by common decision. The analogy of the consul in the senate is drawn, and appeal is made to the writings of Jerome and others.[34] In this way, the bishop is a *primus inter pares*, a first among equals, who is appointed by pastors and whose office differs only by virtue of his being set aside to carry out particular functions. This functional view of the bishop is in contrast to theologies which view the episcopal office as a divinely appointed condition for the constitution of the church.

Councils of the church may be useful for the teaching of God's Word and the extirpation of error. Nonetheless, their validity is determined neither by their size nor the office-bearers present, but by the presence of Christ in their midst. Calvin warns against the defection of pastors and the errors of councils as if to caution his readers of their fallibility. At the same time, he attributes an authority to the decisions of the councils of Nicaea, Constantinople, Ephesus and Chalcedon. Authority, however, rests upon their teaching being 'the pure and genuine exposition of Scripture'.[35] This points to the Achilles' heel of the Reformed position. Who is to judge the scriptural authenticity of conciliar decisions? Yet Calvin is confident that the plain sense of Scripture in matters of fundamental importance will be apparent to sincere believers under the guidance of the Spirit. (Later Protestantism formalized this position in its doctrine of the perfection, necessity, sufficiency and perspicuity of Scripture.) Moreover, he agrees that the best method for resolving doctrinal dispute is for a gathering of a synod of bishops, invoking Christ's Spirit, to reach agreement. Their decisions will carry more weight than those of the private individual. Their common deliberations will militate against diversity and congregational fragmentation.

With the doctrine of ordination in place, and its supplementation by lay orders of ministry, the way is now open for an orderly approach to ecclesiastical discipline. This is one of the most contentious aspects of Reformed doctrine. If the saving doctrine of Christ is the soul of the church, argues Calvin appealing again to an anthropological analogy, so discipline serves as its sinews by holding together the members of the body each in its own place.[36] The first purpose of discipline is to root out the ungodly from within the church, and especially to prevent the unworthy partaking of the Lord's Supper. Its second function is to prevent the corruption of the faithful by bad company. Its third is to restore those who have lapsed by bringing them to repentance. Thus the integrity of the church, the purity of its members, and the reclaiming of those who have strayed are the reasons why the church must exercise godly discipline.

Calvin seems to have envisaged a scale of offences which required punishments proportionately ranging in severity. A mild and paternal chastisement may be sufficient in the face of minor faults. More serious crimes may require public rebuke and repentance, together with temporary suspension from the Lord's Table. This regime must apply equally to princes and common people alike.[37] Nonetheless, discipline must always be tempered by a gentleness of spirit and an acknowledgement of God's mercy. 'For God, whenever it pleases him, changes the worst men into the best, engrafts the alien, and adopts the stranger into the church.'[38] The power of the keys enables the church in circumstances of serious wrongdoing to excommunicate. However, this too can have a remedial function if it recalls the wrongdoer to the way of salvation.

In discussing the scope of ecclesiastical jurisdiction, Calvin both distinguishes and relates it to the role of the civil magistracy. The church has the power to admonish, rebuke, discipline and even excommunicate. But it does not have the power of the sword, or the sanction of fines, imprisonment and execution. These belong to the civil magistrate. Nonetheless, both civil and ecclesiastical rulers work together for the same end of peaceful, harmonious and godly living. In distinguishing the secular and religious authorities in this way, Calvin shows himself to be innocent of the charge of theocracy. Indeed he argues strongly in an anti-theocratic vein that ministers should not hold political office in the civil realm. Here much of Calvin's thought reflects the context of Strasbourg, Geneva and other Swiss cantons. His distinction between the jurisdiction of church and state is self-consciously sharper than the more theocratic model that characterized the Reformed movement in Zurich.[39] All citizens were subject both to civil and ecclesiastical law. The Consistory comprised ministers and elders, the latter group including prominent members of Genevan society nominated by the magistracy. It was intended to meet weekly with the purpose of enforcing ecclesiastical discipline in the entire community. Its remit was extensive and it developed a reputation for being unnecessarily inquisitorial and prying.[40]

The distinction between civil and religious government was built into Calvin's account of political authority.[41] The office of the magistrate was ordained by God for the maintenance of peace and justice within the territorial boundaries of the state. The magistrate was authorized to exercise force in carrying out this task. By contrast, the government of the church was spiritual and was exercised by the office-bearers appointed from within the church. In relating yet distinguishing political and ecclesiastical rule, Calvin establishes a position which rejects anabaptist withdrawal from civil society on the one side and state control of the church on the other. His model also contrasts, as already noted, with tendencies in the Zurich reformation whereby civil and ecclesiastical jurisdiction were fused.[42] Nonetheless, in both his theology and Genevan ministry, it is clear that Calvin desired a partnership between church and state. The state was also responsible for enforcing the first table of the law. For Calvin, this entailed the protection of the Reformed church, the suppression of Roman Catholicism and the prohibition of the mass. The partnership here envisaged represented a Reformed commitment to social transformation. This is less evident in Lutheranism which was dominated by the doctrine of the two kingdoms.[43] The ideal of social transformation is one which characterized Reformed churches at other times and places, although from the early modern period onwards there was a perceived need for a greater distancing of the state from the church, and a for a stronger account of religious liberty. [44]

In Scotland, the *First Book of Discipline* (1560) [45] reveals an attempt not only to reform the life of the church, but to create a godly society in which there is a symbiotic relationship between the religious and the civil authorities. State recognition and defence of the Reformed church was sought, while the church resolved to participate in a system of comprehensive education, poor relief and the moral discipline of all citizens. In cases of serious criminal offence, the state was expected to act in order to supplement the disciplinary function of the church. The presbyterian form of church government took shape after the *Second Book of Discipline* (1578). [46] There emerged the now familiar hierarchy of church courts comprising the Kirk Session at the parochial level, the Synod at the regional level, and the General Assembly at the national level. The Presbytery emerged as a more significant court between the levels of the Synod and Session, and in recent times has replaced the former altogether. All lower courts of the church were made subject to the decisions of the national body. The local Session comprised elders and the parish minister who acted as its moderator, while the Presbytery and General Assembly were formed by an equal number of elders and ministers. Although never co-extensive with the Reformed tradition, the presbyterian system of church government became its most common expression. It reflects several features of much Reformed ecclesiology: the office of the ruling elder who is a layperson entrusted with powers of church government; the synodical nature of church government through courts and councils of men (and later women) who represented their local congregations; and the parity of ministers. Although at the regional and national levels, a minister would be elected to preside at the meeting of the court, it was made clear that he or she was always a *primus inter pares* who held this function only temporarily. Thus Reformed churches generally eschewed the episcopal office, the exception being the Reformed church in Hungary which to this day appoints bishops. In countries like Scotland, the rejection of episcopacy was compounded by the suspicion that bishops would inevitably become the appointees of a monarch generally unsympathetic to the cause of the Reformed religion. In this respect and others, the forms of church government adopted by the Reformed churches were closely allied to the emerging democratic spirit. [47]

THE DEVELOPMENT OF THE REFORMED CHURCHES

From the seventeenth century onwards the Reformed movement developed in a variety of circumstances, and revealed a heterogeneity not displayed by either Roman Catholicism or Lutheranism. In countries such as Scotland, Switzerland and the Netherlands, it became the majority religion. The Reformed church was here in effect the national and established church. In other European countries, Reformed churches were more often in a minority situation, while Dutch and Scottish immigration ensured that Reformed Christianity was a powerful force in the USA from the late seventeenth century.[48] Unlike the Lutheran church which everywhere adopted the *Augsburg Confession* (1530) as an authoritative standard, the Reformed churches tended to draft new confessions appropriate to the changing circumstances in which they found themselves. Thus the *Scots* (1560), *French* (1559) and *Belgic* (1561) *Confessions* were adopted in these countries, although the *Heidelberg Catechism* (1562) exercised a wider influence. The Synod of Dort (1618–19) was the nearest thing to an international Reformed council but its canons, although of wide impact, were not formally adopted by all Reformed churches. The *Westminster Confession* (1647) was originally designed for a united British Reformed church but was adopted only in Scotland and later in the Presbyterian churches of the USA. It reflects a temperate, consensus statement of Reformed orthodoxy and was the most significant confession of the seventeenth century. The accompanying statement on *The Form of Presbyterial Church Government* (1645) outlines a system of church order which was generally adopted in Scotland.

The *Westminster Confession* follows the magisterial Reformation in its teaching on the role of the civil magistrate. Although distinguishing the role of the civil and religious authorities, it concedes to the magistrate the power and even the duty to maintain the purity of the church in its doctrine, worship and government.[49] This was to prove unacceptable to a variety of Reformed groups, not least in the USA where the aforementioned chapter was rewritten by John Witherspoon, the only clergyman to sign the American Declaration of Independence. In England, the *Savoy Declaration* (1658) modified the *Westminster Confession* in opting for a greater degree of spiritual independence while also reflecting a more explicitly congregational model of church order.[50]

Eighteenth-century scruples about the role of the civil magistrate continued to be felt, although these were overshadowed in
the following century by reaction to the major doctrinal controversies. During this period issues pertaining to the interpretation
of Genesis 1, the role of biblical criticism, the rise of modern
science, and the moral difficulties attaching to the doctrines of predestination and hell led to various intellectual crises and heresy
trials within the Reformed churches. This situation is poignantly
evoked in the portrayal of Clarence Wilmot, the American Presbyterian pastor of John Updike's novel, *In the Beauty of the Lilies*.
Such theological upheaval had the effect of loosening affiliation
to the classical Reformed doctrinal standards and creating a
greater theological pluralism within the Reformed churches. It
was to have a profound effect upon ecclesiology in the twentieth
century, as will be shown.

Yet ecumenical impulses within the Reformed churches can be
detected from the sixteenth century onwards. Bucer had sought
to mediate between the Swiss Zwinglians and the Lutherans.
Calvin tried not only to unite the churches of the Swiss Reformation but also to overcome the differences with Lutheranism. In a
letter to Bullinger in 1540 he could write,

> We must purposefully and carefully cherish association and
> friendship with all true ministers of Christ ... in order that
> the churches to which we minister the Word of God may
> faithfully agree together ... As for me, so far as in me lies I
> will always labour to that end.[51]

This desire for friendship and co-operation throughout the Reformation was present in Calvin's dealings with other leading
figures including Luther, Melanchthon and Cranmer. The *Zurich
Consensus* of 1549, although unsuccessful in securing Lutheran
agreement, managed to unite the different sections of the Swiss
Reformation. In a circular letter of 1560, Calvin even harboured
the hope of there being a general church council which would be
attended by the Pope and other Roman Catholic bishops for the
sake of healing the divisions within Christendom.[52]

The subsequent history of the Reformed churches confirmed
this interest in unity. Under the guidance of Beza, a *Harmony of
Confessions* was drawn up in 1581. This includes material from
Lutheran, Reformed and Anglican confessional documents and is

designed to display an underlying agreement on doctrinal essentials. It also ventured the hope that political circumstances might permit the convening of a council which would lead to greater Christian unity throughout most of Europe. This irenic spirit can be found in several Dutch theologians of the seventeenth century. Junius, Arminius and Grotius all sought the greater unity of the church and at least an international Protestant consensus. The Westminster Assembly similarly sought theological unity and harmony throughout the churches of the United Kingdom. In nineteenth-century Prussia, the union of Lutheran and Reformed churches was effected, partly through the contribution of Schleiermacher, thus creating the largest single Protestant church in the world. In diverse ways, therefore, the Reformed churches have displayed repeated moves towards unity since the sixteenth century.

Nonetheless, these impulses towards ecumenical reconciliation have often been negated by the more fissiparous tendencies within the Reformation. The theological disputes involving Amyrauld and Arminius fractured the early unity of the Reformed church. Scottish Presbyterianism was split by the secessions of the eighteenth century, and then by the disruption of the nineteenth century when around a third of all ministers and members under the leadership of Thomas Chalmers left the established church over the issue of patronage. American Presbyterianism has similarly revealed numerous splits and divisions. Only in the twentieth century have some of these earlier divisions been overcome, and even here the success rate has been modest.[53] Compared to Lutheranism, Anglicanism, Methodism and Roman Catholicism, the Reformed churches have been characterized for much of their history by a regrettable fragmentation.

Both the centrifugal and centripetal tendencies of the Reformed churches can be explained by aforementioned features of their ecclesiology. The pattern in Switzerland, France, the Low Countries, the Palatinate, Scotland and in Eastern Europe was for the Reformed churches to group around different confessions in varying circumstances. They thus lacked the doctrinal cohesion of Lutheranism and the organizational homogeneity of Roman Catholicism. Efforts to create greater unity were often impeded by political circumstances. On the other hand, the doctrine of the church espoused by the Reformed confessions implied that where there was consensus on doctrinal essentials, unity was to be respected. This is reflected in Calvin's remarks about agreement on such matters and is implicit in the two notes of the visible church. As with Melanchthon's 'satis est' in the *Augsburg Confession*,[54] the Reformed were likewise convinced that there should be no obstacles to church union where the Word was preached and the sacraments correctly administered. They had never set out with the explicit aim of creating a new denomination. Their goal was ecclesiastical reform in accordance with apostolic teaching and the example of the early church. Thus the oneness, holiness, catholicity, and apostolicity of the church were presupposed in their account of the two marks by which the true church was known.

THE REFORMED CHURCHES IN THE ECUMENICAL MOVEMENT

Modern Reformed commitment to ecumenical endeavour is reflected in the formation of the World Presbyterian Alliance (1875) and the International Congregational Council (1891) which in 1970 merged to form the World Alliance of Reformed Churches.[55] It now comprises over 200 member churches from over 100 countries. Their combined membership exceeds 75 million. Admission to the Alliance is open to any applicant church 'which accepts Jesus Christ as Lord and Saviour; holds the Word of God given in the Scriptures of the Old and New Testaments to be the supreme authority in matters of faith and life; acknowledges the need for continuing reformation of the Church catholic; whose position in faith and evangelism is in general agreement with that of the historic Reformed confessions, recognizing that the Reformed tradition is a biblical, evangelical and doctrinal ethos, rather than any narrow and exclusive definition of faith and order.'[56]

As one might expect from the development of Reformed Christianity, the Alliance embraces a diversity of churches. Many are presbyterian but some are congregational in their style of church government. Hussite and Waldensian churches are indebted to figures of reform prior to the sixteenth century. Many are committed not only to historic confessions but also to more recently composed doctrinal statements.[57] Some member churches are the result of recent transconfessional unions. Most though not all now ordain women. The preponderance of member churches is now in the southern hemisphere, and only a minority are state or national churches. Today the largest presbyterian churches are in South Korea. In 1982 the Alliance declared as *status confessionis* its opposition to apartheid, thus suspending from membership, until recently, the white Dutch Reformed Churches in South Africa. The Alliance is committed both to the work of the World Council of Churches and to the pursuit of a range of bilateral dialogues with other communions. It has contributed much to the theological and administrative leadership of the WCC in the twentieth century.[58] The following samples of bilateral dialogue may serve to illustrate current themes in Reformed ecclesiology.

The Leuenberg Agreement (1973)[59]

This was drawn up by Reformed and Lutheran theologians in Europe as a basis for church fellowship, further doctrinal explorations and mutual commitment to wider ecumenical activity. In seeking to minimize traditional differences over christology, the Lord's Supper, predestination and church order, it begins by affirming the marks of the church founded upon Christ. 'The church is founded upon Jesus Christ alone. It is he who gathers the church and sends it forth, by the bestowal of his salvation in preaching and the sacraments. In the view of the Reformation, it follows that agreement in the right teaching of the gospel, and in the right administration of the sacraments, is the necessary and sufficient prerequisite for the true unity of the church.'[60]

This account of the church is set within a framework of the universal purposes of God. 'The gospel is the message of Jesus Christ, the salvation of the world, in fulfilment of the promise given to the people of the Old Covenant.'[61] It is to this cosmic salvation that the Christian bears witness in a life of worship, gratitude and service. The church is thus dependent upon Jesus Christ and lives between the time of his saving work and his final redemption of the world. With agreement secure on this point, it is argued that there is sufficient common ground on christology, the nature of the real presence in the Lord's Supper, and the doctrine of predestination to seek full ecclesial fellowship. In its comments on predestination, Leuenberg reveals the extent of the Reformed shift that has taken place since the seventeenth century.

In the gospel we have the promise of God's unconditional acceptance of sinful man (sic). Whoever puts his trust in the gospel can know that he is saved, and praise God for his election ... The witness of the Scriptures to Christ forbids us to suppose that God has uttered an eternal decree for the final condemnation of specific individuals or of a particular people.[62]

The ecclesiological significance of this revision of the classical Augustinian-Reformed doctrine of election should not be under-estimated.

The Presence of Christ in Church and World (1977)[63]

The report of the dialogue between Reformed and Roman Catholic representatives reveals some convergences which at least reduce in significance many of the standard disagreements between these groups. The *loci* include Scripture and tradition, the nature of the eucharist, the office of the ordained ministry, church government, and the concept of apostolic succession. By es-tablishing agreement on the trinitarian action of God, the person of Christ, creation and the end of all things, the dialogue is able to position the doctrine of the church in such a way as to establish im-portant common ground. What is significant in this repositioning of ecclesiology is the way in which it represents an advance on both classical Reformed and Roman Catholic views. The goal of God's action in creation and redemption is the restoration and completion of all things. This is grounded in Jesus Christ through whom God creates, redeems and perfects the world. The final scope and object of God's action, therefore, is not the church but the world. This enables the report to describe the church in a series of highly significant images derived from Scripture. It is the 'visible witness and sign of the liberating will of God, of the re-demption granted in Jesus Christ, and of the kingdom of peace that is to come'.[64] The church in its knowledge of Christ through the Spirit lives as a community, a *koinonia*, which comes together to worship, to be edified, and to be nourished by the sacrament. It is also described as 'the pilgrim people of God on the way through the world'.[65] As such it bears witness to Christ as the Lord not only of the church but also the world. Through worship, witness and service, therefore, the church is directed towards the entire creation and its salvation in Christ.

God's Reign and Our Unity (1984)[66]

Similar ecclesiological themes can be found in this Anglican–Reformed dialogue. It has a strong missiological impetus which informs much of what it says about the church. 'The goal of church unity is the reconciliation of all humanity and the whole universe to God.'[67] In grateful acknowledgement of this as God's gift in Christ and in service to it, the church exists as God's apostolic people. Here again we encounter images of the church as an eschatological sign, a foretaste, and a pilgrim people.

> It is essential to approach the question of unity among Christians in this missionary and eschatological context. The Church is sent into the world as sign, instrument and first-fruits of a reality which comes from beyond history – the Kingdom, or reign of God. The unity of the Church is not simply an end in itself because the Church does not exist for itself but for the glory of God and as a sign, instrument and first-fruits of the divine purpose to reconcile all things in heaven and earth through Christ.[68]

This understanding of the church informs subsequent discussion of preaching, eucharist and the ministry. In both the proclamation of the Word and the celebration of the sacraments, Christ is actively present by the power of the Holy Spirit. The church can thus look forward in its worship, fellowship and witness to his future reign. The report insists, moreover, that the eucharist, as 'fundamental to and constitutive of the life of the church'[69] is the proper form of worship each week on the Lord's Day. On the issue of ministry, the report in many ways follows the movement of *Baptism, Eucharist and Ministry* (1982). It locates the ordained ministry of Word and sacrament within the context of the ministry of the whole church which in turn is dependent upon the ministry of Christ, the eternal Son. The ministry of leadership is perceived as essential to the life of the church but neither as prior to nor apart from the ministry of the whole people of God. On the subject of the apostolic succession of bishops, the report in affirming a threefold order of ministry argues that episcopal succession provides a 'ground of assurance' that the church's teaching is that of Christ and the apostles. This seems to move in the direction of claiming that a historical episcopate contributes to the well being (*bene esse*) rather than the essence (*esse*) of the church.[70]

The ecumenical advances of these bilateral dialogues reveal important shifts in Reformed ecclesiology. These have been brought about by widespread revisions of historical teaching on predestination, the scope of salvation, and the kingdom of God. The doctrine of election attests not so much an eternal separation grounded in the divine will between the elect and the reprobate, as God's decision in Christ to redeem the whole creation.[71] The anticipation of the eschatological kingdom renders the church, not so much an ark of salvation, but as the people of God who witness, signify and anticipate its coming. This gives ecclesiology a stronger missiological impetus and a political, world-affirming orientation. While one can find analogous shifts in the teaching of other churches, most notably in Vatican II, it is necessary in this context to consider what it entails for Reformed theology.

The setting aside of the doctrine of double predestination in favour of a more Barthian approach with universalist strains has had a profound impact upon ecumenical dialogue and ecclesiology. The church is no longer co-extensive with the body of the elect but is rather the sign of a salvation effected in Christ which is yet to become universally known and appropriated at the end of the world. The kingdom of God is a final eschatological reality whereas the church is surpassable. The church's task is to bear witness, to anticipate and to look for the coming of the kingdom. This account of the church as a penultimate reality which attests a more ultimate eschatological *polis* is present in ecclesial images such as sign, foretaste, and the pilgrim people of God. These have important ramifications for any contemporary Reformed doctrine of the church.[72]

One virtue of this shift in ecclesiological focus is the way in which it enables a rethinking of the church's relationship to Judaism. The Reformed churches are not alone in seeing a radical revision of earlier supersessionist theologies as a priority for contemporary ecclesiology, but within discussions of Reformation theology this has been acutely felt.[73] Renewed attention to the image of the church as the pilgrim people of God makes possible greater continuity with Judaism. Similar images are applied by the Old Testament to Israel. At least in some strands of Scripture, the divine vocation of the Jews is to be a light to the nations, a witness to the nature and purposes of God for all creation. Where the church is likewise conceived, its unity with Israel, as for example in Romans 9–11, becomes more apparent. Reformed theology with its traditional perception of the oneness of the covenant, and the unity of law and gospel is well placed to integrate the histories of Israel and the church. Attention has already been drawn to the manner in which the Reformed confessions perceived the church as the community of the elect under Christ's headship from Adam onwards. The church thus comprehends Jews and Gentiles. On the other hand, the distinction between the invisible and the visible church now becomes problematic. As Lindbeck points out, the concept of an invisible Israel looks very odd.[74] As the pilgrim people of God who signify the coming kingdom, the church is inherently visible. Moreover, the notion that the invisible church constitutes the elect of all ages must now give way to the concept of the eschatological kingdom. So too must the doctrine of Cyprian, appropriated by the Reformers, that outside of the church there is no ordinary possibility of salvation. Any remaining sense in which the church can be regarded as invisible must derive not from notions of election or the delimiting of salvation but only from the continuity of the pilgrim people across time and space.

The missionary focus of recent ecclesiology also draws attention to the relative lack of interest in this theme in the Reformed confessions of the sixteenth and seventeenth centuries. This has doubtless to do with a political context in which all citizens, apart from Jews and heretics, were adjudged to be members of the church and subject to its discipline. This view is now anachronistic as is the accompanying configuration of church and state. Although there are dangers of exaggerating this, here the model of the church as the pilgrim people of God can accommodate a greater dissociation of church and civil society. It is more appropriate to minority churches, and to national or established institutions overburdened with guilt about the loss of mass membership and social influence. A more dialectical relating of church and society may even make for effective prophetic witness and counter-cultural protest.

Finally, the model of the church as the people of God may convey a greater sense of the mobility of church structures and patterns of worship over the ages. Its adaptation and assimilation to a wide range of contexts can explain the lack of any single pattern of life forms across time and space. Greater sense can be made of change and revision to earlier institutional expressions now found wanting. Thus the recognition that ordination should no longer be restricted to men can be welcomed as an innovation in church order, but as one sanctioned by the central message of Scripture. On the other hand, the need for identity and continuity in widely divergent circumstances may also provide an argument for institutions like the historical episcopate which can provide focus and a sense of continuity with the pilgrim people throughout the ages.[75] It may serve to remind the church of its identity based upon the gospel of Christ as attested by the apostles. The church's well being may thus be promoted by the succession of bishops, even if it has survived and prospered at times without them.

This last argument of course is not widely accepted throughout Reformed communities. In this respect, it draws attention to a range of problems which have to be surmounted if further ecumenical convergence is to take place. In conclusion, I shall select three of those problems which are amongst the most pressing and which reveal something of the pluralism and fragmentation of Reformed Christianity in today's world. This diversity within the modern Reformed tradition accounts for much of the frustration expressed by our dialogue partners when they fail to receive clear delineation of the Reformed position on any given doctrine.

The doctrine of ministry

Within the writings of the magisterial Reformers, we can detect an understanding of ordained ministry as set within the church and as providing leadership of God's people through Word and sacrament. This is viewed as a divine gift to the church from the time of Jesus' calling of the twelve, and it is prefigured by Old Testament models of leadership. Such an account of the ordained ministry is held in conjunction with the doctrine of the priesthood of all believers, it being important to understand that the latter does not entail the negation of the former.

Yet it is doubtful whether this commands widespread confidence throughout Reformed communities today. One hears repeated complaints that such a high doctrine of ordination is crippling the ministry of the whole people of God. In creating a sharp distinction between minister and people, it occludes a proper emphasis upon the ministry of the whole church and the range of charisms imparted to its membership. This is exemplified in calls for persons outwith the ranks of the clergy to administer the sacraments and to conduct public worship. It has been pointed out that even in formal bilateral dialogues several different and conflicting Reformed theologies of ministry operate. These range from positions which emphasize congregationalist themes through those which articulate classical Reformed approaches to others which adopt something approaching a traditional Catholic model of ministry.[76] It seems likely that with the rise of independent Protestant church groups, the understanding of ministry found in Calvin and the confessions is likely to be questioned if not ignored.

The significance accorded the sacraments

We have already noted the importance assigned to the eucharist in *God's Reign and Our Unity*. Here it belongs with the proclamation of the Word at the heart of the weekly diet of worship. While there is support for this in the writings of Calvin and others, it is hard to deny that priority was generally attached to the preaching of the Word over against the sacraments which tend to confirm the former in more visible and tangible forms. The view thus emerged that the weekly gathering of God's people must always involve the speaking and hearing of the Word, but not always the dispensing of the sacraments. Although the latter as divine gifts are not to be neglected they are largely annexed to the proclamation of the gospel. Ecumenical theology, however, tends to move in the direction of juxtaposing Word and sacraments to the extent that the celebration of the Lord's Supper becomes an integral part of the weekly diet of worship. Yet this is still largely foreign to the worship of most Reformed communities in the world today, and, if ecumenical progress is to be achieved, a commitment to the more frequent celebration of the Lord's Supper is probably required alongside a reassessment of its theological significance.[77]

Other problems attach to the doctrine of baptism. Reformed theologians such as Barth and Moltmann have been in the vanguard of those who have expressed doubts about the theology underlying the practice of infant baptism. Is it a sacramental act? Did the Reformers err in trying to unite baptism and the Lord's

Supper under a single generic concept of sacramentality? Does it belong to an outmoded Christendom model by virtue of which a person was effectively born into both membership of civil society and the church? The increasing call for dual practice – infant baptism and believers' baptism – within the Reformed churches threatens to destabilize much of the ecumenical consensus that has been achieved in this area.

The office of the bishop

Although some ecumenical rapprochement has been achieved between Lutheran and Episcopalian ecclesiologies on the subject of the historic episcopate, this is viewed with a degree of scepticism amongst Reformed communities. While a personal episcopal office may bear witness to the apostolic faith, the Reformed complaint is that it also carries the risk of distraction through the elevation of individuals to a higher and non-parochial ministerial function.[78] A threat to the principle of the parity of ministry and to conciliar models of church government involving the eldership is still deeply felt at this point, even where it is conceded that presbyterianism is inherently weak in providing personal oversight at the regional level.

These concluding remarks are raised not to support any Reformed retrenchment or through a desire to ignore genuine ecumenical progress. They merely indicate the spectrum of views that can be found throughout Reformed congregations and are intended to caution against the assumption of a growing homogeneity which leads towards ecumenical convergence. Nonetheless, the cherished principle of *ecclesia semper reformanda* should remind us that a vigorous reassessment of historical practice and contemporary trends in the light of God's Word is an ongoing task.

FURTHER READING

Avis, Paul, *The Church in the Theology of the Reformers*. Marshall, Morgan & Scott 1981.
Leith, John, *Introduction to the Reformed Tradition*. John Knox Press, Atlanta, 1977.
McGrath, Alister, *Reformation Thought*. 3rd edn, Blackwell 1999.

McGregor, Geddes, *Corpus Christi: The Nature of the Church According to the Reformed Tradition*. Macmillan 1959.

McKim, Donald, ed., *Major Themes in the Reformed Tradition*. Eerdmans, Grand Rapids, 1992.

McNeill, John T. and Nichols, James Hastings, *Ecumenical Testimony: The Concern for Christian Unity within the Reformed and Presbyterian Churches*. Westminster Press, Philadelphia, 1974.

Rohls, Jan, *Reformed Confessions: Theology from Zurich to Barmen*. Westminster John Knox Press 1998.

Sell, Alan P. F., *A Reformed, Evangelical, Catholic Theology: The Contribution of the World Alliance of Reformed Churches, 1875–1982*. Eerdmans, Grand Rapids, 1991.

Wendel, F., *Calvin*. Collins 1963.

NOTES

1. Cf. Pelikan, Jaroslav, *Reformation of Church and Dogma (1300–1700)* (Chicago, University of Chicago Press, 1984), pp. 173ff.
2. The extent to which the Reformation doctrine of the invisible church generated problems of institutional expression is explored in detail by Avis, Paul, *The Church in the Theology of the Reformers*. Marshall, Morgan & Scott 1981.
3. *Augsburg Confession* VII.
4. Rupp, G. E. and Drewery, B., ed., Martin Luther (Edward Arnold 1970), pp. 167–9.
5. *Institutes* IV. i.1. All references are to the Ford Lewis Battles translation in the Library of Christian Classics, edited by J. T. McNeill, Philadelphia, Westminster Press, 1960.
6. *Institutes* IV.i.2.
7. Cf. Stephens, W. P., *The Theology of Huldrych Zwingli* (Clarendon Press 1986), pp. 260ff.
8. E.g. *Scots Confession* V. Cf. Rohls, Jan, *Reformed Confessions: Theology from Zurich to Barmen* (Louisville, Westminster John Knox Press, 1998), pp. 166ff.
9. *Second Helvetic Confession* XVII.
10. Rohls, Jan, *Reformed Confessions*, p. 171.
11. *Institutes* II.vi.1.
12. *Westminster Confession* X. In this respect, the Westminster divines were merely repeating the teaching of the *Scots Confession* XVI.

13. *Institutes* IV.i.4. Calvin's frequent use of organic metaphors for the church is noted by Milner, Benjamin C. Jr., *Calvin's Doctrine of the Church* (Leiden, Brill, 1970), pp. 7ff. This expresses the manner in which the church is extended over time and has a history of growth though not without its traumas and ailments.
14. *Institutes* IV.i.11.
15. *Institutes* IV.i.8.
16. *Institutes* IV.i.19.
17. *Commentary on I Corinthians 3.11*. Cf. Wendel, F., *Calvin* (Collins 1963), p. 311.
18. Calvin, John and Sadoleto, Jacopo, *A Reformation Debate* (New York, Harper Torchbooks, 1966), p. 60.
19. *Institutes* IV.ii.1.
20. *Institutes* IV.ii.2.
21. *Westminster Confession of Faith* XXV.v & vi. The *Westminster Confession* remains the subordinate standard of the Church of Scotland. In 1986, however, the General Assembly passed a declaratory act explicitly dissociating itself from these references.
22. *Institutes* IV.ii.12.
23. This is argued, for example, by McGrath, Alister, *Reformation Thought* (2nd edn, Blackwell 1993), p. 198.
24. Wright, David F., ed., *Common Places of Martin Bucer* (Sutton Courtenay Press 1972), p. 205.
25. *Scots Confession*. Chapter XVIII cites as the third note of the church, 'ecclesiastical discipline uprightly ministered, as God's Word prescribes, whereby vice is repressed and virtue nourished'.
26. Cf. the discussion in Wendel, *Calvin*, p. 302.
27. Cf. McKee, Elsie, 'The Offices of Elders and Deacons in the Classical Reformed Tradition', in McKim, Donald K., ed., *Major Themes in the Reformed Tradition* (Eerdmans, Grand Rapids, 1992), pp. 344–53.
28. Cf. Milner, Benjamin J. Jr., *Calvin's Doctrine of the Church*, pp. 134ff.
29. *Institutes* IV.iii.2.
30. *Institutes* IV.iii.15.
31. *Institutes* IV.iii.1.
32. *Second Helvetic Confession* XVIII.

33. Cf. Ainslie, J. L., *The Doctrines of Ministerial Order in the Reformed Church of the Sixteenth and Seventeenth Centuries* (T. & T. Clark 1940), pp. 34ff.
34. *Institutes* IV.iv.2.
35. *Institutes* IV.ix.8.
36. *Institutes* IV.xii.5.
37. *Institutes* IV.xii.7.
38. *Institutes* IV.xii.9.
39. 'The relation of church and state in Zwingli is dramatically symbolised in the statue by the Wasserkirche in Zurich, where he stands with the bible in one hand and a sword in the other.' Stephens, W. P., *The Theology of Huldrych Zwingli*, p. 282.
40. Cf. the discussion in Wendel, *Calvin*, pp. 69ff.
41. Busch, Eberhard, 'Church and Politics in the Reformed Tradition', *Major Themes in the Reformed Tradition*, pp. 180–95.
42. Cf. McGrath, Alister, *Reformation Thought*, pp. 196f.
43. The two-kingdoms doctrine, however, was interpreted in various ways, not all of which were radically different from Reformed views. Cf. Moltmann, Jürgen, 'Luther's Doctrine of the Two Kingdoms and Its Use Today', *On Human Dignity* (SCM Press 1984) pp. 61–78.
44. Cf. Little, David, 'Reformed Faith and Religious Liberty', *Major Themes in the Reformed Tradition*, pp. 196–213.
45. Cameron, J. K., ed., *The First Book of Discipline*. St Andrew Press 1972.
46. Kirk, James, ed., *The Second Book of Discipline*. St Andrew Press 1980.
47. McNeill, John T., *The History and Character of Calvinism* (Oxford University Press 1954), pp. 411ff.
48. For an analysis of the Dutch Reformed influence in the USA see Hesselink, John, 'Some Distinctive Contributions of the Dutch-Arminian Reformed Tradition', in Willis, David and Welker, Michael, ed., *Toward the Future of the Reformed Theology* (Grand Rapids, Eerdmans, 1999), pp. 421–43.
49. *Westminster Confession* XXIII.
50. 'The Savoy Declaration', in Schaff, Philip, ed., *Creeds and Confessions of Christendom* III (Hodder & Stoughton 1877), pp. 707ff.
51. Quoted by McNeill, John T., and Nichols, James Hastings, *Ecumenical Testimony: The Concern for Christian Unity within the*

Reformed and Presbyterian Churches (Philadelphia, Westminster Press, 1974), p. 18.

52. Cf. McNeill and Nichols, *Ecumenical Testimony*, p. 24.
53. The two large Presbyterian churches of Scotland were reunited into a single Church of Scotland in 1929, whereas the Presbyterian Church in the United States and the United Presbyterian Church in the USA were united in 1983. Other unions within Protestant traditions took place in Canada, Australia and New Zealand this century. Cf. McNeill and Nichols, *Ecumenical Testimony*, pp. 235ff.
54. 'For it is sufficient for the true unity of the Christian church that the Gospel be preached in conformity with a pure understanding of it and that the sacraments be administered in accordance with the divine Word.' *Augsburg Confession* VII.
55. Information extracted from WARC website: http://warc.ch/
56. Cf. Sell, Alan P. F., *A Reformed, Evangelical, Catholic Theology* (Grand Rapids, Eerdmans, 1991), p. 2. Sell's book provides the most comprehensive discussion of the theological work undertaken by WARC.
57. Many of these are collected in Vischer, Lukas, ed., *Reformed Witness Today: A Collection of Confessional and Statements of Faith Issued by Reformed Churches*. Evangelische Arbeitsstelle Ökumene Schweiz, Berne, 1982.
58. This has even resulted in complaints that the WCC has been too dominated by Anglo-Saxon, Reformed influences: Institute for Ecumenical Research, Strasbourg, *Crisis and Challenge of the Ecumenical Movement* (Geneva, WCC Publications, 1994), p. 6.
59. The English translation of the text is reprinted in Rusch, William G. and Martensen, Daniel F., ed., *The Leuenberg Agreement and Lutheran-Reformed Relationships* (Minneapolis, Augsburg Fortress, 1989), pp. 139–54.
60. *The Leuenberg Agreement and Lutheran–Reformed Relationships* para. 2, p. 145.
61. *The Leuenberg Agreement and Lutheran–Reformed Relationships* para. 7, p. 146.
62. *The Leuenberg Agreement and Lutheran–Reformed Relationships* paras. 24–5, p. 150.
63. 'The Presence of Christ in Church and World: Final Report of the Dialogue Between the World Alliance of Reformed

Churches and the Secretariat for Promoting Christian Unity, 1977', in Meyer, Harding and Vischer, Lukas, ed., *Growth in Agreement: Reports and Agreed Statement of Ecumenical Conversation on a World Level* (New York, Paulist Press, 1984), pp. 33–463.

64. 'The Presence of Christ in Church and World' para. 54, p. 447.
65. 'The Presence of Christ in Church and World' para. 60, p. 448.
66. *God's Reign and Our Unity: The Report of the Anglican-Reformed International Commission 1981–1984.* SPCK 1984.
67. *God's Reign and Our Unity* para. 25, p. 16.
68. *God's Reign and Our Unity* para. 29, p. 19.
69. *God's Reign and Our Unity* para. 71, p. 44.
70. This is the claim of the Lutheran-Anglican Porvoo Declaration: *Together in Mission and Ministry: The Porvoo Common Statement with Essays on Church and Ministry in Northern Europe.* Church House Publishing 1993.
71. Karl Barth's doctrine of election is clearly a significant ecumenical influence in this respect: *Church Dogmatics II/2.* T. & T. Clark 1957.
72. In much of what follows I am indebted to Lindbeck, George, 'The Church', in Wainwright, Geoffrey, ed., *Keeping the Faith: Essays to Mark the Centenary of Lux Mundi* (Philadelphia, Fortress, 1988), pp. 179–208.
73. The most recent Leuenberg report addresses this issue. Schwier, Helmut (ed.), *Church and Israel: A Contribution from the Reformation Churches in Europe to the Relationship between Christians and Jews* (Lembeck: Frankfurt am Main, 2001). See also Vischer, Lucas, 'The Church – Mother of the Believers', in Willis, David and Welker, Michael, ed., *Toward the Future of Reformed Theology* (Grand Rapids, Eerdmans, 1999), p. 269.
74. Lindbeck, George, 'The Church', p. 183.
75. This is argued sensitively by Lindbeck, 'The Church', pp. 196ff.
76. This is shown by Andre Birmerlé in an unpublished paper. I owe the reference to Fries, Paul R., 'Fundamental Consensus and Church Fellowship: A Reformed Perspective', in Burgess, Joseph A., ed., *In Search of Christian Unity* (Minneapolis, Fortress, 1991), pp. 152–3.
77. For a Reformed defence of a 'higher' doctrine of the sacraments and the need for frequent celebration see MacGregor,

Geddes, *Corpus Christi: The Nature of the Church According to the Reformed Tradition* (Macmillan 1959), pp. 176–98.

78. This is reflected in the reaction of many Reformed churches to the teaching of BEM. Cf. Thurian, Max, ed., *Churches Respond to BEM: Official Responses to the 'Baptism, Eucharist and Ministry' Text*, Vol. 1. Geneva, World Council of Churches, 1986.

3

The Methodist Churches
David Carter

INTRODUCTION

To the question, 'Is there a Wesleyan ecclesiology?', Albert Outler, doyen of the American renaissance of Wesleyan theology, gave the response: 'The answer "Yes" says too much; "No" says too little. Others have argued that there is no Wesleyan doctrine of the Church as such, since John Wesley never undertook a systematic exposition of his theology or ecclesiology.' Many have regarded Methodist ecclesiology as purely pragmatic, if not also downright ambiguous.

It will be contended that there is an authentic Methodist ecclesiology, despite the fluidity and complexity of its historical development. It still awaits the attention of a systematic theologian capable of discerning its total vision and drawing all its strands together. There is, however, clear continuity between the form of ecclesial awareness that developed in the earliest Methodist societies and the ecclesial sense of present day Methodists. A renewed sense of ecclesial belonging was important from the beginning of the Methodist Revival; as James Rigg (1821–1909) put it, Methodism was as much a revival of primitive church life as of primitive doctrine.[1] Nevertheless, the complex evolution of Methodism from 'society' to 'church' and the empirical, ad hoc nature of so much Methodist theology both at the time of the Wesleys and subsequently, make difficulties for the work of the systematic ecclesiologist. One should not exaggerate the importance of the Church–society tension in Methodism. As Benjamin Gregory (1820–1900) emphasizes, the Church, in Methodist consciousness, is a society.[2]

The particular contribution of Methodism to ecclesiology is the 'Connexional Principle', which well illustrates the difficulty of making any hard and fast distinction between pragmatic and theological elements in Methodist ecclesiology. Originally a pragmatic device for missionary and disciplinary effectiveness, the 'Connexion' came to be valued by Methodists as reflecting their sense of the interlocking, interdependent nature of the Church at every level. They believed its spirit reflected the inter-dependence of the apostolic churches as recorded in Scripture.[3] With the exception of a few smaller bodies that have embraced an effectively Independent ecclesiology, Connexionalism is still the principle underlying Methodist polities, however much they may differ in fine detail. Methodists may claim to have been the first in modern times to rediscover and practise the concept of the Church as *koinonia*, before the revival of *koinonia* ecclesiology in the Roman Catholic Church under Möhler and its general ecume-nical reception in the present century.

METHODIST SELF-UNDERSTANDING

Methodism began as a religious society, intended to promote reli-gious revival in eighteenth-century England within the Church of England. The Wesleys had no desire to create a separate church. They saw the fellowship of their societies as complementing the religious life and nourishment that the Methodists should find in the established Church. They particularly expected the Metho-dists to receive the sacraments and to attend the offices of Morning and Evening Prayer at the parish church. Many Metho-dists, however, from early on, preferred the 'preaching services' and the other means of grace of their own societies. From the beginning, Methodism was an *ecclesiola*, or 'mini-church' within a wider church and this brought complex tensions. John Wesley's own frustration with the limitations of the Anglican system and action increasingly drove him to behaviour that threatened a possible split.

In 1784, believing that the pastoral provision made by the Anglican bishops for America was totally inadequate, Wesley felt compelled to provide for the creation of a new church there, pro-viding it with a threefold ministry and a version of the Prayer Book.[4] From then on, American Methodism developed quite separately as a church from Anglicanism. In England, a split came more gradually. In 1795 the Conference authorized its itinerant preachers to celebrate the sacraments where the people and trustees of the societies wished it. This clear breach with Anglican discipline led ineluctably to Methodism becoming a separate church.[5] However, for a generation and more after this, many Methodists continued to attend both Anglican services and their own. Many cherished continuing regard for the 'old church'. The Conference regretted the breach and did not restore the sign of the laying on of hands in presbyteral ordination till 1836.

The language of a society rather than a church continued to characterize much Methodist terminology and practice. The local churches continued to be called societies till very recently. The use of the expression Wesleyan Methodist *Church* only became official in 1897. In the ecumenical era, some Methodists have argued that Methodism should seek, once again, to become a society with a particular vocation to preaching and Christian holiness within a reunited church. Methodism has, perhaps, a particularly deep sense of needing the complementary witness of other traditions in order to fulfil its catholic potential.

Methodism also continued to require certain disciplines of its members that were societal rather than obligations of churchmanship *per se*. Such was the requirement to 'meet in class', which was enforced until the late nineteenth century. When other Free Church people accused Methodism of enforcing a discipline that was not demanded by Scripture, Methodists riposted that this was an aspect of their discipline involved in the decision to be a Methodist rather than to join another branch of the Church.

The vast majority of Methodists are aware of belonging to a distinct ecclesial body with a very distinctive and cherished ethos of its own. The use of Charles Wesley's hymns, the connexional system, the constant itinerancy and interchange of ministers, the practice of particular Methodist forms of devotion such as the Covenant Service, as well as the importance of the class meeting, have given Methodism a tremendous sense of cohesion.

In the Deed of Union of 1932, British Methodism staked out its essential ecclesial claim. 'The Methodist Church claims and cherishes its place in the Holy Catholic Church, which is the Body of Christ.'[6] This clarifies Methodism's claim to authentic churchly status, while affirming quite clearly the recognition of other traditions. In general, the Methodist attitude to other Trinitarian churches has been tolerant and eirenic, though in the nineteenth century, despite Wesley's great regard for the holiness of many Roman Catholic saints, there was deep suspicion of 'Roman superstition' and Tractarian 'Romanizing errors'. The combined effect of the Oxford Movement and the later movement for Free Church co-operation was to bring most Methodists much closer to the other Free Churches and make them less enthusiastic about their Anglican heritage. However, since the 1920s relationships with Anglicans have greatly improved, as they have also with the Roman Catholic Church since Vatican II.[7] British Methodism has affirmed its recognition of the orders and sacraments of its sister Trinitarian churches.

The famous Liverpool Minutes of 1820 deprecated a partisan spirit among Methodists and called for 'the kind and catholic spirit of primitive Methodism' to be displayed to all who held the Headship of Christ.[8] Both British and American Methodism experienced considerable schism in the nineteenth century. These splits have largely since been healed, but have left a heritage in differing attitudes to central authority within the Connexions and towards ecumenical partners. Broadly speaking, those in the original Wesleyan tradition tended to emphasize the importance of strong connexional discipline and often maintained the regard for Anglicanism of the early Wesleyans. The inheritors of the more populist traditions of the non-Wesleyan churches tended to prefer weaker central authority, more local autonomy and closer relations with the other Free Churches rather than with Anglicans.

Many Methodist churches are now involved in Local Ecumenical Partnerships, principally with Anglican and United Reformed churches. British Methodism looks especially for closer relationships with those two churches. Most modern Methodists have a wider awareness of the general Christian tradition than their predecessors, who often had little contact with other churches.

THE SOURCES OF METHODIST ECCLESIOLOGY

The ultimate source of Methodist ecclesiology is the reflection of the Methodist people on their own experience in the light of their reading of the New Testament. This was particularly clear in the writing of Benjamin Gregory and W. F. Slater.

Wesley claimed to be *homo unius libri*, a man of one book, the Bible. It is clear, though, that his ecclesiology was influenced by tradition, reason and experience. Ted Campbell shows it is often difficult to distinguish between when Wesley was influenced by a lesson he derived from the primitive Church and when he looked for precedents to justify what he had already decided, from experience, was good practice.[9] Nor is it always easy to distinguish between when Wesley was providing for ecclesial necessities and when he was merely providing for the Society.

Wesley was influenced by his Anglican inheritance and by his sense of the exigencies of mission. His practice, if not always his theory, was driven by the latter. In a famous statement, he said that he regarded the salvation of souls as 'the end of all ecclesiastical order'.[10] The element of pragmatism in Wesley was often in tension with his regard for tradition. He often felt impelled to part company with Anglican discipline (e.g. in his disregard of parochial boundaries). His pragmatism was governed by his faithfulness to the mission of the Church as he discerned it in the New Testament.

One can see this as dominant in Methodist ecclesiology if one sees the mission as including not merely evangelism but nurturing in the faith. The Methodist societies came into being when some of his first converts asked Wesley to help them grow in faith. Modern scholarship has emphasized 'accountable discipleship' as at being the heart of the Methodist discipline, determining the structure of the society classes, where people accounted to each other, and to the leader, for their spiritual growth.[11] The early Conferences frequently discussed ecclesiological questions, but little systematic ecclesiology was formulated. The most important expression of ecclesial awareness available to ordinary Methodists was in the hymnody of the Wesleys. Charles wrote many hymns descriptive both of the life of the early Church and of the societies. Several of these hymns have remained perennially popular in Methodism. They lyrically describe the mutual care exercised in the societies and their lively sense of the presence of Christ in their meetings.

In the mid-nineteenth century, Wesleyan Methodism faced considerable hostility, from Independents and internal dissidents who alleged that the authority of the ministry was excessive and unscriptural, and from Tractarians who denied the churchly status of Methodism. Several able Wesleyan scholars wrote considerable apologias for their system. They contended that, though no one ecclesial system could be deduced as prescriptive from Scripture, Scripture nevertheless showed that the Wesleyan system was nearer in spirit to the apostolic church than any other system.[12] They also argued that, on the global scale, Methodism was incomparably more effective in evangelism. Alfred Barrett defended the polity of Methodism and the exercise of ministerial authority within it and James Rigg defended the connexional system, while Benjamin Gregory provided a biblical ecclesiology which implicitly pointed to the appropriateness of the Wesleyan system.

In the early years of the twentieth century, Methodist ecclesiology became more severely biblical, particularly in the work of two New Testament scholars, Newton Flew and Harold Roberts. Flew's *Jesus and His Church* (1937) was an up-to-date exposition of the New Testament doctrine of the Church. Flew also masterminded the ecclesiological statement of the British Conference of 1937, *The Nature of the Christian Church* (hereafter cited as NCC),[13] which defended Methodist church principles as consistent with the New Testament and justified the claims in the Deed of Union. At this stage, Methodism made it clear that it stood on the Protestant side of the great ecclesiological debates in the interwar Faith and Order Movement, to which NCC was intended as a contribution. Later, Roberts examined the relationship of Church and Kingdom.

The Nature of the Christian Church was the first official British Methodist ecclesiological statement after reunion. Coming at a time when Methodism was entering the ecumenical movement and had also drawn much closer to the other Free Churches, it gave little attention to the peculiarities of Methodism, and, strikingly, said nothing about Connexionalism. In 1999, a new ecclesiological statement, *Called To Love and Praise* (hereinafter cited as CLP) was approved to the Conference.[14] It addressed the issues that had arisen in the intervening sixty years since the production of NCC and aimed at giving a clearer account of Methodism to ecumenical partners. It also gave the fullest account yet of ecclesiological methodology and presuppositions. It emphasized the triangular relationship of Scripture, tradition and experience in ecclesiology. Scripture is the most important witness to Christ, but Scripture is always Scripture interpreted. Tradition is the context that shapes our use of Scripture, while Scripture is also 'the resource by which the tradition is deepened and purified'. Finally, 'experience and discernment, nurtured, stimulated and corrected by the witness of Scripture and tradition help to confirm the truth that is in Christ.' In such a way Christians may have sufficient authority, or light, by which to travel (CLP 1.2.10). The treatment of *koinonia* in CLP particularly exemplifies these traits (CLP 3.1.5–11).

Two issues now need further attention in Methodist ecclesiology. The first is the nature of the 'reception' process by which Methodism can assimilate and own ecclesiological insights from other Christian traditions. The second is the nature of the authority of Conference statements. To what extent does Methodism have a formal teaching office or magisterium?

THE NATURE AND MISSION OF THE CHURCH

The Methodist understanding of the nature and mission of the Church has developed constantly since the beginning. The complexity of the transition from Society to Church complicates any analysis, as does the more recent assimilation of insights received from modern scholarship, other traditions and the Ecumenical Movement. However, certain emphases can be regarded as having persisted throughout Methodist history. They are the emphases on the Church as called to mission and evangelism, on the Church as a body for the nurturing of people 'pressing on to full salvation' and on the interdependent *koinonia* of the Church at every level.

Wesley's understanding of the nature of the Church naturally took its point of departure from his Anglican heritage. One can emphasize the importance, for him, of Anglican Article XIX with its Lutheran-style assertion of the centrality of the due administration of word and sacraments. Wesley stood in the tradition of Hooker and Jewel with his emphases on apostolic doctrine and subordination to Scripture, unity in essential doctrines, a functional episcopacy and the notion that paradigms for the Church's life should come from the patristic age. He regarded the Anglican constitution and liturgy as the best and most scriptural in Christendom.

Colin Williams sees a tension in Wesley's understanding of the holiness of the Church between the classical Protestant and more recent, pietistic emphases. He saw the holiness of the Church as residing in the objective means of grace, which continued to work even in an imperfect church. Simultaneously, he stressed that the

Church was holy in all its members, albeit in varying degrees, and that no person who lacked holiness could be a true member of the Church. Wesley acted out this tension in his own dual allegiance to the Church of England and in his cherishing of Methodism as an *ecclesiola in ecclesia*, or mini-church within the Church. He wanted no breach with the Church of England despite his condemnation of so many of its ministers and members for their lack of real faith and practice.[15]

Wesley saw the salvation of souls as 'the end of all ministerial order'. He was thus concerned with the practical effectiveness of the Church in both evangelism and nurture. The disciplinary function of the Church in the latter was a key concern. It explains the whole complex of the Methodist discipline, especially that of the class meeting, the ultimate *ecclesiola in ecclesia* of accountable discipleship, later described by Rigg as the germ cell of the Church.[16] However, neither Wesley nor later Methodists claimed that the peculiar aspects of the Methodist regime were essential to authentic ecclesial life, even though they regarded them as exemplifying, albeit in somewhat differing forms, vital aspects of the life of the apostolic and primitive churches. Nevertheless, Benjamin Gregory asserted of the Church Universal that 'the aim of all its ministrations is to present every man perfect in Jesus Christ'. He also argued that the Church continued all the work of Christ save that of his finished atonement. He taught that 'the Church is to be the continuator on earth of Christ's work of invitation, of teaching, of restoration, of sympathy and consolation ... the organ of his highest action upon the world, and that not only by authorization, but, still more by the derivation of life from Him and by the fact that the Holy Spirit is its animating principle'.[17] Gregory argues that Ephesians 1.22–3 implies a 'most real and realisable, a sensitive, intimate, loving union between Christ and His Church'. 'Not only is He her fullness, but she is His fullness'. He also emphasizes the indwelling Spirit as soul of the Church and the Church as the organ of eternal praise of God. In this, one sees a mature reflection on the doxological nature of the Church, fruit of over a century of the ecclesial awareness of the prodigality of divine love, focused and expressed in the Wesleyan traditions of preaching and hymnody.

The classical Wesleyan understanding of the Church was, thus, not purely functional, but strongly trinitarian, pneumatic and christological. Gregory contended that 'Christ Himself declared

that the unity of the Godhead in the three Persons of the Trinity
was at once the Archetype, the Basis and consummation of the
unity of the Church' (HCC, p. 152).

Gregory's profoundly eschatological sense of the destiny of the
Church as agent in the universal work of redemption was linked
to his understanding of its vocation to promote holiness. The
sense of the sheer breadth of the Church's universal catholic
vocation was broadened by the overseas missionary movement
and developments in home missions pioneered by such as Hugh
Price Hughes. Twentieth-century Methodist ecclesiology built on
this. NCC spoke of the life of the Church becoming 'progressively
richer as more and more peoples were added to it' (p. 7). CLP
cleverly integrated an emphasis on the frailty and fallibility of the
Church with a strong emphasis on the sign, even iconic, nature of
the Church in its total life. 'The Church is called to mirror, at
a finite level, the reality which God is in eternity' (CLP 2.1.9).
Trinitarian doctrine is essential to an adequate ecclesiology, it
said. The understanding of God as outgoing communion of love is
said to be 'authenticated when the Church shares in God's
mission to the world' (CLP 2.1.9). CLP endeavours to overcome
the tension between primarily functional concepts of the Church
and primarily iconic ones. It seeks to avoid the twin dangers of a
quasi-Monophysite ecclesiology, which ignores the human
weakness of the Church and endows it with an infallibilist or tri-
umphalist glory, and a quasi-Nestorian ecclesiology which makes
a radical differential between an all too human and fallible
Church and an idealized, purely spiritual, invisible Church. The
Church is simultaneously both fallible and indefectible. It is 'far
from being wholly open to God', yet to the extent of its faithfulness
to God, it can be seen to be iconic of God's future kingdom (CLP
2.1.9). Harold Roberts stresses, in line with both biblical and ecumenical theology, the link between Church and kingdom. The
Church is 'organ of the kingdom of God's rule in the world'.
Because of its corporate nature, it is necessarily structured,
though not after any absolutely rigid pattern, and visible. Its life
anticipates, in part, that of the kingdom.[18]

UNITY, CATHOLICITY AND APOSTOLICITY

The stress in the Wesleys' teaching on unity was on the moral and
spiritual unity of the societies as a result of their common call to

holiness and their common experience of life in Christ. Time and time again in his hymnody, Charles talks of our 'common' Lord, the 'common' peace that we feel and the shared joy of salvation, as in this well-known couplet,

> We all partake the joy of one,
> The common peace we feel.[19]

The unity of the Church is a natural result of the experience of unity in the Spirit and is strictly dependent on it (Gregory, HCC, pp. 152–3).

From the beginning, Methodists have had a lively sense of being part of the greater whole of the one Church of Christ, though the exact consequences of this in the search for unity were not universally agreed in either the nineteenth or the twentieth centuries. Some Methodists construed the unity of the Church as involving mutual recognition by the denominations but not organic unity. Such views rested on the concept of unity as primarily 'spiritual'. They received reinforcement from the movement towards closer, but essentially federal, Free Church co-operation at the turn of the century. Benjamin Gregory, the greatest of the classical Wesleyan ecclesiologists, clearly believed that John 17 entailed movement towards final organic unity. He argued that the growth in holiness and unity of the Church must go hand in hand. 'To despair of the holiness and unification of the Church is to despair of the regeneration and reconciliation of the human race' (HCC, p. 189). This strikingly anticipates the modern emphasis on the Church as sign and first-fruits of the kingdom. Rex Kissack also stressed that Methodist belief in the unity of the Church as possible within time rather than as a purely eschatological phenomenon follows logically from the doctrine of Christian perfection.[20]

In the present century, Methodist understanding of unity has been profoundly influenced by contemporary ecumenical debate. Thus, CLP's understanding of the unity of the Church reflects both particularly Methodist and ecumenical insights. The former influences the statement that unity 'involves the closest possible communion, a unity of will, character, purpose, function and love', while the latter influences the understanding of unity as gift involving a response (CLP 3.1.1, 3.1.2). The nature of unity is understood in the light of the oneness of God and the essential nature of the Church as *koinonia*. 'The Church is one because God is one. This is not simply an aspiration, but a God-given reality. The Church, however, reflects the unity of God most fully when its search for unity goes hand in hand with the search for and realisation of unity in its own life. Indeed, one of the tests of the Church's unity with God is the unity which the Church enjoys in its own life' (CLP 2.4.2).

Many Methodist ecumenists of the immediate post-war era were profoundly influenced by the reunion in South India (1947). They believed that organic unity should involve churches in dying to denominational identities and making real sacrifices in order to rise to new life. For them unity without such death was unity without the Cross. In recent years, positions have become more nuanced. The British Methodist response to 'Called To be One' testified that some Methodists continued to favour organic unity, whereas others favoured a more federal approach. Other approaches, such as that of unity in reconciled diversity and that of conciliar unity, in which denominations keep some separate identity while being bound closely through obligations to consult on all key matters through agreed conciliar structures, are now being considered. The present emphasis on unity in diversity and upon the Trinity as the ultimate model of unity both appeal to elements deep rooted in the Methodist consciousness.

CATHOLICITY

Methodism understands catholicity within the context of the generous love of God. 'The Church is catholic because of the one universal God who has declared his love for all creation in Jesus Christ' (CLP 2.4.4). Catholicity implies universality, temporal and geographical, and authentic fullness of faith and life. In his sermon 'On the Catholic Spirit', Wesley emphasized the importance of the recognition of the same essential core of faith and life in other Christian churches, while not remaining indifferent to diverse opinions on secondary matters, which, however, should not exclude fellowship. Wesley's views made him loath to unchurch any other trinitarian church, however many his disagreements with it. Thus, he even said that he could bear with the 'gross superstition' in the Roman Church because of its trinitarian doctrine and the holiness of so many of its members. Benjamin

Gregory followed him in this, arguing that any attempt by a trinitarian church to exclude another from catholic recognition was, in
itself, a serious sin against the catholicity of the Church. The Liverpool Minutes of 1820 warned Methodists against any sectarian
spirit and called on them to manifest 'the kind and catholic spirit
of primitive Methodism towards all denominations of Christians
holding the Head'.[21]

In the early twentieth century, H. B. Workman and others
vigorously asserted the catholicity of Methodism in terms of
doctrine, life and its maintenance of a distinctive ethos and style
that was nevertheless a distinct *typos* of Christian life (to use the
later phrase of Cardinal Willebrands). NCC identified the ever ex-
panding inculturation of the Church in new communities as a
sign of the catholic vigour of the Church (NCC, p. 7). The 1936
Covenant Service called Methodists to 'new ventures in fellowship', an implicit call to catholicity. Such catholicity in no way
implies uniformity; rather it implies rich diversity, which has
been present as a gift of the Spirit since apostolic times.

APOSTOLICITY

In important respects, Methodism has long anticipated the
current broad ecumenical consensus on apostolicity. Apostolicity
and apostolic succession imply continuity in doctrine and essential
aspects of church life as well as continuity in transmission of
ministry. In the last resort, Methodism rates continuity in
doctrine and life above ministerial succession as such, while
accepting that the latter can be a valuable 'sign, but not guarantee'.[22] NCC stressed doctrine and added: 'true continuity is continuity of experience . . . this is our doctrine of apostolic succession'
(NCC, p. 32). James Rigg regarded apostolicity as involving
teaching, living experience and fellowship. 'Methodism was as
much a revival of primitive church life as of doctrine.'[23]Benjamin
Gregory, in his exegesis of Acts 2.47, regards the apostolicity of
the Church as constantly renewed and re-experienced. 'What is
meant by giving themselves to the Apostles' doctrine is very
plain. They devoted themselves to the learning, to the experimental realisation and to the assiduous practice of those truths that it
was the principle work of the apostles to teach' (HCC, p. 76).
The Wesleys esteemed the first three centuries more for the purity

of their life than for establishing doctrinal norms. They saw their ideals for the societies exemplified in the early communities and especially in the descriptions given in Acts. Charles Wesley's hymn 'Come and let us sweetly join' captures this ethos in such lines as

> Hands and hearts and voices raise,
> Sing as in the ancient days,
> Antedate the joys above,
> Celebrate the feast of love.[24]

In recent years British Methodists have emphasized mission as sharing in God's mission with the emphasis on 'As the Father sent me, so I send you'.[25] Apostolicity is not just an inheritance; it is a constantly renewed experience in the life of the Church. It cannot stand or fall purely by the mechanics of ministerial succession which is not to say that a ministry of *koinonia* is not a vital part of the Church's lived apostolicity (Gregory, HCC, p. 103).

METHODIST STRUCTURES OF MINISTRY, LEADERSHIP AND CHURCH GOVERNMENT

Methodist structures have clear origins in those improvised by John Wesley for the original Methodist Movement in the eighteenth century. They are based on the Connexional Principle which was a device for ensuring the greatest possible missionary flexibility in sending preachers where they were most needed, and for ensuring disciplinary effectiveness both among preachers and members. The annual Conferences, the stationing of itinerant ministers, the linking of churches in interdependent groups (still called circuits in British Methodism) all go back to the time of Wesley.[26]

In the two centuries since the death of Wesley, changes have inevitably occurred. There are now over one hundred separate Methodist churches in fellowship with the World Methodist Council. Their structures vary in detail, while still reflecting the broad presuppositions of the Connexional Principle.

Wesley totally dominated both British and American Methodism until 1784. In 1784 he ordained Coke as superintendent for America. Coke promptly assumed the title of bishop and the Americans began to act independently of 'our old Daddy, Mr

Wesley'. The Baltimore Conference of 1784 set up the structure for the future Methodist Episcopal Church of the USA. In 1791 Wesley's death forced reorganization in British Methodism. Wesley had already provided for a hundred preachers to inherit corporately his responsibilities (the 'Legal Hundred'). In 1791 the Conference provided for the election of an annual President to exercise the powers of presiding at the Conference. However, it was made clear that it was the Conference as a whole that succeeded to Wesley's authority. The preachers, corporately, were to exercise *episkope* over the Connexion and over each other.

From the two original churches of Britain and the USA stem, whether by missionary activity, independent imitation (as was really the case with the Primitive Methodists and Bible Christians in the UK) or schism, all the other Methodist churches. Those churches that split from the original two generally aimed at more democratic systems of church government, with greater lay participation and more local autonomy. The two original connexions, while allowing considerable lay involvement in local church courts, held a very strong doctrine of the Pastoral Office and kept the national Conferences exclusively ministerial till 1872 in America and 1878 in Britain.

The ministry

The present day ordained ministry has its origins in the travelling preachers employed by the Wesleys. They were sent to preach and to administer the societies but not to administer the sacraments unless, as was the case with a few, they were already Anglican priests.

Wesley failed in his original hope to persuade the Anglican bishops to ordain men to help him. He came to believe that, as a presbyter, he had a right to ordain in emergencies. Thus, he appointed Coke and Asbury as 'superintendents' for his mission in America. He provided the threefold ministry of deacons, elders and superintendents, believing that this traditional pattern was the best and that he was properly establishing a church where none had previously existed. He left the Americans to 'the Scriptures and the Primitive Church' as sources for their future practice.[27]

Thus in US Methodism, with the exception of a few smaller groups, episcopacy and the threefold ministry exist. Bishops were and are seen as responsible for evangelistic initiative and over-sight, a job they discharged on the Frontier with great energy in the nineteenth century. They still 'station' elders in their areas. However, the bishops share their authority with their area conferences and are subject to the final authority of the General Conference, which meets only every four years. Elders are the ordinary local pastors and ministers of word and sacrament. Deacons until very recently were the equivalent of British Proba-tioner Ministers. The US Church has recently created a perma-nent diaconate.

In Britain Wesley ordained, towards the end of his life, a very small number of elders, mainly for work in Scotland. He had regarded itinerant preachers as 'extraordinary ministers of the word', 'designed to provoke to jealousy the ordinary ministers', but he did not believe they should administer the sacraments.[28] All itinerant preachers had to spend a period on trial, before being solemnly admitted by vote of their brethren at the Confer-ence to full connexion. In 1818 ordination by prayer and the laying on of hands was restored for overseas missionaries and in 1836 for ministers in the work at home. The idea of a British Methodist episcopate was rejected in the 1790s. The preachers thought it would destroy their brotherhood, preferring corporate, mutual *episkope* in the Conference. Ministers were accounted as presbyters, the term officially appearing in the liturgy in 1975, though used from the nineteenth century in defence of the authen-tic status of ministers in full connexion.

In the late nineteenth century, an order of deaconesses was created in British Wesleyan Methodism. They were not, however, seen as ministers, although ordained. In the late 1980s the diaconal order was opened to men as well and is now seen as an order of ministry, focusing the servant nature of the Church.

Wesley regarded *episkope* as a key function of both the 'ordinary' ministers of the Church, episcopal and presbyteral, and of his 'extraordinary' preachers in their societies. The British Wesleyans considerably developed the doctrine of the pastoral office, believ-ing it to be of divine institution and necessary for the good order of the Church.[29] A rather exclusive emphasis on this and on the strictly subordinate authority of lay leaders was a key factor in some of the schisms of the nineteenth century. The non-Wesleyan Methodists had a much lower doctrine of the ministry. The influ-ence of both traditions can be seen in the Deed of Union and the

1937 ecclesiology statement. The former calls ministers 'stewards in the household of God', but argues that they hold no priesthood 'differing in kind' from that common to all the Lord's people and that they have 'no exclusive cure of souls'.[30] NCC though talks of ministry as gift to the Church as well as arising within it (pp. 26–7). From theologoumena traceable to George Findlay, modern Methodism has developed its doctrine of ministers as representative persons, in whom the ministry of the Church is focused. In the ecumenical era this has been seen as an attempt to transcend the functional/ontological divide on the nature of presbyteral ministry.[31]

Neither Wesley nor his successors believed that any one form of ministry was prescribed in the New Testament. Wesley revered the Anglican pattern, but did not believe the uninterrupted episcopal succession could be proved.[32] World Methodism has been divided between those churches keeping three orders of ministry and those retaining only one (sometimes more recently two, with the restoration of diaconate). The difference does not impair their communion. British Methodists are not anti-episcopal on theological principle and their response to the Lima statement talked of 'awaiting the moment for the recovery of the sign of the episcopal succession'.[33] Methodism believes in orderly succession in transmission of ministerial responsibilities. Methodist presbyters and bishops are seen as having responsibility both for the general discipline and *koinonia* of the Church and for the particular disciplines of Methodism. They are regarded both as presbyters (or bishops in the US case) of the Universal Church and members of a preaching order. In Britain presbyters are still received into full connexion by a standing vote of the Conference, in which it is also resolved that they be ordained. Ordination usually follows later the same day.

In the early nineteenth century, the Bible Christians and Primitive Methodists were pioneers in appointing some female travelling preachers. Later in the century the practice died out. In 1974, the British Conference opened presbyteral ministry again to women. They are also eligible for all levels of the ministry in the United Methodist Church of the USA. World Methodism sees its ordination of persons of all races and both sexes as enhancing the catholicity of the Church and its sign nature (CLP 4.5.14).

Lay ministry

From its societary origins British Methodism has made extensive use of lay people in both administrative and pastoral roles in the societies. Rigg believed Methodism made fuller use of the gifts of its laity than any other church. He argued that the widespread use of lay or 'local' preachers was a sign of the vitality of the Church. Three categories of lay workers date back to very early days. The class leaders were responsible for the classes or mutual fellowship groups, attendance at which was then obligatory. They were responsible to the preachers for the classes. The stewards looked after the administration of the societies, again under ministerial aegis. Local preachers, lay, unpaid preachers, were 'planned' by the superintendent ministers of each circuit to lead worship at stated times and places. In the nineteenth century, lay officials became increasingly associated with the courts of the church at every level. In 1878, they were finally admitted to the national Conference, though matters of ministerial oversight were still dealt with in ministerial synods and sessions of the Conference. Many disputes centred round the role of the laity. All the non-Wesleyan churches in Britain gave a greater role to layfolk, and in the United Methodist Free Churches a layman could even be President of the Conference. Today, the theology and practice is one of partnership, with lay people being represented on committees dealing with ministerial stationing and doctrinal matters.

Structures

At the apex of the structure of each Methodist Church is its Conference, usually meeting annually. The conferences originated with Wesley's habit of calling his preachers together to take counsel on strategy and teaching. In Britain, the annual Conference has final authority over the discipline and teaching of the church. The enormous United Methodist Church of the USA, which also includes many overseas daughter churches, has a series of area and regional conferences, with final authority being in the hands of the quadrennial General Conference to which representatives come from the USA and from overseas. In both main branches of Methodism, the Conference/General Conference has ultimate *episkope* or oversight. Changes to the constitutional law of Methodism, the *Book of Discipline* (US) and *Constitutional Practice and Discipline* (Britain) must be approved in the Conference. Since 1976 the British Conference has had authority under the Methodist Church Act 1976 to alter the previously entrenched doctrinal clauses of the Deed of Union. Conference is the interpreter of doctrine within Methodism. Both ministers and lay people are represented in the conferences. In Britain, they are mainly chosen by the district synods. The conferences have ultimate *episkope*, but accept the principle of subsidiarity. In practice, local churches and circuits have more autonomy than in theory. Thus, in theory, the Conference still 'stations' ministers; in practice, arrangements are made between ministers and circuits with an increasing role for the District Chairmen. Only occasionally does the Stationing Committee of the Conference override local arrangements in the overall interest of the Church.

Between conferences a smaller body, of recent origin, the Methodist Council, takes emergency decisions and does key planning work. Routine servicing of the Connexion and its agencies, such as the World Church Department (formerly the Methodist Missionary Society) is done by the Connexional Team of specially appointed ministers and lay people.

Working up from the local level, each 'society', now normally called and thought of as a 'local' church, is under the guidance of a circuit minister. It has its Church Council, composed of stewards and others with specific responsibilities. The Council is assisted by committees, the nature of which is determined by the size of the membership.

Local congregations are grouped in circuits which share ministerial and local preacher resources, all ministers and local preachers belonging officially to the circuit rather than to one particular local church. The superintendent minister and the circuit meeting have individual and corporate *episkope* over the affairs of the Circuit. The circuit levies an assessment on each church for its contribution to circuit and higher level funds. Lay circuit stewards play a key role in planning and invitations to ministers. Circuits are grouped into thirty-four separate Districts, most with their own 'separated' Chairman who presides at the twice yearly synod and has particular oversight of all the ministers in the District.

METHODISM, *KOINONIA* AND CONNEXIONALISM

A strong sense of *koinonia* has always been at the root of popular Methodist ecclesial consciousness. Methodists experience *koinonia* as gift and calling resulting from a common experience of divine grace, from the common call to holiness and from the practical outworking of these in the life of worship and mutual care in the societies. '*Koinonia*, then, denotes both what Christians share and *that* sharing is at the heart of Christian life' (CLP 3.1.8). It is fundamentally a lived experience. It implies togetherness, mutuality and reciprocity, requiring mutual recognition and a common acceptance of each other's identity. Though it is a fundamental element in their experience, Methodists have gained a renewed and enlarged vision of *koinonia* through ecumenical pilgrimage and insights.

The sense of *koinonia* was especially vividly encapsulated in the hymns that Charles Wesley wrote 'for the society meeting and parting', many of which are still regularly sung. They express a strong sense of *koinonia* across geographical boundaries, across time and eternity and *koinonia* in the essential experience of the apostolic church. Some stress the life of mutual care within the local societies. Perhaps most expressive of all is 'All praise to our redeeming Lord', with its call for mutual edification, and its sense of the common eschatological pilgrimage, and the contribution of individual charisms to the whole. The couplet 'The gift that he on one bestows we all delight to prove' contains a delightful ambiguity. Does it refer to a gift, given to one, which is then communicated to all the others, or is it a special charism given to one alone, which nevertheless edifies the whole?[34]

For Methodism *koinonia* is supremely communion in the grace of God, vividly experienced in the corporate life of the believers at every interlocking level of the Church. Methodists see the Connexional Principle as the most appropriate embodiment of this universal sense of *koinonia*. Wesley originally hit upon connexionalism as a disciplinary and evangelistic device. He was always concerned that the societies should have a global sense of priorities, dictated by their understanding of the needs of others rather than by their purely domestic convenience. Ministers were to itinerate where they were most needed rather than where the richest or most powerful churches could corral them! Hence, naturally, the overriding authority of the Conferences. However, this overriding authority is not about centralization. The local churches are represented in the synods and conferences which listen to their concerns and respect their proper local autonomy. Connexionalism is about mutual responsibility and accountability at every level (CLP 4.6).

The classical Wesleyan ecclesiologists believed that the essence of connexionalism was implied in apostolic practice. The apostles itinerated, conferred regularly on matters of common concern and commended the needs of particular churches to others. Paul expressed the ultimate purpose of 'apostolic connexionalism' in Romans 1.12, mutual encouragement in faith and the circulation of love and insight throughout the whole. Through this, individual churches were reminded of the foundation in Christ and the universal Church of their local *koinonia*. It is the privilege and duty of each local church to adhere to, draw from and to contribute to the richness of life in Christ. Some modern Methodists see connexionalism as a vital contribution to emerging ecumenical ecclesiology. An interesting question, which has never been fully discussed, is the extent to which Methodists might claim that the principle of connexionalism, as opposed to any one embodiment of it, is of the *bene esse* of the Church. Connexionalism is seen as excluding the extremes of independency and autocracy in church government (CLP 4.6.6, 4.6.9). It expresses a delicacy of balance between local and universal, due ministerial authority and lay co-responsibility which can be lacking both in Independent and hierarchical systems.

The logic of connexionalism would seem to point to a global connexionalism, a point often made by Americans, since the practice of the United Methodist Church has been to encourage its overseas daughter churches to stay under the umbrella of the General Conference, while devolving decision-making in many matters. The British Conference has devolved absolute autonomy to many former missionary daughter churches.

Bishop Nacpil of the Philippines has recently spoken of the universal 'connectedness', in divine providence, of creation. He sees connexionalism as an Arminian, inclusive concept. Bishop Etchegoyen of Argentina says that connexionalism involves 'moving beyond ourselves in meeting others, to dialogue with them, to plan together and to travel on the same road together' (Robbins/Carter). British Methodists have recently asserted: 'The Church of Christ is an interdependent whole, because ultimately there is one Lord, one faith, one baptism, one God and Father of all, who is over all, and through all and in all' (CLP 4.6.3). Similarly, 'to speak of God as a loving communion of three co-equal persons suggests that the Church should be a community of support and love in which there is no superiority or inferiority' (CLP 2.1.9).

METHODISM AND DIVERSITY

Despite the rigidity of its early internal discipline, Methodism has always affirmed the legitimacy of considerable diversity within the life of the Universal Church. While regarding the Church of England as the most scriptural of churches, the Wesleys were not afraid to borrow from the spiritual traditions of the Puritans, the Moravians, the Lutherans, the Counter Reformation and the early eastern Fathers, and to commend their treasures both in the *Christian Library* and in the hymn book.

Wesley held to what Geoffrey Wainwright has called a 'generous orthodoxy'. For him Trinitarian theology and orthodox christology were non-negotiable. His supposed indifference to dogma, based on such aphorisms as that doctrine is only a very small part of religion, is more apparent than real. Wesley's main point in making such statements was to highlight the importance of 'experimental divinity' and its consequences in practical Christian living. It was not to deny the importance of the presuppositions of Nicene orthodoxy that necessarily underlay such experimental divinity. Wesley granted that there were theological matters on which Christians could hold differing 'opinions'. He did not regard all such opinions as equally valid and he expected all good Christians to adhere loyally to their opinions conscientiously held (Wainwright, 1995, pp. 231–6).

In the order of practice, Wesley made a distinction between the 'covenanted' means of grace, prescribed in Scripture and, therefore, binding on all Christians, and the 'prudential' ones which included forms of devotion of later origin. For Methodism, these comprised meeting in society, class and bands, the lovefeasts, the Covenant service and other forms of the Methodist discipline. These were regarded as binding on Methodists, as part of a discipline voluntarily accepted, but not on others. This distinction helps to explain what would otherwise seem paradoxical, the acceptance by Wesley and later Methodists of very considerable diversity within the Church universal, along with a rigid insistence, until late in the nineteenth century, on the observance of traditional disciplinary norms within Methodism.

However, an element of diversity was built into Methodism from the beginning, as a result of Wesley's expectation that the Methodists would benefit both from the worship of the parish church and that of the society. Methodists thus became accustomed, as in varying degrees they have been since, to a mixture of liturgical and extempore prayer within their worship.

Doctrinally, early Methodists were strict. Methodist preachers were expected to be able to affirm regularly that they 'believed and preached our doctrines'. These consisted of the orthodox doctrines of the Trinity and christology, belief in the atoning death of Christ and the 'Methodist emphases' on the universal availability of salvation, the witness of the Spirit and the doctrine of Christian holiness or perfection, the preaching of which, according to Wesley, was the purpose for which God had raised up Methodism. Study of certain of Wesley's standard sermons was and is required of all preachers. While not unchurching certain churches, with which they disagreed vigorously on certain finer points, Methodism expected strict doctrinal conformity from its preachers. In the late nineteenth century, Wesleyan Methodists prided themselves that their discipline made impossible the doctrinal wrangling that occurred in the other Protestant churches.

At the beginning of the twentieth century, the ethos of Methodism changed rapidly. Liberal Protestantism became influential on both sides of the Atlantic. The Deed of Union interpreted Methodist theological standards less rigidly than had the old Wesleyan Church. It declared that Wesley's sermons and *Notes on the New Testament* were not intended to impose a speculative or systematic approach to theology. The 1930s also saw the beginnings of a recovery of the neglected sacramental dimension of the Wesleys' teaching, and the emergence, with the Methodist Sacramental Fellowship, of an element in Methodism distinctly more favourable to the catholic tradition than hitherto. The trend was paralleled in US Methodism. Both churches were influenced by the ecumenical and liturgical movements. From the 1960s onwards sections of Methodism were also influenced by the charismatic movement.

The result of all these trends has been a considerable increase in the diversity of Methodist churchmanship and worship on both sides of the Atlantic. However, the existence of the connexional system, the itinerancy of ministers, the corpus of Wesleyan hymnody, better preserved in Britain than in America, and the common acceptance of Wesleyan teaching on sanctification, have all helped safeguard an overall sense of cohesion. Methodism has not suffered as much as have Baptists and Anglicans from the extremes of antagonistic forms of churchmanship.

The Methodist acceptance of diversity has been reinforced by modern biblical scholarship which has endorsed the Wesleyan view that no one form of church organization was normative in the New Testament. CLP endorses the view that diversity is legitimate and enriching. However, it argues that three central common convictions establish norms for later times: first, the conviction that the paschal events and the coming of the Spirit determine the identity and central message of the Church; second, that the Church and Israel share a common heritage; and third, that the common life of the people of Christ expresses itself in worship and fellowship, mission and service. It concludes: 'The unity of the New Testament precludes the view that anything goes, whether in belief or practice.' Contrariwise, it also holds that the Bible itself testifies by its diversity against any narrowly construed biblicism. 'In the end the ecclesiology of the New Testament is not a mass of conflicting ecclesiologies, but a rich variety and that very variety is the norm by which the life of the whole Church is directed, purified and enriched' (CLP 2.3.18). Thus the classical Wesleyan insight, encapsulated in Gregory's statement that the Church cannot be too rigidly defined, is lent support from a modern biblical and ecumenical perspective.

THE VISION OF THE ECUMENICAL FUTURE

There is no one Methodist vision of the ecumenical future. Methodists have long held differing views about ecumenical strategy and the ultimate shape of unity. Some have envisioned an ultimate federation of churches, in communion with each other, but retaining differing structures and styles of Christian life and worship. Others have argued strenuously for organic unity. This continuing tension was present in Methodist responses to the recent Called To Be One process. Increasingly, however, most agree that growing unity will be the product of a convergent pilgrimage, the exact nature of the end of which none can forecast.

Methodists have, perhaps, too rarely stood back and looked at the portrait of unity in terms of the whole Wesleyan experience and tradition. This, I think, yields the following insights. Methodists believe that the 'Coming Great Church' will be a conciliar and connexional church. The former principle involves situating all focal ministries clearly within the context of the *koinonia* of the whole people of God and not above it, in separation. It implies collaborative ministry and synodical authority at every level. Methodists have several times endorsed the principle first enunciated at Lausanne that the government of the Church will include episcopal, presbyteral and congregational elements.[35] These principles could be reconciled either with organic unity or some form of conciliar fellowship as more recently widely advocated. It will also be a connexional church, though future structures adopted may vary greatly from any current in world Methodism. Even if denominations retain separate identities, the logic of connexionalism is that there will need to be procedures for mutual consultation and accountability. The churches will owe it to each other and to their common mission to consult over priorities and needs. As Brian Beck puts it, 'Churches cannot pretend to be united until they are prepared to submit their autonomy to others in matters of mutual concern'.[36]

The ultimate purpose of connexionalism is the circulation of love and insight within the whole body. Romans 1.12 was a favourite text with Gregory, as it is with John Paul II. In ecumenism, all have a duty to contribute and to 'receive'. Methodism will need to do both. It may 'receive' certain personally focused ministries at present lacking in parts or all of Methodism, commended by sister churches, the three most significant being the episcopate, the Petrine ministry and the tradition of eldership (as known in the reformed tradition). When Methodists become convinced of their value to the unity that Christ wills, they will wish to 'receive' them in a manner consistent with their developing understanding of connexionalism and *koinonia*.

Methodists will see all of this in the light of mission and of the Church as sign, foretaste and first-fruits of the Kingdom. Unity is 'that the world might believe' and the Church is called to mirror, 'as clearly as is possible for the church of fallible human beings, the reality which God is in eternity' (CLP 2.1.9).

FURTHER READING

There is no full, up-to-date survey of Methodist ecclesiology. The best general survey of the British tradition is Kissack, R., *Church or No Church*, Epworth, London, 1964. The best introduction to the United Methodist Church, USA is Frank, T. E., *The Polity, Practice and Mission of the United Methodist Church*, Abingdon, Nashville, 1997.

There is no really thorough survey of Wesley's ecclesiology, though there are useful summaries of aspects of it in Williams, C., *John Wesley's Theology Today* (Epworth 1960) pp. 141–66; and in Carter, C. W. ed., *Contemporary Wesleyan Theology* (Grand Rapids 1983), pp. 571–682 (article by David L. Smith). The sermons of Wesley directly relevant to this topic are: 'On the Church', 'On Schism' and 'The Catholic Spirit': see, respectively, Outler, A., ed., *Works of John Wesley* (Nashville, 1986, vol. 3, no. 74, pp. 45–57; no. 75, pp. 58–69; and vol. 2, no. 39, pp. 79–96. For ecclesiological motifs in the hymns, see Osborne, G., ed., *The Poetic Works of John and Charles Wesley*, London 1869; for those still used by modern British Methodists, see *Hymns and Psalms*, Methodist Publishing House 1983, especially nos 752–63.

The best general surveys of Methodism to provide a total context for the historical development of the ecclesiology are: Davies, R. E., *Methodism*, Penguin 1963; Rack, H., *Reasonable Enthusiast*, Epworth 1989; and the four volumes of Davies, R. E., George, A. R., Rupp, G., eds, *History of the Methodist Church in Great Britain*, Epworth 1965–86. On the significance of the class meeting, see, Watson, D. L., *The Early Methodist Class Meeting*, Nashville, Discipleship Resources, 1992.

The standard British Methodist ecclesiological statements are 'The Nature of the Christian Church', 1937, now in *Statements of the Methodist Church on Faith and Order, 1933–1983*, Methodist Publishing House 1984, pp. 5–43, and *Called To Love and Praise* (statement approved by Conference), Methodist Publishing House 1999. For the earlier Wesleyan Conference statement on the nature of the Church, adopted in 1908, see Simon, J. S., ed., *Summary of Methodist Law and Discipline* (Methodist Publishing House 1923), pp. 9–14. See also *The Ministry of the Whole People of God*, Methodist Publishing House, 1988 (report presented to the Methodist Conference).

Other important major ecclesiological works include Shrewsbury, W. J., *An Essay on the Scriptural Character of the Wesleyan Methodist Economy*, 1840; Barrett, A., *Ministry and Polity of the Christian Church*, 1854; Gregory, B., *Holy Catholic Church*, 1873, and *Handbook of Scriptural Church Principles*, 1888; Rigg, J., *The Connexional Economy of Wesleyan Methodism*, 1852 and 1878, and *A Comparative View of Church Organisations*, 1887 and two later editions; Pope, W. B., *A Compendium of Christian Theology* (1880), vol. 3, pp. 259–359; Slater, W. F., *Methodism and the Early Church*, 1885; Quick, W. A., *Methodism, a Parallel*, 1891; Findlay, G. G., *The Church in the New Testament*, 1893; Beet, J. A., *The Church and the Sacraments*, 1907; Lidgett, J. S., *God, Christ and the Church*, 1927; Flew R. N., *Jesus and His Church*, 1937; and Roberts, H., *Jesus and the Kingdom* (Epworth 1955) pp. 84ff. In addition to these specifically, or mainly, ecclesiological works, there are important ecclesiological observations in the sermons and/or works of Hugh Price Hughes, G. G. Findlay, J. S. Lidgett, W. F. Lofthouse and R. E. Davies.

On questions particularly relating to ministry, see Lawson, A. B., *John Wesley and the Christian Ministry*, SPCK 1963; George, A. R., 'Ordination' in *History of Methodist Church*, Epworth 1965, vol. 2, ch. 4; also the relevant sections of the ecumenical documents (see above) and the British statements of 1960 and 1974 on ordination (see *Statements*, already cited above, pp. 124–49) and on episcopacy (*Statements*, pp. 202–37). On the Petrine ministry see Carter. D., 'A Methodist Reaction to *Ut Unum Sint*', *One in Christ*, 1997/2; and Wainwright, G., 'The gift that He on one bestows, we all delight to prove', in Puglisi, J., ed., *Petrine Ministry and the Unity of the Church*, Liturgical Press, Collegeville, 1999.

For a statement in the Wesleyan tradition on ecumenism, see Outler, A., *The Christian Tradition and the Unity we Seek*, New York, Oxford University Press, 1964. For Methodist responses to the *Baptism, Eucharist, and Ministry* process of the World Council of Churches, see Thurian, M., ed., *Churches respond to BEM* (Geneva, WCC, 1986), vol. 2, pp. 177–254.

Important dialogue statements include, from the Roman Catholic–Methodist dialogue, *Towards a Statement on the Church*. Lake Junaluska, World Methodist Council, 1986; and *The Apostolic Tradition*, Methodist Publishing House 1991; and from the dialogue with the Anglicans, *Sharing in the Apostolic Communion*,

Lake Junaluska, World Methodist Council, 1996. Wainwright, G., *Methodists in Dialog*, Abingdon, Nashville, 1995, surveys the whole field of Methodist international dialogues with other churches.

Significant recent articles include Beck, B., 'Some Reflections on Connexionalism', *Epworth Review*, May/Sept 1991; Carter, D., 'A Methodist Contribution to Ecclesiology' (a comparison of Rigg's and Gregory's ecclesiologies), *One in Christ*, 1994/2; Beck, B., 'Connexion and *Koinonia* – Wesley's Legacy and the Ecumenical Ideal', in Maddox, R. L., ed., *Rethinking Wesley's Theology* (Abingdon, Nashville, 1998), pp. 129–40; Carter, D., 'Some Methodist Principles of Ecumenism', *Epworth Review*, October 1998; Robbins, B./Carter, D., 'Connexionalism and *Koinonia*', *One In Christ*, 1998/4; Chapman, D., '*Koinonia* and Connexionalism', *Epworth Review*, April 1999. 'Uniting in Vision', The annual review from the Connexional Team for 1989–99, Methodist Publishing House, 1999, summarizes the structure of the current connexional departments.[37]

NOTES

1. Rigg, J., *Principles of Church Organisation* (1887), p. 207.
2. Gregory, B., *Handbook of Scriptural Church Principles* (1888), vol. 2, p. 256.
3. Rigg, J., *Connexional Economy of Wesleyan Methodism* (1878), pp. 1–23.
4. Turner, J. M., *Conflict and Reconciliation* (Epworth 1985), pp. 22–9.
5. Davies, R. E., *Methodism* (Penguin 1963), p. 130.
6. Brake, G., *Policy and Politics in British Methodism* (Edsall 1984), p. 829.
7. Turner (1985), pp. 146–93.
8. Simon. J. S., *Summary of Methodist Law and Discipline* (Wesleyan Conference Office 1923), p. 269.
9. Campbell, Ted, *John Wesley and Christian Antiquity*. Nashville, Abingdon, 1991.
10. Cited in Wainwright, *Methodists in Dialog*. Nashville, Abingdon, 1995, p. 73.
11. Watson, D. L., *The Early Methodist Class Meeting*, Nashville, Discipleship Resources, 1992.

12. Rigg, *Connexional Economy*, pp. 1–23.
13. See n. 31, below.
14. *Called to Love and Praise*. Methodist Publishing House 1999.
15. Williams, C., *John Wesley's Theology Today* (Epworth 1960), pp. 141–66.
16. Rigg, *Connexional Economy*, pp. 169–90.
17. Gregory, B., *Holy Catholic Church*, (1873), p. 15, hereafter cited as HCC.
18. Roberts, H., *Jesus and the Kingdom*, (Epworth 1955), pp. 84–101.
19. *Hymns and Psalms* (Methodist Publishing House 1983), no. 753.
20. Kissack, R., *Church or No Church* (Epworth 1964), p. 146.
21. Simon, J. S., ed., *Summary of Methodist Law and Discipline*, (Methodist Publishing House 1923), pp. 268–9.
22. Thurian, M., ed., *Churches Respond to BEM*, vol. 2 (Geneva, WCC, 1986), p. 227.
23. Rigg, *Comparative View*, p. 207.
24. *Hymns and Psalms* (1983), no. 756.
25. Cf. Davidson, L., *Sender and Sent*. Epworth 1969.
26. Davies, *Methodism*, p. 89.
27. Gregory, *Handbook*, vol. 2, p. 102.
28. Lawson, A. B., *John Wesley and the Christian Ministry* (SPCK 1963), pp. 47–70.
29. Bowmer, J., *Pastor and People*. Epworth 1975.
30. Deed of Union, cited in Brake (1985), p. 829.
31. *Statements of the Methodist Church on Faith and Order 1933–1983*, (Methodist Publishing House 1984), pp. 5–43.
32. Lawson, A. B., *John Wesley and the Christian Ministry* (SPCK 1963), pp. 48–78.
33. Thurian, M., ed., vol. 2, p. 215 (see n. 22).
34. *Hymns and Psalms*, no. 753.
35. *Statements*, p. 206.
36. Beck, 'Some Reflections on Connexionalism', *Epworth Review*, May/September 1991, p. 49.
37. The permission of the Methodist Publishing House to use material in the copyright of the Trustees for Methodist Church Purposes is gratefully acknowledged.

4

The Roman Catholic Church

Cecily Boulding OP

ORIGINS OF CATHOLIC ECCLESIOLOGY[1]

Roman Catholics share with other Christians a concept of the Church which finds its origins in the Christian groups described in the Acts of the Apostles, who met together in their homes for 'the breaking of bread and the prayers' (Acts 2.42),[2] and in the gatherings of converts, such as those at Ephesus, whom St Paul exhorted to 'maintain the unity of the Spirit in the bond of peace' (Ephesians 4.3). The evolution of structures for precisely this purpose is attested by the end of the first century in the letters of St Ignatius of Antioch:

> All of you, follow the bishop as Jesus Christ followed the Father, the presbytery as the Apostles, respect the deacons as the ordinance of God. Let no one do anything that pertains to the church apart from the bishop. Let that be considered a valid Eucharist which is under the bishop, or one whom he has delegated.[3]

From its very beginning therefore, the Church is seen to have had both a visible and a spiritual dimension. The visible dimension naturally and inevitably reflected human social and political structures. The earliest form of ecclesiology (long before the word was coined), as can be seen in the discussion preceding the appointment of the seven 'deacons' recorded in Acts 6, was therefore the consideration of what structures were, or were not, appropriate vehicles and instruments of the invisible, spiritual reality of grace and salvation.

With the conversion of the Roman Empire to Christianity in the fourth century, and the much closer link between political and ecclesiastical life, that question became more acute. For the next thousand years or so, especially in the West, ecclesiology – the study of what the Church is – tended to focus mainly on its external, visible structures, and to be formulated in a polemical context of claim and counter-claim by civil and ecclesiastical rulers. This was most obviously exemplified in the evolution of the power of the papacy, whose aggressive claims to supremacy over the Patriarch of Constantinople were a major cause of the schism which opened between the Eastern Orthodox Churches and the Western Latin Church in 1054, and which still endures. Similarly sacramental theology, a vital aspect of ecclesiology, was not infrequently developed in response to various heresies which controverted the value and validity either of specific sacraments, or of the whole concept of a sacramental economy. Consequently, by the later Middle Ages such ecclesiology as there was tended (with a few honourable exceptions like the work of Aquinas in the thirteenth century) to focus almost exclusively on the visible, structural dimension of the Church. It was the sixteenth-century Reformers' very necessary reaction to this approach that really generated ecclesiology in the modern sense of a serious, disciplined pondering on the question, 'What is the Church?'

The Reformation splintering of medieval Christendom into various 'churches' compelled the Roman Catholic Church (which as we know it today is largely the outcome of the Counter Reformation) to face that question, and it was answered in largely reactionary terms. The popes of the time and the theologians of the Council of Trent (1545–64) knew no other categories than 'catholic', 'schismatic' and 'heretic'. They therefore saw those who rejected some or all aspects of the visible, structured mediaeval Church as 'heretics', and proclaimed that those who remained in full communion with the See of Rome constituted the surviving 'Catholic Church' in the West, identified now by the sacramental and hierarchical structure so fully and clearly defined by the decrees of the Council of Trent. This concept found explicit formulation in the writings of the late sixteenth-century Jesuit theologian Robert Bellarmine as 'a perfect society subject to no other, and lacking nothing for its own institutional completeness'.[4] Clearly the intention was to secure the permanent emancipation of the Church from the control of secular rulers, but the unfortunate effect of thus describing the Church in quasi-political terms was to perpetuate the over-emphasis on external structures. While the Pauline concept of the Church as the Body of Christ was retained, the role of the Holy Spirit in constituting and animating the Church was virtually lost sight of altogether. As a result reaction to political developments and upheavals in Europe from the seventeenth to the nineteenth century stimulated a theology of the Church as a visible kingdom, constituted by hierarchical and especially papal authority, with grossly inadequate attention given to the dimension of spiritual reality.

In the mid-twentieth century the Second Vatican Council (1962–5) explicitly set out to correct this situation with a much more profound and nuanced ecclesiology, the fruit of various trends and streams of influence which developed both inside and outside the Catholic Church in the nineteenth and twentieth centuries.

The foundational document produced by that council is its dogmatic *Constitution on the Church* (commonly known by the opening words of the Latin text in *Lumen Gentium* [*Light of the Nations*], and so referred to as LG). Its position is reflected and further developed in a number of other Council documents, notably:

> *The Church in the Modern World* (*Gaudium et Spes* [*Joy and Hope*]: GS)
>
> *The Role of Bishops in the Church* (*Christus Dominus* [*Christ the Lord*]: CD)
>
> *Life and Ministry of Priests* (*Presbyterorum Ordinis* [*Priestly Order*]: PO)
>
> *Apostolate of the Laity* (*Apostolicam Actuositatem* [*Apostolic Activity*]: AA)
>
> *Missionary Activity of the Church* (*Ad Gentes* [*To the Nations*]: AG)
>
> *Ecumenism* (*Unitatis Redintegratio* [*Restoration of Unity*]: UR)
>
> *Non-Christian Religions* (*Nostra Aetate* [*Our Times*]: NA)
>
> *Revelation* (*Dei Verbum* [*The Word of God*]: DV)
>
> *The Liturgy* (*Sacrosanctum Concilium* [*This Holy Council*]: SC)

Lumen Gentium is really the first comprehensive statement of Roman Catholic ecclesiology from the highest source of authority – a General Council – since the decrees of the Council of Trent were specifically concerned with concrete issues rather than with the fundamental concept of ecclesiology. Consequently LG is the basic and primary source, but it does not of course come out of the blue. Rather it subsumes in a fuller vision perennial truths about the Church previously enunciated only partially or in isolation; its sources are evident in the scriptural, patristic, conciliar and theological references and quotations that are found throughout the documents mentioned – now to be read in a Vatican II perspective. While the character and content of *Lumen Gentium* will be presented here, this can be no substitute for reading the text itself; the material is dense, with every word well weighed, but not unduly complex.

THE NATURE AND MISSION OF THE CHURCH

Lumen Gentium opens with a programmatic phrase which defines the theme of the whole document: 'The Church in Christ is in the nature of a sacrament, that is, a sign and instrument of communion with God and union among all people' (LG, 1), a phrase re-echoed towards the end of the document: 'Rising from the dead Christ sent his life-giving Spirit upon his disciples, and through them set up his body which is the Church as the universal sacrament of salvation' (LG, 48). This sacramental concept of the Church is expounded with precision in article 8 of *Lumen Gentium*, which makes clear the Roman Catholic conviction that the earthly, visible structures of the Church are not just political arrangements but, having in some sense a divine origin, are in themselves sacramental:

> The one mediator, Christ, established and ever sustains here on earth his holy Church, the community of faith, hope and charity as a visible organisation through which he communicates truth and grace to all. But the society structured with hierarchical organs and the mystical body of Christ, the visible society and the spiritual community, the earthly Church and the Church endowed with heavenly riches, are not to be thought of as two realities. On the contrary they form one complex reality which comes together from a human and a divine element. For this reason the Church is compared, not without significance, to the mystery of the incarnate Word. As the assumed nature, inseparably united to him, serves the

Divine Word as a living organ of salvation, so in a somewhat similar way does the social structure of the Church serve the Spirit of Christ who vivifies it, in the building up of the body.

The intertwined treatment of the one complex reality which is the Church is pursued throughout the entire document in the very manner in which the contents are arranged.

Chapter one, 'The Mystery of the Church', treats of its spiritual, unseen dimension originating in the Trinity itself, in the light of God's fundamental plan to share his own life with the human race he has created (LG, 2–4). The incomprehensible depth of this mystery is brought to light in God's revelation of his plan in the Old Testament, where a variety of familiar images – flock, sheepfold, field, olive tree, vine, temple – foreshadow the definitive establishment of the Church on earth by Christ (LG, 5–6). That Church is seen to be constituted by the Holy Spirit as the mystical body of Christ, where 'the life of Christ is communicated to those who believe, and who through the sacraments are united in a hidden yet real way to Christ in his passion and glorification ... He has shared with us his Spirit who being one and the same in head and members, gives life to, unifies and moves the whole body. Consequently the work of the Spirit could be compared by the Fathers of the Church to the function that the principle of life, the soul, fulfils in the human body' (LG, 7).

Chapter two, 'The People of God', is linked to chapter one by article 8 quoted above, and deals essentially with the outward and visible aspect of the Church: the human beings who compose it. The implication of the title is taken up in finding the origin of the visible Church in the covenant people of the Old Testament, with its emphasis on the coherent and closely interrelated character of that community of salvation. 'The people of the new covenant, however, has Christ as its head ... its status is that of the dignity and freedom of the children of God ... its law is the new commandment of love ... and its destiny is the kingdom of God.' It is established by Christ as 'communion of life, love and truth, and taken up by him as the instrument of salvation for all' (LG, 9).

The practical working out of this salvation is then detailed in relation to each of the seven sacraments:

Incorporated into the Church by baptism the faithful are appointed to the duty of Christian worship. More perfectly bound to the Church by confirmation they are obliged, as true witnesses of Christ, to spread the faith by word and deed. Taking part in the eucharistic sacrifice they participate in Christ's offering of himself to the Father and offer themselves with him. In the sacrament of reconciliation they obtain God's merciful forgiveness, and are fully reconciled again with the community which is wounded by the sin of any of its members. The sacrament of anointing assures the sick of God's merciful love and their continued inclusion in the community of the Church. Ordination to the sacred ministry empowers those so chosen by God to serve the body of the Church by providing leadership and sacramental ministrations; while the sacrament of matrimony not only establishes what is aptly called the 'domestic church', but is itself the sacramental sign of the faithful love which unites Christ to his spouse, the Church. (LG, 11)

The implications of the title of chapter two, 'The People of God', remind us of the earthiness of this reality which is the visible aspect of the Church. A pilgrim people like the Israelites of old, it must experience constant movement and change, despite its attachment to eternal realities. It is inevitably influenced by structures, trends and events in human history, and it is subject to ignorance, error and sin. This aspect, briefly alluded to in *Lumen Gentium* ('The Church . . . at once holy and always in need of purification, follows constantly the path of penance and renewal' (8)), is brought out more fully in another document. *The Church in the Modern World* (GS) opens with a re-emphasis on the solidarity of the Church with the whole human family, and goes on to consider 'the aspirations, yearnings and often dramatic features of the world in which we live', the crises and problems produced by social and technological progress, and the implications of globalization (GS, 4–5, 8). It asserts the essential dignity of human nature made in the image of God, but recognizes the reality of sin in its social and universal as well as in its individual and personal dimensions (GS, 12–17). The communitarian nature of the human vocation and the interdependence of person and society is considered, along with paragraphs on the common good, respect for the human person, equality and social justice, responsibility and participation (GS, 24–31). The value of human activity and the rightful autonomy of human affairs are affirmed, together with the assertion that these have been affected by sin and need to find their ultimate fulfilment in the paschal mystery of Christ's redemptive death and glorification (GS, 34–8).

> Far from diminishing our concern to develop this earth, the expectancy of a new earth should spur us on, for it is here that the body of a new human family grows, foreshadowing in some way the age to come. That is why, although we must be careful to distinguish earthly progress from the increase of the kingdom of Christ, such progress is of vital concern to the kingdom of God in so far as it can contribute to the better ordering of human society. When we have spread on earth the fruits of our labour – human dignity, fraternal communion and freedom – according to the command of the Lord and in his Spirit, we shall find them once again, cleansed from the stain of sin, illuminated and transfigured when Christ presents to his Father an eternal and universal kingdom. (GS, 39)

A further aspect of the earthly dimension of the Church, touched on in *Lumen Gentium* chapter two, is its comprehensiveness and actual spread among the peoples of the world. Catholic or universal in intent, the catholic unity of the Church is seen, historically, as only partially and progressively realized. The concept of *koinonia*-communion gives rise to an exterior description of various categories, graduated in terms of the clarity and visibility of their relationship to the historic Church on earth. Thus Roman Catholics who accept its entire organization together with all the means of salvation offered, are fully incorporated into the visible structure of the Church. Catechumens are joined to that visible structure by their explicit desire for baptism. All the baptized, honoured by the name of Christian, though not professing the full Roman Catholic faith and not in full communion with the See of Rome, are seen as 'joined to the Church in many ways', that is, by many bonds of shared faith, sacramental and spiritual life and liturgy, devotion and virtue (LG, 15).

Those who have not yet received the Christian Gospel 'are related to the People of God in many ways': by the covenant and the promises of the Old Testament in the case of the Jewish people; by faith in the Creator, 'the one merciful God, mankind's judge on the last day' in the case of Islam; by their conscientious actions moved by grace in the case of those who sincerely seek an, as yet unknown, God, or who have not yet attained any explicit consciousness of God (LG, 16). A further document of Vatican II, *The Church's Missionary Activity* (AG) asserts the obligation of the Church, 'in obedience to the command of its founder' (Matthew 16.15) and because of its essential universality, to endeavour to spread the Gospel to all people (AG, 1). This principle is coupled with extensive treatment of the appropriate manner in which this should be done, in order to maintain respect for human dignity and freedom of conscience, as well as appreciation for the real values inherent in diverse religious and human cultures.

The aspect of the historical visibility of the Church is further developed, notably in the documents on *Ecumenism* (UR) and on *Non-Christian Religions* (NA). *Ecumenism* opens with the uncompromising statement, 'Christ the Lord founded one church and one church only, yet many Christian communions present themselves as the true inheritors of Jesus Christ . . . such division openly contradicts the will of Christ.' It continues: 'The Lord of Ages wisely and patiently follows out the plan of his grace on our behalf, sinners that we are' (UR, 1), and provides an extensive treatment of the Catholic involvement in the ecumenical movement. *Non-Christian Religions* opens with a generalized description of the phenomenon of religious consciousness and of world religions, and continues:

> The Roman Catholic Church rejects nothing of what is true and holy in these religions. It has a high regard for the manner of life and conduct, precepts and doctrines which, though differing in many ways from its own teaching, often reflect a ray of that 'truth which enlightens all people'. Yet it is in duty bound to proclaim Christ who is 'the way, the truth and the life' (NA, 2).

The two sides of the one complex reality which is the Church are further brought together in the placing of chapters three and four of *Lumen Gentium*, which deal respectively with the ordained and lay members of the Church. Chapter two pointed out that all baptized members of the Church share in the priestly, prophetic and kingly roles of Christ himself; and further that, while the 'common priesthood' received at baptism and the ordained or 'ministerial priesthood' are different modes of participating in the one priesthood of Christ, they are essentially related to each other in terms of service for empowerment, in fulfilment of the Christian vocation of all (LG, 10–13). Chapter three treats of the hierarchical structure of the Church; that is to say, it is mainly concerned with how the sacramentally ordained ministry provides the framework or skeleton which gives foundation and shape to the ecclesial life of the People of God. Chapter four deals with how the non-ordained actually live out their own participation in the priestly, prophetic and kingly role of Christ. Incorporated into Christ by baptism, their secular character is specific to the vocation and mission of lay people, who seek the kingdom of God precisely by engaging in temporal affairs. Appointed to this apostolate by the Lord himself in baptism and confirmation, they are called upon to make the Church present and fruitful especially in those circumstances or places where only they can bring the Gospel (LG, 31–3). Participating in the Eucharist and worshipping everywhere by their holy actions, they consecrate the world to God. Established as his witnesses and provided with a supernatural instinct for the faith (*sensus fidei*) they proclaim Christ by their words and by the testimony of their lives in the ordering of the circumstances of this world. They play a part in the advance of the kingdom of God by recognizing the inner worth of created things, impregnating culture and human works with moral values and so directing them according to the plan of the Creator and to the praise of God (LG, 34–6).

The theme of the goal and purpose of the Church is further pursued in chapter five on *The Universal Call to Holiness*.

> The followers of Christ . . . called by grace and justified in the Lord Jesus have been made children of God in the baptism of faith . . . and so are truly sanctified. They must hold on to and complete in their lives that sanctification they have received (LG, 40).

God has poured his love into our hearts through the Holy Spirit (Romans 5.5); so the most necessary gift is charity, by which we love God above all things and our neighbour for his sake. If this charity is to grow and flourish in the soul, the faithful will gladly hear, and obey the word of God, take part in the Church's liturgy, frequent the sacraments, especially the Eucharist, and apply themselves constantly to prayer, self-denial, active fraternal love and the exercise of all virtues (LG, 41–2).

The Church, however, will achieve its final perfection only in the glory of heaven when the sacraments and institutions of this age have passed away. When the Lord comes again in glory death will be no more, and all things will be subject to him. Until then some of his disciples are still pilgrims on earth; others have died and are being purified, while still others are in glory, in full light contemplating God as he is. Our belief in the communion of saints means that there is no interruption in the full communion of the wayfarers with those who sleep in the peace of Christ (LG, 48–9).

MINISTRY, LEADERSHIP AND CHURCH GOVERNMENT

In the Roman Catholic Church lay and ordained ministry differ from each other 'in essence, not only in degree' (LG, 10). While both share, each in its own proper way, in the one priesthood of Christ, the ordained ministry is not just an extension or fuller share in that 'royal priesthood' which all receive at baptism; rather 'it belongs to another realm of the gifts of the Spirit'.[5] This distinction is in line with Christian tradition as articulated by St Augustine of Hippo in the fifth century in relation to the Donatist schism, which recognizes sacramental ordination as lifelong and unrepeatable, in a manner analogous to baptism.[6] This view of the nature and function of ordained ministry is seen as the divinely inspired evolution of the apostolic ministry described in the later books of the New Testament, and witnessed to in the post-apostolic writings:

> Christ has, through his Apostles, made their successors the bishops ... sharers in his consecration and mission. These in turn have legitimately handed on to different individuals in the Church various degrees of participation in this ministry. The divinely established ecclesiastical ministry is exercised by those who have from antiquity been called bishops, priests and deacons (LG, 28, Abbott translation).

The purpose of this ordained ministry within the People of God is twofold: to provide leadership in continuity with Christ's own ministry as prophet, priest and king for the teaching, sanctifying and shepherding of his disciples; and to establish the sacramental structure of that *koinonia*-communion which is the Church. The overall function of leadership devolves on all three levels of ordained ministry, in a way proper to each:

> Bishops ... receive from the Lord the mission of teaching all peoples and preaching the Gospel to every creature ... They are authentic teachers ... endowed with the authority of Christ ... witnesses to divine and catholic truth ... who do proclaim infallibly the doctrine of Christ when ... in communion with each other and the successor of St Peter ... they agree that a particular teaching concerning faith or morals is to be definitively and absolutely held ... a position most clearly seen in the teaching of an ecumenical council (LG, 245).

The document on *The Role of Bishops* (CD) provides extensive discussion of the content and characteristic manner of their teaching, with notable emphasis on respect for the human person in all circumstances, contemporary human as well as spiritual relevance, and up-to-date methods and accessibility (CD, 12–14). Bishops exercise this teaching role personally by public preaching on all suitable occasions, and by frequent pastoral letters addressed to their clergy, the people of their diocese or specific groups within it. In practice they share this role with very many other ministers of the Church, both ordained and lay; so they also discharge their responsibility indirectly by promoting and overseeing the religious training and education of such other ministers – priests, deacons, catechists, teachers of religion and others – as well as by monitoring the content and practice of religious education in Catholic schools and institutions.

Deacons, whose liturgical service specifically includes the solemn proclamation of the Gospel, are also authorized to give catechetical instructions and so sometimes fulfil this function at the liturgy or in other suitable circumstances. However, the regular duty of teaching the faith, both within the Church and in unevangelized missionary contexts, falls chiefly on priests as the principal assistants of the bishop:

> Associated with the bishop by reason of their sacerdotal dignity and in virtue of the sacrament of orders, after the image of Christ the supreme and eternal High Priest, they are consecrated to preach the Gospel and shepherd the faithful,

as well as to celebrate divine worship as true priests of the New Testament (LG, 28).

The role of the priest is further developed in the document on *The Ministry and Life of Priests* (PO), in a spiritual, pastoral and practical manner which emphasizes that they owe it to everyone to share the truth of the Gospel in which they rejoice, 'presenting all aspects of the Christian message in various ways according to need, and in a manner that can be effective in moving the minds and hearts of their hearers' (PO, 4). It is they who are responsible for the initial introduction of the newly baptized, whether adults or children, to the truths of the faith, and for the provision of suitable catechesis to assist them to grow in that faith. Priests in official charge of parishes, or in comparable positions, are obliged to preach publicly on Sundays and all greater feasts which are 'holy days of obligation', and to ensure that those who present themselves for the sacraments of baptism, confirmation, Eucharist and matrimony are sufficiently instructed in the faith.

Again at this level the role of teaching is widely shared, with other priests serving the Church in various capacities, and with very many lay teachers and catechists – particularly members of religious orders – both in schools and in the mission field. All these are in some way authorized by the bishop. In practice a very large proportion of the Church's teaching function is carried out by school-teachers, mostly lay people, and by parents who are 'the first heralds of the faith to their children' (LG, 11).

A primary function of the ordained ministry is to provide for the sanctification of the whole of the People of God by celebrating the sacraments with and for the lay members of the Church. Sacramental ordination of priests and deacons is confined to the bishop, who shares his own priesthood, in differing degrees, with these fellow ministers. He is also the original minister of confirmation, which confirms the initial admission, by baptism, of new members to the Church. Baptism itself is normally celebrated in the solemn manner by a priest or deacon, but in circumstances of exceptional need anyone, believer or not, can baptize if the explicit intention is to do what the Church intends to do and a minister in priestly orders only can confirm, for whoever the human minister, it is Christ who is the ultimate minister of all the sacraments.[7]

The centre and summit of the Christian life is the celebration of the Eucharist 'in which the victory and triumph of Christ's death are again made present'.[8] At the Last Supper our Saviour instituted the eucharistic sacrifice of his body and blood as a 'sacrament of love, a sign of unity, and a bond of charity'.[9] It is the paschal banquet in which the feast of the body and blood of Christ 'is eaten, the mind is filled with grace, and the pledge of future glory is given to the faithful'.[10] Bishops, as the successors of the Apostles, were the first presidents of the eucharistic celebration, but very early in the Church's history it became necessary to provide additional ministers for this purpose, which seems indeed to have been the origin of an ordained ministry of the second, or priestly, rank. The Eucharist can only be celebrated under the presidency of a validly ordained priest but – despite centuries of stifling custom resulting from both inertia and inadequate awareness – the lay faithful are not, as Vatican II has pointed out, merely silent spectators (SC, 47). Rather they offer the eucharistic sacrifice not just through the hands of the priest but together with him, as an essential part of the worshipping Church, which is the mystical body of Christ the head. They offer themselves, along with Christ, to the Father, and seal their participation in this offering by receiving the eucharistic body of Christ in Holy Communion, which can also be carried to those who are absent by the deacon or other duly appointed lay ministers.

The ordained bishops and priests of the Church are also empowered to pronounce God's forgiveness of sin, in the words of absolution used in the sacrament of reconciliation or 'confession', which restores the baptismal holiness of the individual sinner, and of the Church community wounded by all such sin. Those prevented by sickness or frailty from joining the common public worship of the Church are sacramentally included therein by the sacrament of the sick, in which they are anointed with blessed oil to the accompaniment of prayer, by the ordained priest as official representative of the Church.

In Christian marriage the two baptized spouses confer the sacrament on each other, but in keeping with the tradition going back to the end of the first century, such a marriage must be sanctified by a public contract made in accordance with the conditions laid down by Church authority.[11] This normally requires the use of a prescribed form in the presence of the Church's officially recognized witness, usually a priest or deacon. The Catholic understanding of the sacramental nature of marriage arises from the participation of husband and wife in showing forth the mystery of the union between Christ and his Church (cf. Ephesians 5.32).

In providing for the sacramental structure of the Church, the ordained ministry is intimately associated with perpetuating, visibly on earth, Christ's role as shepherd of his flock. He described himself as the 'good shepherd' who laid down his life for his sheep, but after his resurrection he conferred real authority on those whom he commissioned to teach all nations (Matthew 28.19). He had declared that 'he who hears you hears me, and he who rejects you rejects me' (Luke 10.16) and told them that 'whatever you bind on earth shall be bound in heaven' (Matthew 18.18). Obviously the Church's ordained ministers should exercise Christ's authority with Christ's own gentleness and wisdom, but the fact that such authority was conferred on fallible and sinful men who frequently fall far short of that ideal, does not radically destroy their right and duty to make authoritative decisions for the life of the Church.

The authority rests primarily with the bishops who share it in due measure with the priests ordained by them. Over the centuries it has all too often been seen in political terms, since the human measures taken to select and appoint bishops are inevitably similar in many ways to those employed in other areas of human life. Moreover, the early development of a second rank of ministers, empowered to celebrate the Eucharist and pronounce absolution, tended to suggest that the difference between priests and bishops lay only in the extent of their respective spheres of authority. Vatican II put a decisive end to this misconception by its solemn affirmation that 'the fullness of the sacrament of orders is conferred by episcopal consecration . . . which is thus the acme of the sacred ministry' (LG, 21).

This firm teaching is concerned not so much to emphasize the power of bishops, as to make clear that the hierarchical structure of the Church as a whole is the product not merely of human political and administrative arrangements, but of the sacramental transmission of divine grace. In the face of a long period of inadequate understanding and perception, Vatican II was concerned to reassert that sacred power and authority in the Church are not so much 'possessed by' any individual of whatever rank, but rather that it is still Christ's own authority and power that are 'shared in' by various grades of ministry in various ways. This participatory nature of authority is further emphasized by the collegial character of the episcopate, in which bishops are not isolated and autonomous individuals; and by the fact that priests are seen to constitute with their own bishop a unique sacerdotal college or *presbyterium*. Moreover, as local representatives of the bishop, it is their function to 'assemble the family of God as a brotherhood fired with a single ideal' in each parish or equivalent part of the diocese, for teaching and worship (LG, 28).

As in the New Testament Peter emerges clearly as the head and spokesman of the college of apostles, so too the college of bishops, under Christ, has a visible head on earth in the pope. Catholics believe that Christ intended this primatial role of Peter to continue in his Church. The nature and function of the papacy as the centre and guardian of unity in the Church emerged gradually in history. In the early centuries, especially during persecution, local churches looked after their own affairs under the direction of their own bishops, and recourse to the Bishop of Rome seemed called for only in cases of major dispute. Two such early disputes concerned the terms on which apostates, who had denied their faith under persecution, should receive absolution – a matter of sharp disagreement among some leading bishops in the third century, and the correct date for the celebration of Easter, which divided the eastern and western regions of the Church in the fourth.

By the end of the second century St Irenaeus of Lyons had articulated the function of papal primacy:

We will refute all unauthorised assemblies . . . by pointing to the tradition of the greatest and oldest church . . . founded and established at Rome by the Apostles Peter and Paul . . . This tradition the Church has from the Apostles and their faith has been proclaimed to all men . . . For this church has a position of leadership and authority; and therefore every church, the faithful everywhere must needs agree with the Church of Rome; for in her the apostolic tradition has ever been preserved by the faithful from all parts of the world. The blessed Apostles, after they had founded and built the Church of Rome, handed on to Linus the office of bishop . . . He was succeeded by Anacletus . . . In this order of succession the apostolic tradition of the Church, and the preaching of the truth have come down to our own time.[12]

As with the episcopate, so the role and function of the papacy in the Church can be, and has been, subject to abuse and sometimes understood and exercised in human and political terms too far removed from those appropriate to a sacred office modelled on Christ himself. With the fourth-century Christianization of the Roman Empire, the Bishop of Rome was in fact encouraged to become a powerful political figure by the action of the Emperor Constantine in 'leaving' the City of Rome to the Church and building himself a new capital at Constantinople. In the fifth-century barbarian invasions, the bishops of Rome, like other bishops throughout the Empire, had to assume political and even military leadership. In the middle ages, when kings and emperors (like Henry II of England who instigated the murder of St Thomas of Canterbury) not infrequently usurped what were considered to be the rights of the Church, popes and bishops increasingly asserted – and sometimes exaggerated – those rights, consolidating their own positions in legal and political terms, so that it was difficult at times to distinguish between spiritual and political authority. In the later middle ages, when 'Christendom' was synonymous with Europe, the distinction was blurred even in theory, since the pope was theoretically accepted as the feudal overlord even of kings and emperors – a position that was recognized, for his own advantage, by King John of England at the time of *Magna Carta*.

While such abuses did not invalidate the doctrine of primacy, they certainly obscured it, rendering it unconvincing and eventually unacceptable, as became apparent in the East–West schism of 1054, and the sixteenth-century European Reformation. This did however provoke extensive reforms in papal practice. By the nineteenth century a different political and social climate suggested that the time had come to define and delimit clearly the nature and authority of the papacy, a task undertaken by the first Vatican Council in 1869–70. The language of that definition still reflects the stance of legal claims, but the claims made are confined exclusively to the spiritual and ecclesiastical sphere, with no remaining political overtones.

Vatican I's decree, *Pastor Aeternus* [*Eternal Shepherd*],[13] has four sections compiled in the manner which had become customary in the late middle ages: a chapter of theological reasoning is followed by a 'canon' or brief propositional statement of belief; only these canons are binding on catholic faith, though they should of course be interpreted in the light of the preceding chapters. Canon one requires belief that:

> Blessed Peter the Apostle was ... appointed prince of the Apostles and visible head of the whole Church militant; that he directly and immediately received from the same Lord Jesus Christ not just a primacy of honour only, but true and proper jurisdiction.

This proposition is based chiefly on the words of the risen Christ recorded in St Matthew's Gospel (16.16–19) and St John's Gospel (21.15–17).

Canon two declares:

> It is by the institution of Christ the Lord, by divine right, that Blessed Peter should have a perpetual line of successors in the primacy over the universal Church; and that the Roman Pontiff is the successor of Blessed Peter in this primacy.

Obviously no New Testament text can be adduced for this intention of Christ. It is supported, as to its permanence, by the historical witness of the Council of Ephesus in 431, and from the sermons of St Leo the Great, Pope from 440 to 461; and as to its collocation with the See of Rome, by the words of St Irenaeus already quoted, and those of St Ambrose of Milan at the Synod of Aquileia in 381.

Canon three declares that:

> The Roman Pontiff has the office not merely on inspection and direction, but of full and supreme power of jurisdiction over the universal Church, not only in matters which belong to faith and morals, but also in those which relate to the discipline and government of the Church throughout the world; and that he possesses not merely the principal part, but the fullness of this supreme power; further that this power is 'ordinary' and 'immediate' over each and all of the churches and each and all of the pastors and faithful.

The theological chapter preceding this canon makes clear that this extensive authority is seen as the necessary implication of Christ's commission to Peter to feed and govern his flock. It does not however prejudice the real authority of other bishops over their own particular churches. As *Lumen Gentium* says, 'Bishops, as vicars and legates of Christ, rule the particular churches assigned to them ... nor are they to be regarded as vicars of the Roman Pontiff, for they exercise the power which they possess in their own right' (LG, 27). While papal power is described in canon three as 'episcopal' this is not meant in a sacramental sense, but in the radical sense of the verb *episcopein*, to oversee.

Canon four, which was at the time of the subject of much greater debate, proclaims:

> Faithfully adhering to the tradition received from the beginning of the Christian faith ... with the approval of the Council we teach that it is a dogma divinely revealed that: the Roman Pontiff, when he speaks *ex cathedra*, that is, in discharging the office of pastor and teacher of all Christians, by virtue of his supreme apostolic authority, he defines a doctrine concerning faith or morals to be held by the universal Church, by the divine assistance promised to him in Blessed Peter, is possessed of that infallibility with which the Redeemer wished his Church to be endowed ... and therefore that such definitions are irreformable of themselves, and not because of the consent of the Church.

What is noticeable here of course is that the pope is formulating and expressing not his own personal faith, but the faith of the Church as such; he is the authentic mouthpiece of the Church in view of the doctrine of primacy defined above.

These canons reflect not only the papacy's vicissitudes but also the Church's problems with the democratic mood and prevalent philosophical and theological liberalism of late nineteenth-century Europe. But their formulation, far from precluding it, positively required that further analysis and development that was prevented at the time by the outbreak of the Franco-Prussian war in 1870. Official presentation of such contextual development had to wait for Vatican II, which firmly located this seemingly too powerful papacy within, and not above, the college of bishops (LG, 22). While the Bishop of Rome is recognized as head of the college, it is this college that exercises supreme authority over the whole Church, and papal primacy does not confer on the bishop of Rome any new sacramental power or authority. When he acts as pope, even on his own initiative, it is as head of the college of bishops that he acts.

A number of studies and reflections in the latter half of the twentieth century have gone on to explore how the doctrine of primacy might be more fruitfully entertained, if it could be more effectively distinguished from many historical aspects of its exercise in practice, now widely recognized as neither essential, nor in some cases even justified by that doctrine. Notable among these is the work of the Anglican–Roman Catholic International Commission expressed in the agreed statement, *The Gift of Authority*.[14]

UNITY, CATHOLICITY, APOSTOLICITY

The Church is universal in intent: 'Go therefore and make disciples of all nations' (Matthew 28.19). It is to be 'the universal sacrament of salvation' (LG, 48). This role necessarily implies both unity and catholicity. Moreover, as the Church is the *sacrament* of salvation, its unity must be visible in this world, secured by recognizable bonds of union. In the post-Reformation period such bonds were expressed in the *Catechism of the Council of Trent* as agreement in one faith, sharing in the same sacrifice and sacraments, and union under one head – the pope. In the twentieth century these bonds are more commonly expressed in somewhat more ecumenically friendly language as: a common profession of faith, common sacramental life and the acceptance of a common ordained ministry. But Catholics would still specify the sacrificial character of eucharistic worship, and the precise nature of the authority exercised by the ordained ministry, including papal primacy, which is indeed intended to be at the service of unity. Until the mid-twentieth century this service was seen mainly in its canonical or juridical aspect of speaking the final word on disciplinary or doctrinal matters. With the advent of Pope Paul VI in 1963 a new dimension became apparent in papal visits to many parts of the world, so that the ministry took on a more obviously personal quality, of interest and concern, a practice maintained by Pope John Paul II who, by the time of the millennium, had visited eighty-six different countries.

The role of the Church as the sacrament of salvation for all necessarily implies its real rootedness in all human cultures, and the consequent diversity of appearance, language and customs in which salvation will be preached, ministered and celebrated. This point was well made by Cardinal Ratzinger, Prefect of the Congregation for the Doctrine of the Faith, in connection with the publication, in 1994, of the *Catechism of the Catholic Church*. He pointed out that this universal text should now be transposed into

> local, regional or national catechisms, to give voice to the multiple gifts of the various churches which, in specific ways, welcome, develop and complete what belongs to their specific character and tradition, using their own language, respecting their socio-cultural characteristics, and their own ecclesial character and tradition.[15]

Such catholic diversity is secured by the recognition of the ecclesial reality of the local, particular churches in the dioceses led by bishops throughout the world, which 'are constituted after the model of the universal Church; it is in these and formed out of them, that the one and unique Catholic church exists' (LG, 23). Such local and particular churches cannot, however, be totally independent and self-sufficient; they must be in communion with all the rest if they are to be truly 'church'. Unity and catholicity are essentially correlative. A major sign and instrument of this communion among the churches is the college of bishops. The corporate character of the episcopate has always been apparent from the ancient liturgical custom of having three co-consecrators laying hands on the head of a new bishop at his consecration, though at times it has also been obscured by political or social emphasis on the authority of the individual bishop – the 'local ordinary' according to canon law in his own diocese.[16] Though Vatican II did reiterate that bishops rule the particular churches entrusted to them as vicars and legates of Christ (LG, 27), it also re-emphasized and developed the concept of collegiality:

> As in accordance with the Lord's decree St Peter and the rest of the Apostles constitute a unique apostolic college, so the Roman Pontiff, Peter's successor, and the bishops, successors of the Apostles, are related and united to each other in a similar way ... The holding of ecumenical councils over the centuries points to the collegiate character of the episcopate ...

A man is constituted a member of the episcopal body by sacramental consecration, and by hierarchical communion with the head and members of the college ... This college is the expression of the multifariousness and universality of the People of God, and of the unity of the flock of Christ ... In it bishops exercise their own proper authority for the good of their faithful ... but as members of the college and successors of the Apostles by Christ's arrangement and decree, each is bound to be solicitous for the entire Church. (LG, 22–3)

'That membership of the College which is an essential element of the universal Church, is anterior to the individual bishop's headship of a particular church.'[17]

The practice of such collegiality has been further enhanced since Vatican II by the establishment of national or regional Bishops' Conferences – permanent institutions in which a given grouping of bishops collaborates in the joint exercise of certain teaching or pastoral functions for the greater good of their own people and of the universal Church. While such Conferences do not exercise the solemn authority of the entire episcopate of the Church, they do provide an obvious local and concrete application of its collegial character. 'Their importance is seen in the fact that they contribute effectively to unity between the bishops, and thus to the unity of the Church ... a most helpful means of strengthening ecclesial communion.'[18]

Since the collegial character of the episcopate is derived from the apostolic college, it is in this context that bishops should be seen as successors of the apostles. It is not, now, a matter of tracing a direct linear succession in any particular diocese back to an original apostolic holder of the see, though such linear succession was considered significant in the earliest centuries of the Church, and was cited by St Irenaeus as the guarantee of the authenticity of tradition.[19] Rather the college of bishops, membership of which is anterior to the headship of a particular church, is seen as succeeding collectively as a constituent element of the Church, to the college of Apostles as such; thus it provides the main vehicle and guarantee of the apostolicity of the Church throughout the ages.

It was the primary role of the Apostles to hand on by the spoken word of their preaching, by the example they gave, by the institutions they established what they themselves had received, whether from the lips of Christ, from his way of life and his works or whether learned from the prompting of the Holy Spirit ... This was faithfully done by the Apostles and by others associated with them ... In order that the full living Gospel might always be preserved in the Church the apostles left the bishops as their successors (DV, 7).

While the apostolic succession of the episcopal college provides the main guarantee for the continued apostolicity of the Church, it is evident from the very elements mentioned above as part of the tradition to be transmitted, that even securely established episcopal succession does not comprehend the whole of that quality of apostolicity which must characterize the life of the Church. Apostolic doctrine is formulated in credal statements believed, recited, studied and pondered by all the faithful. The salvation brought by Christ is made accessible in sacraments and worship celebrated by the People of God as a whole, and lived out in the spiritual and moral lives of each and every member of the Church. The apostolic succession of the episcopal college is the visible focus and manifestation of the apostolicity of the whole Church.

KOINONIA-COMMUNION

A limited concept of *koinonia*-communion has been current in the Church for centuries, witnessed to by the practice of referring to the reception of the sacrament of the Eucharist as *Holy Communion*, for in this sacrament the worshipper is offered the closest possible communion with God through the redemptive sacrifice of Christ. As the first Epistle of John says: 'Our communion [*koinonia*] is with the Father and with his Son, Jesus Christ' (1 John 1.3).

The twentieth century has seen both a deepening and a broadening of this concept, notably in a more vivid realization of the essential relationship that must exist between all those who are thus in communion with God through Christ. So the Church itself is seen as an organic communion held together by the life of grace bestowed on all the redeemed. This has encouraged a shift from a mainly structural concept of the Church to a more christological one: Vatican II described the Church as 'a communion of life, love and truth' (LG, 9), and saw the one, unique Catholic Church as 'formed in, and out of particular churches' headed by individual bishops in communion with each other (LG, 23). The reality of this one Church does not consist merely in a federation of individual churches. On the contrary, that communion which is the mysterious, spiritual essence of the Church is prior to the existence of any particular local church, and is visibly secured by communion with the see of Peter.[20]

Such a concept of communion had already appeared in the 1943 encyclical letter of Pope Pius XII, *The Mystical Body of Christ*,[21] which pointed out that 'those oriented towards the mystical body of the Redeemer by some unconscious desire and resolve', are already moved by grace. From this it was a short step to conclude with St Irenaeus that 'where the Spirit is, there is the Church'.[22] That step was formally taken by Vatican II in *Lumen Gentium* in the formulation: 'the sole Church of Christ *subsists in* the Church governed by the successors of Peter' (LG, 8), with its clear recognition that Christ's one Church is not coterminous only with the Roman Catholic Church.

This move has done much to revitalize the life of the Church in many ways. The corollary, that there must be varying levels or depths of communion, according to the intensity of any believer's relationship with Christ, provided the concept of partial or imperfect communion with the visible Church, a concept which has done so much to replace a negative divisiveness with a positive and optimistic outlook in the ecumenical movement. That movement has however sharpened the question of how the nature of the Church as a 'communion of life, love and truth' is related to its structured, visible manifestation, which is constitutive of its very nature precisely as the *sacrament* of salvation. Three aspects, or levels, of communion can be usefully identified:

> Communion in the Holy Spirit with God and with all who enjoy his grace is the gift of God and an objective reality, irrespective of the human consciousness of it. As St Augustine said of the fourth-century Donatists, 'We are brothers whether we like it or not.'[23]

Such communion in the Spirit is of its nature invisible, but also, of its nature, tends towards visible manifestation in and through a community in which the reality can be recognized, expanded and deepened. On this second level such community is made visible and actual by the traditional bonds of communion – profession of one faith, sharing in one sacramental life and the acceptance of a common ministry.

A third level is that of canonical communion – the articulation and acceptance of recognizable, juridical norms, the presence or absence of which can be verified, and the purpose of which is to maintain and protect real communion. For Catholics such norms are found in the visible structure of the Church already described. They must however remember that such structures may protect, but do not of themselves create or guarantee, the inner reality of communion with God. As Vatican II pointed out about Roman Catholics, 'their status results not from their own merits but from the grace of Christ; if they fail to respond in thought, word and deed, they will not merely not be saved, but will be the more severely judged' (LG, 14). On the other hand churches and ecclesial communities lacking some of the visible elements that Catholics consider necessary for the fullest expression of communion 'are not deprived of significance and importance in the mystery of salvation, for the Spirit of Christ has not refrained from using them as means of salvation' (UR, 3).

Ecumenical dialogue has given ample illustration of the reality of partial but imperfect communion between the Roman Catholic Church and various others, as well as the differing configurations each gives to the required exterior bonds of communion. For Catholics these find their ultimate focus in the sacrament of the Eucharist in which 'the unity of believers who form one body in Christ (cf. 1 Corinthians 10.17) is both expressed and brought about' (LG, 3). Eucharistic communion and ecclesial communion are considered to be inseparable,[24] since the Eucharist is a 'church-making sacrament'.[25] 'The bread and wine become the sacramental body and blood of Christ in order that the community may become more truly what it already is, the body of Christ'.[26] 'Receiving communion should always imply a longing to be more closely united with the Church, as members of Christ's body'.[27] For this reason the Roman Catholic Church offers eucharistic hospitality to other Christians only by way of exception, in particular cases.

The Tradition of the early, undivided Church made sharing fully in the same faith the condition for sharing fully in the

Eucharist ... only the full reconciliation of Christians can make normal the full sharing together in the sacrament of unity.[28]

DIVERSITY AND THE ECUMENICAL FUTURE

Increasing appreciation of the nature of the Church as a communion opens the way for a fuller acceptance of the fact that true and full communion need not preclude diversity among the members of the Church. In the aftermath of the sixteenth-century Reformation, security in the truth was sought by a strong tendency towards uniformity in the definition of doctrine, in the mode and expression of sacramental liturgy and in ecclesiastical and moral discipline. Yet there has always been diversity in the Catholic Church. There are twenty-three Catholic rites, each with its own liturgy, sacramental discipline, canon law and spirituality, all in full communion with the See of Rome. Though the Western, Latin rite is numerically the largest, they include communities of Eastern Christians who have maintained or renewed communion with Rome, while preserving their own religious and cultural heritages, which are more closely related to those of the Orthodox Churches. The proliferation of religious orders in the Catholic Church has also meant a great deal of variety in the way the life of the Church is lived out in practice, and the renewed openness of the Church to the world around it since Vatican II has provided the opportunity for a more positive appreciation of such diversity. The tone for this was set by the opening paragraph of *The Church in the Modern World*: 'The joy and hope, the grief and anguish of people of our time ... are the joy and hope, the followers of Christ. Nothing genuinely human fails to find an echo in their hearts' (GS, 1). Real integration with and participation in human history as it is being played out, necessarily demands of the Church a movement away from the static, almost frozen, uniformity of outlook and practice that characterized it, to a large extent, between the Council of Trent in the sixteenth century and the Second Vatican Council in the twentieth. Sent as the universal sacrament of salvation to meet, sanctify and save men and women where they are in everyday life, the Church must constantly learn how to preach the unchanging Gospel in all the varieties of human culture and circumstance.

This need for change and diversity was clearly expressed by Pope John XXIII in his opening speech to the Second Vatican Council:

> We sometimes have to listen, much to our regret, to persons who, though burning with zeal are not endowed with too much sense of discretion and measure ... They say that our era in comparison with the past is getting worse, and behave as if they had learned nothing from history, which is none the less the teacher of life ... We must disagree with these prophets of gloom who are always forecasting disaster ... In the present order of things divine providence is leading us to a new order of human relations, which by men's own efforts and even beyond their very expectations, are directed to the fulfilment of God's designs; and everything, even human differences, leads to the greater good of the Church ... Authentic doctrine should be studied and expounded through the methods of research and literary forms of modern thought. The substance of the ancient doctrine of the deposit of faith is one thing, and the way in which it is presented is another.[29]

Consequently while the ecumenical hope of Catholics is for one visibly united Church in communion with the pope, the successor of St Peter, they realize that that one Church will not be a repetition of past structural uniformity, but a communion which embraces all the gifts of the Spirit present in other Christian churches and ecclesial communities. This will moreover demand further changes in the Catholic Church, notably in the manner in which papal primacy is exercised as a service of unity, a fact strikingly recognized by Pope John Paul II in his 1995 encyclical *Ut Unum Sint* [*That They May Be One*].

> Whatever relates to the unity of all Christian communities clearly forms part of the concerns of the primacy ... I am convinced that I have a particular responsibility in this regard, above all in acknowledging the ecumenical aspirations of the majority of Christian communities and in heeding the request made of me to find a way of exercising the primacy which, while in no way renouncing what is essential to its mission, is none the less open to a new situation ... I insistently

pray the Holy Spirit to shine his light upon us, enlightening all the pastors and theologians of our churches, that we may seek – together of course – the forms in which this ministry may accomplish a service of love recognised by all concerned. This is an immense task which we cannot refuse and which I cannot carry out by myself. Could not the real but imperfect communion existing between us persuade church leaders and their theologians to engage with me in a patient and fraternal dialogue on this subject, a dialogue in which, leaving useless controversies behind, we could listen to one another, keeping before us only the will of Christ for his Church ... 'that they all may be one ... so that the world may believe that you have sent me'.[30]

On the way to that goal of full visible communion, Catholics should, after the example of the pope, look for and encourage opportunities and means of living out in practice the degree of imperfect communion that we already recognize.

Despite the very serious schisms and divisions tearing us apart, in all the communities of the baptised in the East and in the West there is to be seen a surprising vitality ... If it is 'in one Spirit that we have all been baptised into one body', what is the relation between this Spirit of unity which we can be sure is effective, and the division between confessions which however does not cause the wellspring of grace to dry up?[31]

At a significant inter-church gathering in Swanwick, England in 1987 Cardinal Hume, as spokesman for the Catholic Church in England and Wales, said:

I hope that our Roman Catholic delegates will recommend to the members of our Church that we now move quite deliberately from a situation of co-operation to one of commitment to each other. By 'commitment' I mean that we commit ourselves to praying and working together for church unity, and to acting together both nationally and locally for evangelisation and mission ... I would like to see this commitment become official policy.[32]

It has indeed become official policy in many parts of the Church, but the real reception of it by the rank and file, in a way that will permeate the whole of Catholic church life, is a much slower process.

FURTHER READING

ARCIC, *The Church and Salvation*. ACC/CTS 1987.
ARCIC, *Church as Communion*. ACC/CTS 1991.
Congar, Yves, *Lay People in the Church*. Geoffrey Chapman 1965.
Coughlan, Peter, *The Hour of the Laity*. Philadelphia, E. J. Dwyer, 1989.
Dulles, A., *Models of the Church*. Dublin, Gill & Macmillan, 1976.
Farmer, Jerry T., *Ministry in Community*. Louvain, Peeters, 1993.
Hamer, Jerome, *The Church is a Communion*. Geoffrey Chapman 1964.
Ker, Ian, *Newman and the Fullness of Christianity*. T. & T. Clark 1993.
Küng, Hans, *Structures in the Church*. New York, Thomas Nelson, 1964.
Küng, Hans, *The Church*. Burns & Oates 1967.
Montini, G. B., *The Church*. Dublin, Helicon, 1964.
Preston, Geoffrey, *Faces of the Church*. T. & T. Clark 1997.
Thornhill, John, *Sign and Promise*. Collins 1988.

NOTES

1. Throughout this essay the short form 'Catholic' means Roman Catholic unless the context indicates otherwise.
2. Scriptural quotations have been taken from the Revised Standard Version, Reference Edition, Thomas Nelson, London and New York 1952.
3. Ignatius, 'To the Smyrnaeans', 8.
4. Bellarmine, *Disputations*. Tome 2, book 3, *The Church* c.2 (Naples, Giulano, 1857), tr. present author.
5. Anglican–Roman Catholic International Commission [ARCIC], *Final Report*. CTS/SPCK 1982 (Ministry and Ordination: 13).

6. Cf. Augustine, *Against the Writing of Parmenianus*, tr. B. Leeming in *Principles of Sacramental Theology* (Longmans 1960), p. 156.

7. Cf. Augustine, *Homilies on John's Gospel*, tr. J. W. Rettig (Washington, Catholic University of America, 1988), on John 6.1.

8. Council of Trent, *Decrees*, tr. J. A. McHugh and J. F. Wagner (New York, Callan, 1923), *Decree on the Eucharist*, 5.

9. Augustine, on John 6.13 (see n. 7).

10. *Divine Office According to Roman Rite*. Evening Prayer II for the Feast of the Body and Blood of Christ. Collins 1974.

11. Cf. St Ignatius of Antioch, *Letter to Polycarp*, 5, in Bettenson, H., ed., *Early Christian Fathers*. Oxford University Press 1969.

12. Irenaeus, *Against Heresies* 3.3.1–2, in Bettenson.

13. Butler, C., *The Vatican Council*. Longmans 1930.

14. ARCIC, *The Gift of Authority*. CTS/Church House Publishing 1999.

15. Ratzinger, *Catechismo e Inculturazione–Catechesis and Inculturation*. Quoted by J. Komonchak in 'The Authority of the Catechism' in *The Living Light*. Washington 1993.

16. *Code of Canon Law*, tr. Canon Law Society (Collins 1983), no. 135.

17. Cardinal George Basil Hume, 'Effective Collegiality', Address to USA Bishops' Conference, 18 June 1999, in *Briefing*, London, 14 July 1999.

18. Hume, 'Effective Collegiality'.

19. Irenaeus, *Against Heresies* 3.3.1.

20. Cf. Ratzinger, 'Letter on Some Aspects of the Church as Communion'. *Osservatore Romano*, Rome, 17 June 1992.

21. Pius XII, *The Mystical Body of Christ*, English edition. CTS 1943.

22. Irenaeus, *Against Heresies* 24.1.

23. Augustine, *Commentary on Psalm* 32, tr. G. Hebgin and F. Corrigan (Longmans 1961), p. 29.

24. *Directory for the Application of Norms and Principles of Ecumenism* (CTS 1993), 129.

25. Catholic Bishops' Conferences of England and Wales, Ireland and Scotland, *One Bread, One Body* (London 1998), 53.

26. ARCIC, *Final Report, Eucharist, Elucidation*, 6 (see n. 4).

27. *One Bread, One Body*, 53.

28. *One Bread, One Body*, 93.

29. Abbott, W. M., ed., *Documents of Vatican II* (Geoffrey Chapman 1966), pp. 710ff. Other quotations from the Documents of Vatican II have been taken from the Flannery translation (Dublin, Dominican Publications, 1975), except where otherwise indicated, with occasional corrections in the light of the Latin text (Vatican Polyglott Press, 1974) by the present author.

30. John Paul II, *Ut Unum Sint – That They May Be One*, English edition (CTS 1995), 95–6.

31. J. M. R. Tillard, 'From BEM to Koinonia'. Unpublished paper for Faith and Order plenary commission meeting, Moshi, 1996.

32. 'Cardinal's Decisive Intervention', Address to Swanwick Inter-Church Meeting, 1987. In *Briefing*, London, 18 September 1987.

5

The Baptist and Pentecostal Churches

Brian Haymes

Baptist and Pentecostal Churches are both expressions of evangelical Christianity. However, it should not be assumed that they have similar ecclesiologies with only minor differences. Such an assumption would be misguided and this chapter will attempt to show the theological differences.

Two limitations need to be identified. First, the understanding of being Baptist which will be described here reflects the tradition of Baptist Churches in membership of the Baptist Union of Great Britain. While it is Baptist ecclesiology which is the general subject, the fact is that Baptists are a very diverse people and not all who claim the name Baptist will be ready to recognize the portrait painted here. The truth is that Baptists have never been a theologically monochrome people. Today there is considerable diversity among them in understandings of the Faith and its practice, so much so that the ancient joke is often repeated, namely that the person who can speak for all the Baptists has yet to be born and the parents are dead!

Second, even wider diversity is to be found among Pentecostal groups, reflecting the dynamic and spontaneous nature of the movement. A consequence of this is that generalizations are difficult and, whereas there are many fine historical and social studies of Pentecostalism, there is a lack of substantial works of Pentecostal ecclesiology. For the purposes of this chapter, by Pentecostal we shall mean those specific groupings of Pentecostal churches, such as The Assemblies of God, which have taken a denominational form. A distinction is also drawn between denominational Pentecostalism and what is commonly called the charismatic movement. This has impacted all the major denominations and its effect will be mentioned but it will not be further discussed.

Like all denominations, both Baptists and Pentecostalists believe they are part of the one Church of Jesus Christ. Neither sought initially to be separate denominations but rather hoped to be renewal movements within the churches of their day. Both suffered severe criticism, not to say persecution, from the churches they implicitly or directly criticized. For both of them what was at issue was the importance of the Church being the Church. In their beginning and still today they see themselves as belonging to the one Church of Jesus Christ. For example, on Monday 17 January 1905 in London, the Baptist World Alliance formally came to birth. Baptists had come from all over the world under the presidency of Revd Alexander Maclaren. In his inaugural address he invited those present to do something rather unusual for Baptists. He called on the representatives to stand and recite together the Apostles' Creed so that there be no doubt that Baptists belong in the 'continuity of the historic Church'. This was a surprising request because Baptists do not often use creeds in worship. However, the intention was clear enough. Baptists, whatever others have said about them, sometimes in dismissive sectarian terms, have understood themselves to be part of the one Church of Jesus Christ.

Baptist Churches are children of the Reformation. The Reformation raised questions of authority in and out of the Church. The printing and availability of the Bible meant that what had been unquestioned teachings of the Church came under scrutiny. Contrasts were drawn between what the Church had become compared with the record of its life in the New Testament. Questions of power, authority, responsibility, ministry, were all out in the open. What is of no doubt is that it was precisely the doctrine of the Church that was the issue at the centre of Baptist beginnings. Where was the true Church to be found? In their early days and now, Baptists are not able to recognize particular features of some traditions as being true to the Church. They have dissented in the interests of what they believed to be purity of doctrine and practice. Although relationships between Roman Catholic, Anglican and Orthodox Christians have been at times distressingly painful, for which Baptists must bear their share of blame, all this has had to do with the importance of the Church in the calling and purposes of God. Of course, all other denominations will say the same, which is only to affirm that this collection of essays is on a crucial topic.

The desire that the church should be true to the Church of the New Testament is a fundamental tenet of Pentecostalism. It claims not that it is a new movement in itself so much as one inseparably related to what God did on the day of Pentecost when the disciples received the promised Holy Spirit (Acts 2). Pentecostalists argue that God has always kept his Church by the work of the Spirit. 'Baptism in the Spirit' is understood to be normative for all Christians. The outbreak of tongues speaking in Topeka, Kansas in 1901 and the Azusa Street services of 1906 in Los Angeles are taken to be 'initial evidence' of the blessing of the Holy Spirit, the Spirit always at work in all God's people. As in the New Testament, so for Pentecostalists, the key question is, 'Have you received the Spirit?' If the answer is 'No', or a bemused look, then the respondent has still some way to go before they are 'really' a Christian. Of course, this begs the questions about what it means to receive the Spirit, how is the Spirit given, and how can we be sure that this really is the Holy Spirit and not simply the up-rush of religious enthusiasm. However, once again, the issue is the nature of the true Church and where it will be found. Pentecostalists will say it is where testimony to the work of the Spirit is given.

Early Pentecostalism, although it had roots in the Holiness traditions, was sometimes denounced by other evangelicals for its alleged emotionalism and the subordination of the Bible to experience. Likewise, early Baptists also were criticized and persecuted by the established churches. In consequence, relations with other churches have sometimes been fragile. Presently, a number of Baptist Unions are members of national Councils of Churches and of the World Council of Churches. The Baptist Union of Great Britain, for example, is a founder member of both the old British Council of Churches and of the World Council of Churches. However, some large groupings of Baptists still stand outside the ecumenical movement, seeing their participation as a compromise. For example, the numerically enormous Southern Baptist Convention in America initially refused to seek membership of the World Council because it was a Council of Churches and Baptists do not see themselves as a Church. Pentecostalism has also shown anti-ecumenical attitudes citing such reasons as the liberalism of ecumenism and the participation of the Roman Catholic Church. However, local Pentecostal congregations may well be ready to share with other evangelical groups, especially in

evangelistic work, but there remains deep antipathy towards the
Roman Catholic Church for what are taken by Pentecostalists to
be distortions of the gospel of Jesus Christ. The issues are as
serious as that.

One consequence of this is that Pentecostalism, although it has
become so strong, has remained outside the ecumenical movement. Sadly, we have no Pentecostal response to the 'Lima
Document'. There are responses from several Baptist Unions and
Baptists have been involved in interdenominational conversations, for example, with Anglicans, Roman Catholics, Reformed
and Methodists. Surprisingly there has been a limited Pentecostal–Roman Catholic dialogue since 1972 and these conversations
owe a great deal to the Pentecostal leader David Du Plessis.
Increasingly there have been more Pentecostal leaders sharing
these meetings as representatives of their denominations. Some
national Councils of Churches include black churches that often
have a Pentecostal emphasis. None the less, it is a fact of history
that internationally Baptists and Pentecostalists, who have
together been so concerned about the Church, have been part of
the awkward squad as far as ecumenism is concerned.

Baptists and Pentecostalists are more ready to share discussions,
worship and acts of mission with other Christians than used to be
the case. It is possible to find the old hard exclusivist attitudes on
both sides of the divide but these are less and less common. Pentecostalism has shown remarkable growth and in many parts of the
world now exists as a dynamic movement. With growth has come
confidence, not least for self-criticism! The influence of the charismatic movement on other churches has also brought change,
although not necessarily of the kind that enables Pentecostal
denominations to come into partnership. The fact remains that
Baptists and Pentecostalists still believe that there are aspects of
being faithful as Church, drawn from the Bible, to which their
own convictions and history, bear witness.

THE SOURCES OF BAPTIST AND
PENTECOSTAL ECCLESIOLOGIES

The first of the Fundamental Truths, the doctrinal statement of
the Elim Churches made in 1993, reads, 'We believe the Bible,
as originally given, to be without error, the fully inspired and

infallible Word of God and the supreme and final authority in all matters of faith and conduct'. The basic theological principle of the Pentecostal movement is biblical experiential theology, where the experience shows itself physically. Basically, Pentecostalists adhere to the affirmations of evangelical Christianity and the content of the Fundamental Truths is unexceptional at times in this respect. Some Pentecostalists tend towards a basic unreflective and uncritical biblicism. Inevitably, this has led to differences of interpretation and serious theological disagreements, for example, on Christology. Such disagreements are not always resolved and have resulted in further division. Generally speaking the sources of Pentecostal ecclesiology are conservative evangelical doctrine, pre-millennial eschatology and a literalistic fundamentalistic approach to biblical interpretation. The appeal to direct experience of God, of being led by God, and the power of testimony, all these are essentially part of this whole approach. It makes the need for discernment crucial. In this respect, the pastors of Pentecostal churches, as preachers of the Word and church planters, are often figures of significant authority in their congregations. There is evidence however of more nuanced theological responses coming from some Pentecostalists, for example, in the *Journal of Pentecostal Theology* begun in 1992. Generally, theology has not been well thought of among Pentecostals who have prized instead direct practical experience of the Spirit and the gift of faith. Hence Pentecostals have not felt the need to produce comprehensive theological systems and have lived largely within the convictions of evangelicalism.

What about Baptists and the sources of their ecclesiology? Baptists also see in Scripture an authoritative source for faith and practice but not quite as Pentecostalists do. As heirs of the Reformation, Baptists recognize the significance of the tradition of Christian faith and witness but argue that that tradition is always to be tested against Scripture. Likewise, Baptists have honoured the creeds of the Church but have not set them alongside or above Scripture. Historically, Baptists have been more concerned with drawing up confessions of faith. These confessions, usually reflecting in early days a Calvinistic origin, differentiated Baptists from other groups of Christians and attempted to justify their separate existence. But Baptists have been non-credal in that they have not sought to establish binding authoritative confessions of faith on one another. These confessions were often revised as a result of further discussion and many confessions would often acknowledge that what was written had a penultimacy about it because the Lord had yet more light and truth to break forth from out of his holy Word. Baptist confessions often had a clause such as this from the 1646 edition of the London Particular Baptist Confession:

> Also we confess that we now know but in part and that we are ignorant of many things which we desire to and seek to know: and if any shall do us that friendly part to show us from the Word of God that we see not, we shall have cause to be thankful to God and to them.

The quotation illustrates the authority of Scripture, the lesser status of confessions and a humility, which Baptists have sometimes but not always shown before the truth of God. The confessions themselves were heavily marked with Scripture references. It was Scripture that was the guide to recovering the genuine apostolic life of the Church. It was against Scripture that other traditions had to be judged. Any who wrote creeds and sought to compel assent, or insist upon assent, over-stepped the mark as far as Baptists were concerned, for they were claiming for their words an authority which belongs to the Word of God alone. This point is perhaps strongest in its negative aspects. Many Baptists, for example, are not against using the ancient creeds, recognizing that they affirm the faith of the Church. But creeds and confessions are not so final that they cannot be revised and re-expressed. At best, creeds have a penultimacy about them and, of themselves, could never be the basis of Christian fellowship.

THE NATURE OF THE CHURCH AND ITS MISSION

In the Fundamental Truths of the Elim Churches the paragraph on the Church states, 'We believe in the spiritual unity and the priesthood of all believers in Christ and these comprise the universal Church, the Body of Christ.' Later, under the heading of the Commission, it reads, 'We believe that the gospel embraces the needs of the whole man and that the Church is therefore commissioned to preach the gospel to the world and to fulfil a ministry of healing and deliverance to the spiritual and physical needs of mankind.' This is a minimal definition of the Church but links the being of the Church with mission. All this is in keeping with our earlier observation that Pentecostalism is a movement before it is a denomination. The word 'fellowship' is important, for Pentecostalism sees the Church as a fellowship of professed Christians, those 'born again', a community of those who have a personal experience of salvation and so are united in Christ.

Many Pentecostal denominations argue for the autonomy of local congregations, on the basis of the assertion that there is no evidence of organization beyond the local congregation in the Bible. So Danish Pentecostals state, 'The Pentecostals believe that each congregation should be free and independent as were all the congregations mentioned in the Scriptures, and that they reject all kinds of organization and establishment of denominations except the foundation of local churches'.[1] This suggests a congregational system but this is not the case with all for some Pentecostal bodies have the word Church in their title.

The fact is that because of its experiential movement based nature, Pentecostalism has taken many forms. Alongside the congregational types there are others with episcopal or presbyterial forms of organization. There are differences of opinion on baptism, on the necessity of speaking in tongues, the status of pastors and apostleship. Although early hopes were that the movement could be free from doctrinal disputes, these inevitably came and with them ecclesiological issues of authority and doctrine. The result has been the multiplying of denominations, one of the very things against which early Pentecostals turned. Walter Hollenweger comments that 'the distinctive focal point of a denomination is no longer the Pentecostal experience, but Pentecostal doctrine; this has come about since the majority of members and quite a few pastors have no longer undergone the experience of baptism of the Spirit'.[2] Here is the nub of the matter, for Pentecostals hold the conviction that the Church consists of those regenerate by the Holy Spirit and made new in Jesus Christ. This is a lived experience, witnessed to in Scripture, before it is a doctrine. It was because many early Pentecostals did not see this work of the Spirit in other churches that they felt the need to found new congregations of those who had experienced the renewing work of God. Without it there is no Church of God, only a religious organization with its power structures and its methods of control. The life of the Church is grounded in the life of God.

Pentecostalism, as a twentieth-century phenomenon, is a response to the forms of Christianity prevalent at the beginning of the twentieth century. To identify a Baptist understanding we must recall the context of seventeenth-century England. For Dissenters, life was hard and persecution not unknown. The alliance of church and state meant that not to conform to the laws relating to worship was tantamount to being a traitor. Some, reluctantly, felt that under such oppression the only way they could practise their religion was to go abroad. One of those was Thomas Helwys (1550?–1615?), squire of Broxtowe in Nottinghamshire, who went with others to Holland where he met with more dissenters, most particularly John Smyth, and also encountered the Mennonites. Eventually Helwys returned to England and established the first Baptist Church on British soil in 1612. Helwys argued for religious freedom for all. Certainly, if Jesus Christ is Lord, the Church cannot live under the authority of the State. Helwys was imprisoned for this authentic Baptist conviction.

Helwys was a General Baptist, that is, one whose theology was broadly Arminian. A few years later, Baptist churches of a more Calvinist theology were formed, known as Particular Baptists. These were congregations which came out of Separatism and Congregationalism largely on the matter of baptism. Identifying this difference illustrates again that from the earliest times Baptists have never been without different strands of understanding to their life and doctrine.

The group who returned to England with Thomas Helwys wrote a Confession of Faith containing a short crisp paragraph on the Church. It reads,

> That the church off CHRIST is a compainy off faithful People 1 Cor. 1.2 Eph 1.1 seperated fro the world by the word and Spirit off GOD. 2 Cor 6.17. being kint vnto the LORD, & one vnto another, by Baptisme. 1 Cor. 12.13 Vpon their owne confessio of the faith. Act. 8.37. and sinnes. Mat. 3.6 [3]

Here are affirmed two fundamental Baptist ecclesiological convictions. First, the Church is the creation of God. God calls the Church into being and therefore its origin is in the purposes and intention of God. Hence the Church is no accident of history, no optional extra within the divine economy. The Church is a company of people, graciously gathered by God, under Christ the Lord, united in the fellowship of the Holy Spirit. Its existence is always a serious, urgent and theologically crucial matter. The absence of the church, or any grave distortion of its faith and life, is deeply significant, not least for the world. So a Baptist understanding of the Church and its mission begins with God. Central is the person of Jesus, the crucified, risen and ascended Lord, but Baptists draw on the whole biblical story of God calling a people. The call of God is primary as God takes the initiative to fulfil his purposes for all creation. Although some Baptists reduce the concept of God's salvation to almost exclusively individual and spiritualized terms this has not been consistent with the more biblical understanding shared by the majority that the Church is called by God to be a witness to the world and a means by which God will further his purposes in the world.

Second, the call of God is a gracious invitation. It springs from the nature of God's will to fellowship and desire to save humankind. Thus, the Church is composed of those who freely of their own confession have responded to God's grace with faith and repentance. Early Baptists, with their strong Calvinistic influences, were ready to use the language of election, emphasizing the divine purpose and grace which are foundational for the Church. Those who are called and have, by grace, responded are the baptized and the majority of Baptists have said that these alone are the members of the Church. The searching, covenant-making call of God seeks a response, freely given, willingly entered into. No one can make this commitment for and on behalf of another. Faith that is compelled, or simply 'inherited' and not personal, is no faith and discipleship, or worship, which is forced by law is counterfeit. Belonging in the Church involves both grace and faith.

Again, the christological centre is crucial. These two convictions come together in the belief that God has acted in history and, in his sovereign purposes, has done a new thing in Jesus which leads to the bringing into being of a new humanity of which the Church is called to live as a first expression. The Church is called to be a holy people, marked by the character of the triune God. One consequence of this is that the kind of distinctions drawn outside the Church, and on which people can place such store, are to be viewed in another context. For example, in the light of Christ, the Church cannot be defined in nationalistic,

racial, ethnic, educational or economic terms (Galatians 3.28).
Being 'separated out of the world' means, among other things,
that the values of the secular society are not to be determinative
in the membership or description of the Church. What really
matters is Jesus Christ and faithfulness to his will and purpose.
The context of the Church's vocation is the eschatological one of
the Kingdom of God. This is not to say that our present culture
and context have no significance, but it is to say that even such fundamental factors as nationality or ethnicity cannot be decisive in
the community of the new humanity. A national or ethnic church
is a concept that Baptists believe sits uneasily with the New Testament understanding of the Church. It would be something to
claim that Baptists have lived out this conviction for the truth is
that racism, sexism and other forms of human divisiveness have
been and are still known between and among congregations.
Baptists have not always lived out their baptism. As in a natural
family, so the Church cannot choose its members because the foundation call and choice is God's.

Baptists keep the use of the word Church to two clear designa-
tions. One is for the One Holy Catholic and Apostolic Church,
the universal Church of Christ, militant here on earth and trium-
phant in heaven. Its origin is in the gospel.[4] As such, Church is a
singular term. It is theologically misleading to place an adjective
before it, especially of a national, ethic or doctrinal kind, even the
adjective 'baptist'! Thus in the Second London Confession of
1677, the chapter on the doctrine of the church reads,

> The Catholick or universal Church, which (with respect to
> internal work of the Spirit, and truth of grace) may be
> called invisible, consists of the whole number of the Elect,
> that have been, are, or shall be gathered into one, under
> Christ the head thereof; and is the spouse, the body, the ful-
> ness of him that filleth all in all.[5]

The second use for the word is local, where 'church' means the
congregation gathered in a particular place, covenanted together
in Christ. Wherever there are those who have responded to his
call and are intent on living together the life of discipleship, there
is the Church, even if it is only two or three gathered in his name
(Matthew 18.20). Having Christ what more do they need, save
that desire to worship and serve the Triune God made known in

his self-revelation? There may be other matters which help the Church to be the Church in any place but the heart of the Church is Jesus Christ with his gathered people.

So it is that Baptists express their life in local congregations. It is only in this context that they speak of a 'Baptist Church' and that term relates only to the local congregation. Thus there is no British or American Baptist Church. Instead, local churches associate in Unions or Conventions. They do this for reasons of fellowship, mission, accreditation of ministers and other practical purposes. There are other intermediate forms of church life which we shall come to describe later but the careful limitation of the word Church to either the universal or local is important. To see why this is so, let us use the Baptist Union of Great Britain as an example.

First there were local Baptist churches, such as the one in London of which Thomas Helwys and those with him were members. Among the early Baptists there was an implicit and understandable need to keep contact with one another, which they did in Associations. Thus associating is an important feature of authentic Baptist life and it would be erroneous to think of Baptists as being a collection of independent evangelical churches.

It was not until early in the nineteenth century that United Kingdom Baptists sought a more general union beyond that of the regional Associations. In 1832 the core of the present Baptist Union of Great Britain was formed. Several attempts were made to produce an agreed constitution and eventually, along with several practical objects, there emerged 'The Declaration of Principle' which was identified as 'the basis of this Union'.[6] The Declaration was never intended to have the defining power of a Creed, neither was it to be a foundational Confession of Faith but it was designed to hold together, in covenant, a wide family. Its intention, evidenced by the development through several forms, was to be inclusive rather than exclusive.

So what is the basis of the Baptist Union of Great Britain? The Declaration has three main clauses.

First, 'that our Lord and Saviour, Jesus Christ, God manifest in the flesh, is the sole and absolute authority in all matters relating to faith and practice, as revealed in the Holy Scriptures, and that each church has liberty, under the guidance of the Holy Spirit, to interpret and administer His Laws'.

This clause in itself is a key passage for understanding Baptist ecclesiology. When it comes to questions of authority in the Church then Baptists declare that absolute authority belongs to Jesus Christ and him alone. Final authority for the Church is to be found in a person, not a book, nor a creed, nor any human leadership structure. Here Baptists might be distinguished from others in the evangelical tradition of the faith, such as Pentecostalists, who assert that the Bible itself is the final and absolute authority. Their argument is that in the Bible we have the divinely inspired Word of God and these writings bear witness to Jesus Christ. Baptists in contrast have argued that our final authority is Jesus Christ, to whom the Bible bears its witness. This is an important theological distinction with implications about church governance. While it is true that some Baptists can be found among fundamentalist Christians this is not an authentic Baptist stance. Baptists have delighted in the phrase 'the crown rights of the Redeemer'. The living Lord, he who is revealed in Holy Scripture, is the one to whom all authority in heaven and on earth has been given.

In fact Baptists are known for their high regard for Scripture. They value the Bible above all other books and the Declaration, while insisting that authority belongs to Jesus Christ, adds the important clause 'as revealed in the Holy Scriptures'. The Bible is vital, primarily as it serves the authority of Jesus Christ. It is the reliable place where people can expect to hear God's word. Baptists believe that God is manifest in Jesus Christ and Christ is manifest to us in the Bible. Thus it is not a theory about inspiration, nor the letter of the text, nor a generally agreed pattern of doctrinal interpretation which is the authority for Baptist Christians. Jesus Christ is Lord and so relativizes all other claims to authority.

All reading of the Bible is a matter of interpretation. How do you determine the 'correct' and therefore authoritative teaching of Scripture? How do you recognize Christ in his authority without falling into the trap of making him after your own image? This is the same kind of question that Pentecostalists have to face with regard to discernment of the Spirit. It is a question for all in the Church and there is more than enough evidence in history to indicate the crucial nature of this question. Given their ecclesiology, Baptists have no reason to support the extreme individualism which claims a 'right' to personal interpretation, but how do they safeguard against its errors?

The Declaration of Principle, clause 1, goes on to say, 'each Church has liberty, under the guidance of the Holy Spirit, to interpret and administer His Laws'. Three important emphases are embedded in this formula.

The task of interpreting and administering Christ's Laws belongs, in the first instance, to all the members of the local congregation. Baptists, when they are true to their best insights, gather in local congregations to seek the mind of Christ. This listening and seeking is done in Church Meeting and all who are members are expected to share the task together. Mutual waiting on God, listening to Scripture, and to one another, is ecclesiologically significant. It would be wrong to describe it as democracy for that is rule by the people. It is Christ's will that is being sought. Very few votes are taken at Church Meetings, and these mostly relate to decisions that have important legal implications. It is the sense of the meeting in God, seeking the guidance of the Holy Spirit together, that is vital. Of course, there is no guarantee that the mind of Christ will be known. 'The purest Churches under heaven are subject to mixture and error (Second London Confession, 1677)[7] and the decisions of Church Meeting are not themselves final and absolute. The issue may be revisited and a change of the church's judgement noted. Baptists do not see this as a weakness but the inevitable consequence of our humanity, a factor which no pattern of Church government can overlook. Such an approach to being the Church places a considerable responsibility on the membership. The minister, deacons and other leaders will be listened to with special care but they have neither a veto nor an authority that puts them above the search for the will of Christ. This is a corporate responsibility and no voice should be silenced in this search.

Can a local church bear such responsibility? Baptists answer with a qualified 'yes'. The church is gathered by the risen Christ and his sovereign presence is with the disciples. Having Christ, the Scriptures, the tradition of faith, the sacraments, all in the fellowship of the Holy Spirit, what more do they need? This response expresses the conviction that such spiritual resources really are available to the local church. As such, under Christ, each congregation has liberty to interpret and administer Christ's Laws. They are not under the authority of another church, or hierarchy of ministers, let alone the State. Because the Church in that place is Christ being present in his body, each local congregation has the liberty and responsibility to interpret the mind of Christ.

The qualification however is important and can be overlooked by Baptists themselves. It is that in the task of seeking Christ's will, while not being under the authority of other congregations, or Association Councils, or national and international Assemblies, a congregation marked by spiritual wisdom will seek the fellowship and counsel of other members of the one body of Christ. So to quote again from the 1644 London Confession, 'Although the particular congregations be distinct and several bodies, every one a community and knit city in itself; yet are they all to walk by one and the same rule, and by all means convenient to have the counsel and help one of another in all needful affairs of the church, as members of the one body in the common faith under Christ their only head'.[8]

To give an illustration, twice in recent years the Baptist Union of Great Britain has debated and voted on whether or not it should be a member of new ecumenical instruments following the ending of the British Council of Churches. The new Council of Churches for Britain and Ireland, as proposed, had both new structures and a wider membership. Anyone with knowledge of British Baptists would have been aware that membership of the new body, which included Roman Catholics, would require careful thought and prayer. But who would decide and how? Each local church was provided with details of the scheme and was invited to discuss it in Church Meeting. A denomination-wide debate was encouraged. Local Associations of churches arranged for shared discussions among churches until a full debate by the Baptist Union Assembly, to which every congregation could send representatives, was held. In keeping with Baptist ecclesiology, representatives were not mandated to vote but were present to share the worship, the debate, the listening, the praying, and eventually the voting. Upon that decision the Union would act. If there were local churches which disagreed with the decision, then their decision was noted and their conscience was recorded. The Assembly decision would be one that all Baptists would have to take seriously but none were so bound by it that it became a condition of membership. Dissent was not going to be forbidden. Some years later the whole question was revisited by the Assembly and another vote taken. To many other denominations this sounds like a cumbersome, almost impossible process, but it was undertaken as an outcome of our ecclesiology. The faithful were consulted. Each local church was encouraged to undertake its own search for the mind of Christ but this was also done by Baptists together, without infringing the privileges and responsibilities of local congregations. No church which disagreed with the decision was required or expected to leave the Union. Baptist congregations are independent, in the sense that no other church body or person has authority over them but they are more properly interdependent and never isolationist.

The third emphasis in the first clause of the Declaration relates to a Baptist understanding of the Church as a disciplined community. Each Church has liberty, not to make up its own laws, but to interpret and administer Christ's Laws. Baptist Churches discipline their members. They do this following Matthew 18.15–20. If at times the discipline sounds to our modern ears rather petty and unfeeling, we must remember that the desire is to live out the gospel words. There were and are ways of behaving which are inconsistent with Christian living. Paul expressed deep feelings about the apparent willingness of the church in Corinth to tolerate wickedness which even pagans would decry (1 Corinthians 5). It is not impossible for a national Union or local Association to withhold fellowship from a congregation believed to be speaking and living in ways that are an offence to the gospel.

The second clause of the Declaration of Principle builds on the first. It touches on what many outside the denomination think is the distinctive feature of Baptists. We have seen that the decisive issue is the doctrine of the Church, the fellowship of believers, those called by God in Christ who have responded in faith. If the Church of Christ is made up of believers, and the sign of entry into the Church is baptism, then baptism is for believers only. Hence clause two reads,

> That Christian baptism is the immersion in water into the name of the Father, the Son, and the Holy Ghost, of those who have professed repentance towards God and faith in our Lord Jesus Christ, who 'died for our sins according to the Scriptures; was buried, and rose again the third day'.

The candidates for baptism are those who have 'professed repentance towards God and faith in our Lord Jesus Christ'. There is a connection in Baptist minds between baptism, salvation and discipleship. This is evident in the holding together in the clause of Matthew 28.19 and 1 Corinthians 15.3. In most cases the candidate coming for baptism will have undergone a pattern of preparation which has involved teaching about the content of the faith, the life of discipleship and the responsibilities and privileges of church membership. The candidate comes in personal response to the call of God in Christ. They are not baptized against their will nor while they are unable to appreciate what is being done to them. They are not being pressed into the Church, or God's salvation, by the choice of others. Baptism is by total immersion. In so doing Baptists believe they are following the example and command of Jesus and the practice of the early Church. Candidates are baptized into the name of the Trinity and thus Baptists understand that to be baptized indicates an awesome relationship between the believer and the very being of the triune God. It is incorporation into the deep fellowship which is the life of God with all who are Christ's.

This is an appropriate place to comment on sacraments. Pentecostalists avoid the word because of its associations and all the implications in the phrase *ex opere operato*. The Fundamental Truths speak instead of the Ordinances. 'We believe in the baptism of believers by immersion in water in obedience to the command of Christ and in the commemoration of Christ's death by the observance of the Lord's Supper until His return.' Baptism, as an act of obedience, is less than sacramental, as is the commemorative approach to the Lord's Supper. The emphasis appears to be on Christ's death rather than his presence. However, some Pentecostal theologians are reflecting on all this and seeking to move beyond an anti-sacramental polemic, especially considering the role of the Holy Spirit in the ordinances.[9]

While there are some Baptists who share Pentecostalism's anxiety about the word sacrament, there are others who readily use it both with regard to baptism and the Lord's Supper. They understand that baptism is more than an act of obedience and Communion more than a memorial. Both are God-given occasions when God has graciously promised to meet with his people. Thus baptism is into the life of God in Trinity and communion is a feeding upon Christ as God uses the ordinary stuff of creation, bread, wine and water, to be present to us and for us. These are never mere symbols. Baptism and the Lord's Supper are sacraments in that God meets us in them.

The third clause of the Declaration reads, 'that it is the duty of every disciple to bear witness to the Gospel of Jesus Christ, and to take part in the evangelization of the world'. The mission of the Church is to share the mission of the Christlike God. Mission means evangelism, telling the good news of Jesus Christ so that others may respond to the saving love of God. But mission means more than evangelism. It involves all the purposes of God for the world. Thus Baptists are glad to remember among their number William Carey (missionary to India), Billy Graham (evangelist) and Martin Luther King (civil rights leader).

Pentecostalists believe that the work of the Spirit in healing, exorcising, prophesying, giving visions, empowerment for mission, bringing to faith, is evident today in the church. As such, mission is theologically the work of God. It is God who heals, delivers, converts and empowers. Again the emphasis is not on organization but on the freedom of God and the response of women and men to the call of Christ. The mission of the triune God is cosmic in scope. Thus issues of politics, ecology, genetics, justice and peace for all creation are part of the concern of a church sharing the mission of God.

Baptists would particularly mention under the theme of mission the challenge to seek religious liberty for all. Helwys' initial plea was remarkable in that it was a call for freedom for all to practise their religion, or none, with freedom from the state powers. This, with human rights, remains part of the Baptist understanding of what it is to share the mission of God. The Baptist World Alliance has special commissions working on human rights, religious liberty, against racism and ethnic intolerance.

UNITY, CATHOLICITY AND APOSTOLICITY

Both Baptist and Pentecostal traditions find these terms difficult to handle. They have a history with which neither Baptists nor Pentecostals are immediately comfortable. Undoubtedly both movements would say that the Church of Christ knows already in part a unity in the Spirit that is the gift of God. There is only one Body of Christ. This is a real unity because it is in God, as believers are united in Christ. Thus unity is a work of grace.

But, as has been indicated, different responses are made to the ecumenical movement. Many Baptists will argue that since the faith we hold is fundamentally incarnational then the visible form of the church is an important matter. The present obvious divisions are not simply unfortunate. They express a fundamental failure of the church to be the church. Hence the quest for the visible unity of the church is always urgent. Catholicity is always to be expressed at local as well as in trans-local and international ways.

However, there is immediate unease when such unity is first described in terms of structures, recognition of ministries, sacraments, or papacy. This suggests to Baptists and Pentecostals that form is being put before Spirit, institution before movement. In general terms it might be claimed that Pentecostals are not drawn to such discussions since it is the Spirit alone who brings life. Baptists are more ready to work towards visible expressions of unity but are cautious about the terms in which other churches often set the questions because, by that approach, certain answers are already determined, answers to which Baptists and Pentecostalists will not be able to give full assent.

For example, much work towards expressing unity has focused on baptism, eucharist and ministry, resulting in the Lima document. Pentecostalists have not shared in these discussions in great measure because for them the fundamental question is not, 'Have you been properly baptized?' or 'Was the Eucharist celebrated by someone validly ordained?', but 'Have you received the Spirit?' For Pentecostals, the question of the Spirit's vivifying power is more important than issues of orders and sacraments. This is in keeping with Pentecostalism's powerful missionary emphasis and impact.

Baptists likewise have reservations about assumptions other traditions take for granted. Thus, for example, in their response to the Lima document, Baptists raised the question of who is a Christian? They see this as unanswered in the text but it is too important to be overlooked. An answer might be given along the lines that anyone who is baptized is a Christian and thereby a member of the one Church. Thus Baptists come under pressure to acknowledge a common baptism. But even if we could agree on recognition of infant baptism as baptism, Baptists want to ask about the unbaptized disciples of Christ. Must we say the members of the Salvation Army, or the Society of Friends, are not Christians and outside the Church? If baptism is seen as a requirement, then the performance of a rite is being made the basis of Christian fellowship. Can that really be the case in the light of Paul's letter to the Galatians?

If the starting point for definitions of unity is to be what the Church does through its duly accredited agents, then Baptists and Pentecostalists will protest that the wrong direction is being taken. Does the Church imagine that she controls God's grace? Is the Spirit a bird that can be caged by our traditions? Did you receive the Spirit by keeping these traditions or is it really the case that God has his freedom and the wind blows where it wills? These are the kind of rough questions Baptists and Pentecostalists bring to the discussion.

Yet both believe that catholicity is inherent in the church. Baptists and Pentecostalists will agree that the church is found where people are gathered together by Christ in the power of the Spirit. Most Baptists will not dissent from the reformed assertion that the true church is where the Word of God is preached and the gospel sacraments are duly administered, although they will want to add something about the need for faithful corporate discipleship. Perhaps Pentecostalism is suggesting that the accepted criteria for catholicity and apostolicity are not the most appropriate? Perhaps too much stress has been placed on form, order and control and not enough on the disarming creative sovereign Spirit that seeks the glorifying of Jesus and the urgent proclamation of his gospel?

The apostolic nature of the Church means that it shares in the apostolic work of God. The Father sends the Son and the Son sends the disciples, breathing the Holy Spirit on them (John 20.19–23). The church is always in mission, in partnership with the missionary God. If William Carey, Martin Luther King and David du Plessis are not an expression of the apostolic nature of the church, indeed not part of the apostolic succession, then apostolicity has little meaning for Baptists and Pentecostalists. Both traditions long for the church to be faithful in terms of Acts 2.42, being true to the apostolic teaching and practice. This they see as participation in the mission of God.

STRUCTURES OF MINISTRY, LEADERSHIP AND CHURCH GOVERNMENT

Again, Baptists and Pentecostalists begin the discussion other than with accepted ecumenical categories of validity and ordination.

Both would assert the priesthood of all believers, by which they mean not that each individual is their own priest and need no other to come to God, but that each may be a priest to another within the unique and final high priesthood of Christ. Ministry belongs to Christ and is his gift. So, again from the Elim Fundamental Truths, on The Ministry, 'we believe in the ministries that Christ has set in his Church, namely, apostles, prophets, evangelists, pastors and teachers, and in the present operation of the manifold Gifts of the Holy Spirit according to the New Testament'. The Assemblies of God, USA, statement says of the ministry, 'A divinely called and Scripturally ordained ministry has been provided by our Lord for a twofold purpose: (1) the evangelization of the world, and (2) The edifying of the Body of Christ (Mark 16.15–20; Eph. 4.11–13)'.

Both traditions reject any suggestion of a separated priesthood, this being absent from the New Testament. They are unconvinced by historical and theological arguments for the threefold ministry of bishop, priest and deacon and find the attention given to these issues in ecumenical discussions inordinate and stultifying.

This is not to say that Baptists and Pentecostalists do not recognize that God does call some to particular ministry in the Church. The local Baptist church may well have a minister/pastor who will have been trained at a recognized theological college, will have had his/her call tested, will have been called to serve the congregation as pastor, who will have been ordained with the laying on of hands and whose name will be among those formally accredited by the Baptist Union or Convention.[10] Along with the minister or ministers, the local church may also appoint elders and deacons. They share the ministry with the pastors, perhaps with special functions according to their gift, but particularly they share in the distribution of the bread and wine at the Lord's Supper. Baptists have also recognized trans-local ministry in the form of Superintendents or Regional Ministers. However, as described earlier it is the local church members meeting which is the most significant context of leadership and decision-making.

Negatively, no Superintendent can force his or her judgement on a Church. Positively, all members, including the ministers, are under the lordship of Christ, the one to whom all authority is given. The ordained ministry is not constitutive for the life and witness of the Church, although ministers are one of the gifts of the risen Christ to enable all the members of the Church to be built up in their calling.

Jesus is taken to be the model for ministry which is incarnational, kerygmatic and empowered by the Holy Spirit. His ministry found expression in humble service and took the form of caring for, or shepherding, others. Issues of status, title, hierarchies do not fit easily with the One who came as a servant. The Church is an extension of Christ's ministry. Indeed all those who share the life in Christ have their part to play in that ministry (1 Corinthians 12.7). Ministry is not the prerogative of an apostolic elite with the power to pass it down to others. No more is it restricted to the 'called' for all are called in Christ. Thus ministry belongs to the whole Church, although Pentecostals and Baptists recognize the importance of ordination of those set apart for leadership in the Church.

It is probably true to say that, given the nature of Pentecostalism, the church-planting apostles have exercised a great deal of authority in their congregations. There have been tensions in British forms of Pentecostalism between local congregations and the leadership of national leadership teams and General Councils. Pentecostals know, with Baptists, that their form of church government requires a serious quality of spiritual perception. It is not a democratic form, after all, but a corporate seeking of the mind of Christ. Monarchical forms of ministry are rejected because they are not true to the understanding of the Church as a fellowship of believers. The problem is of course that, although we have in the Holy Spirit an infallible guide, none of us has an infallible apprehension of his guidance. That is true of all churches, their leaders and their members.

KOINONIA

As we have seen, Baptists more than Pentecostalists have participated in ecumenical discussions on *koinonia*. To begin to identify a Baptist understanding of this key term it will be helpful to quote from two statements by the Baptist Union of Great Britain.

First from the 'Baptist Reply to the Lambeth Appeal, Adopted by the Annual Assembly, May 4, 1926':

We believe in the Catholic church as the holy society of believers in our Lord Jesus Christ, which He founded, of

which He is the only Head, and in which He dwells by His
Spirit, so that though made up of many communions, organized in various modes, and scattered throughout the world,
it is yet one in Him.[11]

Second, from *The Baptist Doctrine of the Church: A Statement approved
by the Council of the Baptists Union of Great Britain and Northern Ireland,
March 1948*:

> It is in membership of a local church in one place that the
> fellowship of the one holy catholic Church becomes signifi-
> cant. Indeed, such gathered companies of believers are the
> local manifestation of the one Church of God on earth and
> in heaven ... The vital relationship to Christ which is
> implied in full communicant membership in a local church
> carries with it membership in the Church which is both in
> time and in eternity, both militant and triumphant. To wor-
> ship and serve in such a local Christian community is, for
> Baptists, of the essence of Churchmanship.[12]

There have been times in their history when Baptists have so emphasized the significance of the local congregation under Christ
that they have played down or even ignored the essential interre-
latedness of all such congregations in Christ. In many of the basic
documents produced by Baptists on ecclesiology the emphasis on
koinonia is clear. The Church is the one company of those drawn
by grace into the fellowship of Christ.

A recent publication of the Baptist Union of Great Britain has
sought to examine more deeply this relationship between the
local church and churches in Association, Council and Assembly.[13] It argues that concepts of covenant, fellowship (*koinonia*),
and body are crucial in exploring the relationship between the
local and universal understandings of Church. The document
suggests that covenant, fellowship and body may also have application in regional terms. There is still resistance to using the term
Church for anything other than the local congregation or the
universal Church of Christ. However, some regional and national
Assemblies celebrate the Lord's Supper during their meetings,
while this is still resisted by others. Their caution relates to any
suggestion that the Union might think of itself as a Church. The
debate will continue.

Another report on *episkope* among Baptists, entitled *Transforming Superintendency*,[14] deliberately begins its discussion with the triune nature of God as being the key to understanding the being of the people of God. *Koinonia* is of the essence. It is in such biblical terms as communion, fellowship and covenant that Baptists base their thinking on the Church. Recent Trinitarian theology has only confirmed Baptists in this emphasis, rejoicing in the love of God, the grace of the Lord Jesus Christ, and the fellowship of the Holy Spirit. As Neville Clarke has put it:

> Our fellowship is with the Father and with His Son Jesus Christ because there has been granted to us participation (*koinonia*) in the Spirit. As at Pentecost it is the corporate sharing in the Holy Spirit that makes the people of God; and the 'fruit of the Spirit is love', that love which is the very nature of God and which has been 'poured into our hearts through the Holy Spirit'. The Church for God is the fellowship of the Spirit, and therefore the fellowship of love. She exists for worship, to offer to the Father the praise which is his due, to glorify his name, to actualize in her own life and being the kingly rule of Christ, to manifest in space-time the reality of the new creation, to be the abiding pledge in history of the transformation of earth in the age to come, to mirror through communion the love that binds together the blessed Trinity.[15]

VISIONS OF THE ECUMENICAL FUTURE

The ecumenical future is hard to envision for Pentecostalists and Baptists. There remains a strong antipathy towards all things Roman Catholicism but this is undergoing change with growing personal relationships. Protestant evangelicalism is always going to challenge the claims of Rome on what are taken to be fundamental issues of authority, grace, priesthood and salvation. And there are new instances of an old problem as in Eastern Europe, for example, Baptists and Pentecostalists are frustrated, to put it no more strongly, by national churches in partnership with the political state.

Against that, the effect of the charismatic movement has yet to be fully known. People of very different ecclesiastical traditions are being brought together, often to their surprise and disturbance.

The charismatic movement has brought a dimension to ecumenism which, perhaps because it is going beyond the assumptions of the ecumenical movement, has yet to be assessed.

A further point is the increased partnership in mission among evangelicals. While this part of the Church is not free from rivalries, the situation has changed in the last twenty years and, since it is among evangelical Christians that numerical growth is to be found, the situation will go on changing.

Some Baptists will remain committed to the ecumenical movement. Those who do so will have the mission of the Church primarily in mind. The merger plans of the last century had little appeal since the deeper question remains that of the renewal of the Church in the mission of God. That will not happen without a greater sense of unity in Christ and renewal is unlikely while the Church is disobedient in its divisions. But this only raises the question again as to whether the approaches of the past have been radical enough. It is often said that unity plans stumble over questions of order and ministry. Baptists and Pentecostalists want to press the questions about the nature of the Church deeper than the issues of order and ministry, asking theologically how anyone becomes and remains a Christian. Issues of order, ministry, control over the means of grace, hierarchy and priesthood may have their place. But they arose later in the Church's story. They are not of the *esse* (being) of the Church.

In the last analysis, all our ecclesiologies are provisional. This too is a truth about the Church. We all pray for a future not yet achieved, for a fulfilment not yet given. Risking, perhaps unwisely, a crude analysis, the churches which are strong on order, priesthood and creation are churches of the Father; those whose passion is for salvation and the coming of the Kingdom are churches of the Son; those who are less concerned with orders but rejoice in the power and new life from God are churches of the Spirit. How do we become together the Church of the Holy and undivided Trinity?

FURTHER READING

Along with books mentioned in the text, further studies in Pentecostalism include:

Brewster, P. S., ed., *Pentecostal Doctrine*. Greenhurst Press, 1976.

Burgess, S. M., McGee, G. B. and Alexander, P. H., eds, *The Dictionary of Pentecostal and Charismatic Movements*. Zondervan, Grand Rapids, 1988.

Cox, H., *Fire from Heaven*. Cassell, London, 1996.

Further studies in Baptist thinking include:

Cross, A. R., *Baptism and the Baptists*. Paternoster Press, 2000.

Fiddes, P. F., ed., *Reflections on the Water*. Regent's Study Guides 4. Regent's Park College, 1996.

Freeman, C. W., McClendon, J. W. and Velloso da Silva, C. R., eds, *Baptist Roots*. Valley Forge, Judson Press, 1999.

McBeth, H. L., *A Sourcebook for Baptist Heritage*. Nashville, Broadman Press, 1990.

Walker, M. J., *Baptists at the Table*. Baptist Historical Society, 1992.

NOTES

1. Bloch-Hoell, N., *The Pentecostal Movement* (Allen & Unwin 1964), p. 153.
2. Hollenweger, W., *The Pentecostals* (SCM Press 1972), p. 425.
3. Lumpkin, W. L., *Baptist Confessions of Faith* (Chicago, Judson Press, 1959), p. 119.
4. Hayden, R., *Baptist Union Documents 1948–1977* (Baptist Historical Society 1980), p. 5.
5. Lumpkin (1959), p. 285.
6. Kidd, R. L., ed., *Something to Declare* (Whitley Publications 1996), p. 10.
7. Lumpkin (1959), p. 285.
8. Lumpkin (1959), p. 168.
9. Warrington, K., ed., *Pentecostal Perspectives* (Carlisle, Paternoster Press, 1998), pp. 204–22.
10. Hayden, pp.12–95.
11. Payne, E. A., *The Fellowship of Believers* (Carey Kingsgate Press, 1952) pp. 142–7.
12. Hayden, p. 6.
13. Baptist Union, *The Nature of the Assembly and the Council of the Baptist Union of Great Britain*. Baptist Union, 1994.
14. Baptist Union, *Transforming Superintendency*. Baptist Union, 1996.
15. Gilmore, A., ed., *The Pattern of the Church* (Carey Kingsgate Press, 1963), p. 96.

6

The Churches of the Anglican Communion

Paul Avis

INTRODUCTION

The purpose of this chapter is to set the Anglican tradition of ecclesiology in an ecumenical framework. There can be little doubt
that there is in fact an Anglican tradition of ecclesiology.[1] This
may appear to be a statement of the obvious. However, some
well-known exponents of Anglicanism in the recent past (such as
Stephen Neill and H. R. McAdoo and even Michael Ramsey)
would have questioned it. Anglicans have tended to play down
the claim that there is a distinctive set of Anglican beliefs, including beliefs about the Church. Apologists for Anglicanism apparently felt that they needed to deny that Anglicanism entailed any
special doctrines in order to assert its catholicity. Their aim was
to show that Anglicanism was not some sort of ecclesiological
aberration but was an authentic expression of the one, holy,
catholic and apostolic Church. Anglicanism was assumed to be
an undifferentiated expression of Christianity, 'mere Christianity'
in C. S. Lewis' famous phrase. The Church of England was catholicism in the English context (though not usually exclusively so)
and other Anglican churches likewise in their own contexts.[2]

It is not that this view is false. Anglicanism does aim to conform
to the canons of the early, undivided Church. It is orthodox in
faith by the standards of the early ecumenical councils. It is
catholic in its order by the standards of the post-apostolic
Church.[3] It identifies itself with what the Church believes and
does. It does not wish to be different in fundamental doctrine or
basic practice. The question of Anglican distinctiveness arises,
however, precisely when we ask: What is the body that makes
these claims and what right has it to make them? In answering

that question, we find ourselves articulating a distinctive Anglican ecclesiology.

Anglicans who adopted what Stephen Sykes has dubbed 'the no special doctrines' stance could not avoid the question why, if there was nothing special about Anglican beliefs and Anglicans merely professed what the whole Church held, Anglicans were not in communion with either the Roman Catholic Church or the Orthodox Churches, the two oldest and largest Christian families. Denying that Anglicanism had any ecclesial distinctiveness, that it had doctrines of its own, made it impossible to answer this question, except in terms of the sheer perversity of one party or the other in persisting in a state of separation.

This tactic – what we might call the fallacy of misplaced modesty – has been exploded in more recent writing. Sykes (1995) and Avis (1998a; 2000) in particular have shown that Anglicanism needs to set out its ecclesiological credentials, not in tension with its claims to catholicity, but precisely in order to assert that catholicity, to show how it claims its place among the commonwealth of churches in the *oecumene*. And it is above all in the area of ecclesiology that this has to be done. It bears repeating that Anglicans do not want to set up special interpretations of the catholic faith, the dogmas of the Holy Trinity or of Christology agreed by the early ecumenical Councils, or in any sense to 'monkey with the creed' (in Hilaire Belloc's memorable phrase). They would shrink from any such suggestion. As far as these foundational beliefs of Christianity are concerned, Anglicans take their stand on the teaching of Scripture and of the early ecumenical Councils. But it is precisely when it comes to ecclesiology that Anglicanism inevitably has to be different. Anglican ecclesiology is the activity in which the churches of the Anglican Communion engage when they explain what they are as churches. To deny the distinctiveness of Anglicanism at this point is futile: it is to saw off the branch on which you are sitting.

In fact, there are distinctive Anglican tenets in ecclesiology with regard to both faith and order. Faith is concerned with beliefs, with doctrine, and Anglicanism believes and teaches certain distinctive things about the Church. Order is concerned with practice, with structure, with ministry, with authority, and Anglicanism is distinctive in these areas too. In reality, however, faith and order cannot be held apart in ecclesiology. They go hand in hand. Faith is reflected in life. Order is grounded in theology.

These are not two dimensions of the Church's life that can be analysed separately. They are a seamless whole. The exponents of Anglicanism of the 'no special doctrines' school would probably not have denied that Anglicanism exhibits certain distinctive traits in order (we shall look at these shortly). Where they went wrong was in attempting to detach order from doctrine, as though the outward ordering of the Church, its structures of ministry and oversight, did not intend to reflect its essential nature and purpose.

THE ANGLICAN COMMUNION

But where should we look to find this distinctive ecclesiology? Where is it located in an authoritative or definitive way? At this point we immediately come up against the particular character of Anglicanism. Anglicanism is instantiated in thirty-eight national or regional churches (often called provinces, though some of them are made up of more than one province) around the world.[4] The Communion totals some 70 million souls. About 25 million of these are attributed to the Church of England on the basis of its 'baptismal membership' – which everyone knows to be a shaky basis for assessing the strength of a church. (However, the Church of England is not the only church in the world to have a substantial nominal allegiance.) So the Anglican Communion is about the same size as the Lutheran World Federation (LWF), but larger than the World Alliance of Reformed Churches (WARC) and smaller than world Methodism. Of course, the Anglican Communion is tiny compared with the Roman Catholic Church, which has about a billion 'members', and small even in comparison with the Orthodox churches (about 200 million).

No single one of the Anglican churches or provinces – not even the Church of England – claims to be the definitive expression of Anglicanism. There is too much diversity in Anglicanism for that. The Anglican churches do not necessarily have the same statements of doctrine. There are variations in their structure. They also vary in their relation to the state, the Church of England being the only one that is established in the strong sense of the word.[5] The Anglican Communion is not a global church; it is not a church at all in the proper sense of the word, though it has ecclesial characteristics. It has no central governing authority or unified canon law (though it does have global structures of conciliarity and the potential of a core Anglican canon law is currently being explored).[6] What is it then?

The title of this chapter 'The Churches of the Anglican Communion' indicates the slightly elusive reality of Anglicanism. It is a family of churches, all of which are self-governing (autonomous) while being united with each other in fellowship or communion (*koinonia*). This means that their autonomy is certainly not the last word to be said about them. Equally important is the fact that they exist in a relationship of spiritual and pastoral interdependence. There is a state of symbiosis between Anglican churches that is grounded in two factors.

The first factor contributing to the symbiosis of Anglican churches is its common tradition. This is threefold, being expressed in liturgy, spirituality and theology.[7]

The liturgical tradition derives from the Book of Common Prayer, 1662 (BCP), which was universally reflected in Anglican liturgies until recently and is still a powerful, though sometimes unacknowledged, influence (see below for comment on Anglican worship). The BCP is regarded by many Anglicans as unparalleled in the chaste beauty of its elevated language. It is a simplified, reformed liturgy drawn largely from ancient sources but touched with the liturgical genius of Thomas Cranmer and in places with a down-to-earth pastoral wisdom.

The tradition of spirituality stems substantially but by no means exclusively from Caroline divinity, the flowering of Anglican spiritual writing during the reign of Charles I, but in fact throughout the seventeenth century. Its great exponents include Lancelot Andrewes, George Herbert, Thomas Traherne and Jeremy Taylor. Their spiritual writings have enjoyed something of a renaissance in recent years. The biblical, sacramental and practical character of Anglican spirituality reflects the seminal influence of Richard Hooker (d.1600). Perhaps the greatest influence on Anglican spirituality is the BCP itself.

The Anglican tradition of theology is linked to liturgy and closely allied to spirituality. At its best it is a lived, prayed and applied theology. While Anglicanism has not excelled in systematic theology, it has a distinguished record in biblical, historical and, to some extent, philosophical theology. In the Anglican practice of theology, Scripture, tradition and reason have their allotted places and are held in a particular balance and relationship, just as they are in the BCP and the classical Anglican divines. The Bible is the primary source of Christian theology for Anglicans and, in showing the way of salvation, does not need to be complemented by tradition. Even the creeds are to be believed because they are firmly grounded in Scripture. But, in the Anglican understanding, the Bible does not lay down a blueprint for the Church's outward ordering or polity. In that area the witness of the post-apostolic period is to be followed, though nothing is to be required that is contrary to Scripture. The ecclesiological canons of the Church of England rather remarkably understate their claims in this respect, insisting merely that the outward polity of that church is 'not repugnant' to the teaching of Scripture. Both Scripture and tradition are interpreted by means of reason, which is understood, not in the spirit of the Enlightenment, as an individualistic and analytical instrument, but in a cultural, sapiential sense, as the light of God diffused, albeit imperfectly, through human knowledge and experience and to be exercised humbly, collectively and prayerfully.

The second factor that holds Anglican churches in a relationship of symbiosis is made up of the 'instruments of the Communion'. These are fourfold.[8]

First there is the Lambeth Conference (LC) of all the bishops (or at least all the diocesan bishops) of the Communion who come together at the invitation of the Archbishop of Canterbury. The first LC was held in 1867 and the most recent in 1998. They take place at ten yearly intervals and so far have always been held in England (first at Lambeth Palace, the London residence of the Archbishop of Canterbury, and more recently at Canterbury itself). The LC is not the governing body of the Anglican Communion; it is precisely a conference. The bishops come together to confer with one another, to share their experiences, problems and insights. Although the LC tends to pass numerous resolutions, these have only moral authority in the Communion; they are not legally binding on the member churches or provinces until they have been adopted (if at all) by the general synods of those provinces. Since the 1998 LC, the Communion has faced the unprecedented situation of some provinces or their bishops publicly repudiating, by word or deed, particular resolutions of the LC.

The second instrument of the Communion is the Anglican Consultative Council (ACC). This is an elective, representative body made up of laity, clergy and bishops. The ACC meets normally once a year and acts as the standing committee of the LC. It will reflect on major issues, especially matters concerned with mission and with the cohesion of the Communion. Like the LC itself, it does not have any legislative or juridical authority. The ACC may meet in any part of the world.

The third instrument is the Primates Meeting. The Primates are the metropolitans or senior archbishops of the Communion. They are gathered by the Archbishop of Canterbury annually to discuss together issues affecting the life of the Communion. The Primates may meet anywhere in the world.

The fourth instrument of the Communion is the office and ministry of the Archbishop of Canterbury itself. In order to understand Anglicanism, we must grasp this unique role. Canterbury is the first metropolitan see (seat of the bishop or archbishop) of the Church of England, founded by St Augustine of Canterbury in 597, and therefore of the Anglican Communion. The litmus test of membership of the Anglican Communion is to be in communion with the See of Canterbury. Of course, this cannot be the only condition for membership of the Communion. A common faith and order; a shared tradition of theology, liturgy and spirituality; and participation in the instruments of the Communion are also involved. But it is the ultimate criterion. And it is the Archbishop of Canterbury himself who decides whether he is in communion with a given church or a given archbishop or bishop. As we have seen, it is the Archbishop who invites the Anglican bishops from around the world to participate in two of the four instruments of the Communion: the Lambeth Conference and the Primates Meeting. This power of invitation constitutes the only formal exercise of primatial authority that the Archbishop of Canterbury possesses. It can be, and occasionally has been, exercised negatively, though that is a largely untried mechanism for regulating issues of communion among Anglicans. It will be apparent, then, that there is a real, though muted, universal primacy in Anglicanism, located in the pastoral office of the Archbishop of Canterbury. It is spiritual and pastoral and its authority is almost entirely of a moral nature. It is devoid of juridical power. It is a ministry of presidency, carrying a power of invitation to participate in the consultative instruments of the Communion. As such, it carries a faint echo of the Roman Catholic ecclesiological principle of 'hierarchical communion' with the college of bishops and the head of that college, the Pope, though without the element of implicit obedience that Roman Catholic bishops owe to the Pope.

Two of these four instruments – the ACC and the Primates Meeting – are comparatively recent developments. But the essential character of the Communion has been articulated by various Lambeth Conferences. The Conference of 1930, for example, stated that the Anglican Communion is indeed 'a fellowship', made up of properly constituted dioceses, provinces or regional churches that (a) are in communion with the Archbishop of Canterbury and (b) share certain characteristics. These characteristics are: (1) that they maintain 'the catholic and apostolic faith' in the tradition of the BCP; (2) that they are 'particular or national churches' ministering within a given territory and there promoting an inculturated expression of the Christian faith, appropriate to that nation's history and experience; (3) that they are bound together not by a central juridical authority but 'by mutual loyalty sustained by the common counsel of the bishops in conference'.[9]

OTHER RELATIONSHIPS

The Anglican Communion is in communion with several other families of churches: the Old Catholic Churches of the Union of Utrecht, mostly on the continent of Europe, through the Bonn Agreement of 1930–1; the Mar Thoma Church of India; the Philippine Independent Church; and two small churches of the Iberian peninsular. An important litmus test of being 'in communion' is the interchangeability of episcopally ordained ministers.

In addition, member churches of the Communion have entered into communion with other churches (see further below). Episcopalians and Lutherans have achieved 'full communion' in the USA and in Canada. The four British and Irish Anglican churches are now in communion with most Nordic and Baltic Lutheran Churches (through the Porvoo Agreement). Such is the nature of the Anglican Communion, as explained earlier, that there is not automatic transitivity of relationship between the provinces.

The picture of how Anglicans view other churches would not be complete without some reference to agreements that fall short of communion but are seen as a stage on the way to it. The Episcopal–Lutheran agreement in the USA (*Called to Common Mission/Concordat*) had several intermediate stages over a period of decades before 'full communion' was attained in 2001. Similarly, the Church of England has recently entered into agreements, that fall short of communion (with interchangeability of ministers), with other churches: with the German Evangelical Church (EKD, through the Meissen Agreement); with the Moravian Church in England (through the Fetter Lane Agreement); and with the French Lutheran and Reformed Churches (through the Reuilly Agreement). These relationships are premised on agreement in the apostolic faith and on the goal of full visible unity. They involve mutual acknowledgement of one another as churches and a commitment to work towards ecclesial communion including the interchangeability of ministries. But this depends on agreement, which has not yet been attained in these cases, on the theology and practice of episcopal oversight, including ordination.[10]

A variant of this approach is the proposals of the Formal Conversations (1999–2001) between the Church of England and the Methodist Church of Great Britain. This too follows the Meissen model and moves towards mutual acknowledgement coupled with mutual commitment. Since, however, there is agreement in principle between the two churches on episcopal oversight, the Conversations envisage a national covenant that would provide an immediate springboard for the next stage towards organic unity, a stage at which the issue of integrated ministry would need to be addressed.[11]

A common Anglican ecclesiology can be discerned in all these agreements, as well as elsewhere. But, as the 1930 Lambeth Conference recognized, this ecclesiology is embodied, inculturated and worked out in specific contexts which lend a particular colouring to it and mark it out as distinctive, perhaps unique. It follows that there is an element within Anglican ecclesiology that cannot simply be transposed to a different context. Anglicanism is very different in Scotland, Myanmar, the Diocese of Sydney, Australia, or the Southern Cone of South America. And they are all different from English Anglicanism! To some extent, the same must be true of other communions that are not global, centralized churches, as are the Roman Catholic Church and the Moravian Church, to take the two extremes, the one a thousand times larger than the other. And even the Roman Catholic Church wrestles with the tension between uniformity dictated by the centre and inculturation generated by the pressure of context.

To take a specific example of a contextualized agreement: the Porvoo Agreement is largely between national (in some cases established) churches with historic sees that (with the exception of Lutheran and Anglican chaplaincies) are in geographically separate territories, many of which have their own languages. The national extension and established or semi-established status of most Lutheran churches means that they are more relaxed about confessional identity than some other Lutheran churches. The Porvoo relationship is described as 'visible unity' and is seen as a stage on the way to the ultimate goal of the 'full visible unity' of Christ's Church (as portrayed, for example, in the classic statements of the New Delhi and Canberra Assemblies of the WCC).[12]

These are aspects of the Porvoo approach that cannot be transposed to North America. The context of *Called to Common Mission* is markedly different: the two churches share a common territory; there are no historic sees; neither church is established by law; there is only one language; and there is a strong confessional identity among the Lutherans that has to be respected. The result is a model of 'full communion' that would not make a great deal of sense in Northern Europe, where there is greater sensitivity to the anomaly of parallel episcopal jurisdictions when these exist in a relationship of full communion.[13]

HOW ANGLICANS SEE THEMSELVES AND OTHERS

Anglicans believe that they belong to the one, holy, catholic and apostolic Church of Christ. But they do not believe that they are the only ones who so belong. The Anglican churches claim their rightful place in the one Church. But they do not believe that they are the only ones with a rightful claim. The way that Anglicans see themselves is not exclusive. This balanced position tends to be put in various ways which can be illustrated from the official statements of the Church of England.

First, the canons of that church (A1) insist that it 'belongs to the true and apostolic Church of Christ'. Second, the Preface to the Declaration of Assent states that the Church of England 'is part of the One, Holy, Catholic and Apostolic Church' (Canon C15). The recent ecumenical agreements that the Church of England has entered into include the acknowledgement or recognition of 'one another's churches as churches belonging to the One, Holy, Catholic and Apostolic Church of Jesus Christ' (Meissen Agreement between the Church of England and the *Evangelische Kirche im Deutschland* (EKD)). Thus Anglican churches see themselves not as *the* Church, but *a* church within the one Church. How do Anglicans justify this position? As a smallish body in world terms, and one that is not in communion (in the full or strict sense of the term) with either the Roman Catholic or the Orthodox Churches, Anglicans cannot credibly describe themselves as 'catholic' in an unqualified way. The fact that their churches are not recognized as catholic by the largest church to bear that name – in particular that Anglican ministerial orders are held to be null and void and that Roman Catholics are not allowed to receive Holy Communion at Anglican services – is a source of deep and enduring humiliation and embarrassment to Anglicans.[14]

On the other hand, Anglicans have excellent relations with many of the churches that took their rise from the Reformation, and have entered into relationships of varying degrees of communion with Lutheran churches (notably the agreement for 'full communion' between the Episcopal Church of the USA and the Evangelical Lutheran Church in America, 2001). But it is important to note that Anglicans only do this when those Lutheran churches are willing to adopt 'catholic' order, i.e. the threefold ministry of bishops, priests and deacons in visible historical continuity. Anglicans treasure visible historical continuity. They do not believe that the Church of England originated at the Reformation. They maintain that it stands in unbroken continuity with the Catholic Church of the West and, beyond that, with the ancient undivided Church of the Apostles, the Fathers, the martyrs and the bishops in their historic sees. So, although Anglicans did not disdain the name of Protestant for their churches until the Oxford Movement brought a greater consciousness of catholic continuity in the mid-nineteenth century, Anglicans today tend not to define themselves as churches of the Reformation in an unqualified way.

If Anglicanism cannot be described in an unqualified way as either catholic or reformed, how should it be described? Anglicans consistently define themselves as *both* catholic and reformed. On the one hand, they affirm the ecumenical creeds of the early Church and continue the threefold ministry of bishops, priests (presbyters) and deacons from patristic times. They have never held that the outward ordering of the Church requires chapter and verse in the Bible, but acknowledge the authority of the early post-apostolic tradition in this area. Their worship gives a central place to the Eucharist or Holy Communion but maintains a balance and complementarity of word and sacrament. Anglicans maintain, therefore, that they uphold all the essentials of catholicity. But, on the other hand, Anglicanism has been permanently shaped in crucial ways by the Reformation. It affirms the centrality of Scripture (made available to the people in their own language) and that nothing needs to be added to the explicit teaching of Scripture to show the way of salvation. It upholds justification by grace through faith and the sharing of all baptized believers in the royal priesthood of Christ. Its ordained ministers are free to marry and it ordains women as deacons and priests (and in some provinces as bishops). While certainly not advocating a free-for-all in faith, Anglicanism has recognized the claims of conscience and the duty of Christians to arrive at personal conviction of the truth. Anglicanism therefore bears the essential marks of reformed Christianity.

However, the qualifiers 'catholic' and 'reformed' are not adequate on their own to delineate the ecclesial character of Anglicanism. Something needs to be added about the intellectual climate and ethos of Anglicanism as it has developed during the past five centuries. Anglicanism generally has been deeply influenced by the intellectual currents of modernity. It has been hospitable, but always after a protracted, violent struggle, to the contributions of the seminal intellectual movements of western culture: the Renaissance, the Reformation, the Enlightenment, the scientific revolution and the various human and social sciences. Particularly in its British and American expressions, it is responsive to cultural trends in the arts, especially literature. It is, on the whole, a tolerant faith, willing to give fairly generous scope to theological exploration, on the part of its clergy as well as its laity, in dialogue with non-theological academic disciplines. In this respect, Anglicanism is a reasonable faith also, a faith that is open to reason, to exploration and to debate.

The interaction of catholic, reformed and 'reasonable' aspects of Anglicanism can be seen in its attitude to its 'historic formularies'.

These vary from one province or church to another, but they generally derive from three common sources: the Thirty-nine Articles of Religion, the Book of Common Prayer, 1662, and the Ordering of Bishops, Priests and Deacons in its form of 1662. As the Church of England's Preface to the Declaration of Assent makes clear, these are regarded as an 'inheritance of faith', sources of inspiration and guidance, especially for the clergy and licensed lay ministers. There is, however, an acknowledgement that the faith of the Church, as the Church of England has received it, needs to be expressed afresh in each generation. The historic formularies are, of course, subordinate in authority to the Bible and to the creeds and in fact are intended to help Anglicans to interpret Scripture and the witness of the early Church. The formularies are complemented by the canons of each church, which usually include some important ecclesiological material.

STRUCTURES OF MINISTRY AND GOVERNMENT

The churches of the Anglican Communion maintain the historic threefold ordained ministry. That is to say, they ordain bishops, priests (or presbyters) and deacons in conformity with the practice of the primitive Church. The Preface to the Ordinal in the BCP makes the rather risky claim that there have been these three orders in the Church since the times of the apostles. Anglicans today may tend to be unnecessarily defensive about this. The basic forms of the threefold ministry can certainly be traced back to the apostolic age. But they underwent further development in the period that followed. In a rather paradoxical and unresolved way, ministerial order is seen as both single (there is and can be only one Holy Order, for order must by definition be single) and threefold (there are three ministries or orders within it).

Like others within the ecumenical movement, Anglicans have employed and developed the concept of representative ministry. But this is not deployed in a merely 'democratic' sense, as though the authority for ordained ministry were delegated by the faithful to certain spokespersons. The ordained are seen as representing both Christ and his Body the Church in their ministry of word, sacrament and pastoral care. They cannot represent the Body without being related to the Head of the Body; and they cannot represent the Head without being related to the whole Body, for (as the Reformers continually insisted) Christ cannot be without his people and his flock cannot be without their Shepherd. In that respect, Holy Order is said to be a sacramental or ecclesial sign of Christ's presence and work in and through the Church.

Ordination is sequential or incremental, so that one is always ordained to the diaconate first and the presbyterate next. According to the Canons of the Church of England (C1, 2) a person ordained to any order can never lose the character of that order. This suggests that the distinctive nature of the diaconate is carried into the presbyterate and that of each of these into the episcopate. The episcopate gathers up and affirms inclusively the ministry of the deacon and of the presbyter.[15]

It is widely recognized that the integrity of the diaconate is weakened when it is seen as simply a transitional stage or stepping stone on the way to the priesthood. The distinctive diaconate flourishes in several churches of the Communion and is particularly strong in the Episcopal Church of the USA. The Church of England is currently considering a 'renewed' or distinctive diaconate, as a 'go-between' ministry, linking the eucharistic heart of the Church's life with its dispersed mission in the world. Recent research into the classical and New Testament uses of *diakonia*, especially in the work of John N. Collins, has brought out its meaning as commissioned, authoritative agency. In this sense, the diaconate becomes fundamental to all ordained ministry and constitutes a sacramental focus for the commissioning, the apostolic mission, of the whole Church. This understanding will no doubt have implications for how the transitional diaconate itself is viewed and practised.[16]

Anglicanism strongly affirms the ministry of lay people on the basis of the royal priesthood of baptized believers. The laity play leading roles in the life and governance of the Church at every level, from the parish to national synods. The particular forms of lay involvement in ministry will vary across the Communion. In the Church of England, for example, Churchwardens and Readers are associated with the bishop in their lay ministry. Lay ministries that are locally, rather than nationally, accredited include Lay Pastoral Assistants and Evangelists. In Anglicanism bishops have oversight of all aspects of accredited ministry, lay and ordained.

ANGLICAN WORSHIP

In Anglicanism there is a close connection between worship and belief. The ancient saying *Lex orandi lex credendi* ('The rule of worship is the rule of belief') is recognized in the Anglican tradition. The BCP is one of the historic formularies of the Church of England and liturgy has a comparably authoritative place in the polity of the other provinces. Worship in the Church of England has been conducted in the vernacular since 1549, according to one of the fundamental principles of the Reformation, and is liturgical, using a range of authorized forms from the Book of Common Prayer (1662) to *Common Worship* (2000). Worship has, therefore, been in the vernacular throughout the Anglican Communion. Traditionally, Anglican worship revolves around Morning and Evening Prayer (Mattins and Evensong) and the Eucharist or Holy Communion. Other forms of service, such as Family Services, may be authorized by the bishop from time to time. In some Anglican churches in practice, there is considerable local discretion about the form of service to be used.

Only priests and bishops may preside at the Eucharist, though deacons, Readers and others assist. The Diocese of Sydney, Australia, is currently moving towards non-presbyteral presidency at the Eucharist and, if this is finally approved by the Archbishop of Sydney, it will constitute a serious anomaly within the shared faith and common order that undergird the Communion. It will also have major ecumenical implications, especially for relations with the Roman Catholic Church and with the Orthodox Churches. However, the Diocese of Sydney does not feel much of an affinity to those two traditions. The House of Bishops of the Church of England, in its report *Eucharistic Presidency*, has affirmed the link between presidency at the Eucharist and pastoral leadership or oversight in the community. But of course, the position adopted by the Church of England carries no intrinsic authority for any other Anglican province.[17]

Clergy, Readers, choirs and other assistants robe in cassock and surplice, especially for non-eucharistic services and eucharistic vestments are widely used. In Anglican worship, words, music, colour, decoration, sacred imagery, movement (and sometimes incense) are all used to glorify God and uplift the worshipper. There is a balance and complementarity of word and sacrament, as befits a church that is both catholic and reformed.

Modern Anglicanism is both episcopal and synodical in its governance. It has, of course, always been episcopal, but synodical government began in some Anglican provinces in the latter part of the nineteenth century and reached the Church of England in 1919, finally being expressed in the establishment of the General Synod in 1970. It embodies the conciliar principles of constitutional authority, representation and consent that stem from the pre-Reformation conciliar movement. The Anglican Reformers had a great deal to say about the proper role of councils in the polity of the Church. Richard Hooker and Richard Field were opposed to absolutism in either Church or State and were exponents of conciliar thought.

Lay people, clergy and bishops have particular responsibilities in the way that these principles are worked out at every level of the Church's life. In the Church of England, for example, Parochial Church Councils (PCCs) are the very local form of church government. Elected annually by all those baptized worshippers who enter their names on the parish electoral roll (this may include those who are also members of other churches), the PCC shares responsibility with the incumbent and Churchwardens (the latter also being elected annually, but in theory by a wider parish constituency) for church life within the parish, including the church building, parish finances, worship and mission.

All parishes are represented by elected lay persons on the Deanery Synod which has more of a reflective and supportive role and is not directly part of the legislative process of the Church of England. These Deanery Synod representatives form the electoral college for lay representatives on the Diocesan and General Synods. These are made up of houses of laity, clergy and bishops. Bishops have special, but not exclusive, responsibility for matters of faith and order, including ministry and worship. The House of Bishops consults together frequently on matters that are not confined to synodical business and acts collegially.[18] In other churches of the Communion, provincial synods have an important role. For example, in the Episcopal Church of the USA, considerations of geography dictate that the General Convention meets only every three years. Meanwhile, diocesan and provincial synods meet more frequently.

Anglican synodical (conciliar) structures are constitutional bodies. That is to say, the scope and limits of the responsibilities and authority of every constituent part are laid down. Although this can lend itself to apparently labyrinthine procedures that appear to ape parliamentary processes, it does in fact guard against autocracy by a system of checks and balances. As the 1948 Lambeth Conference showed, Anglicans are sensitive to the threat of 'spiritual tyranny' and see authority operating in a dispersed mode before it can come into focus and its decisions can be put into execution. Moreover, those who are uncomfortable about the resemblances between synodical and parliamentary procedures should be aware that both expressions of representative government have developed from the common stock of medieval political thought.

In the Church of England, for example, the system of checks and balances particularly comes into play when controversial issues are being considered. New developments in the life of the church, such as the liturgical provisions of *Common Worship* or the ordination of women to the priesthood, require two-thirds majorities in each of the Houses of the General Synod voting separately. Diocesan synods are consulted about certain issues and they in turn may consult the deanery synods and parishes. The General Synod is elected for a period of five years and is inaugurated in the presence of the Queen, the Supreme Governor (though without executive authority) of the established Church of England. It meets at least twice a year for a period of days. The Archbishops of Canterbury and York are its presidents but it is chaired by a panel that includes lay people. The General Synod includes ecumenical representatives who are non-voting members and it welcomes official guests from other partner churches.

MISSION

The picture that many Protestants and Evangelicals have of Anglicanism is of a spiritually inert church, dedicated to the maintenance of the *status quo* through a steady round of pastoral duties. In reality, however, modern Anglicanism is highly mission conscious. However, that mission is envisaged in a broad sense at the cutting edge of the Church's life as that life is manifested in worship, preaching, teaching, pastoral care and compassionate service. Anglican faith is personal but not private and Anglicans are normally committed to involvement in the local community and in civil society at large. Anglicanism does not lend itself to the gathered church model but is a 'church in the community' type of ecclesiology.[19] Although the Church of England is the only fully established Anglican Church, Anglicans generally look favourably on a working relationship with the state, provided the apostolic authority of the Church is not infringed.[20]

Its position as the Established (that is to say, legally and constitutionally recognized) Church means that the Church of England is committed to a nationwide pastoral ministry, to full involvement in civil society and to making a contribution to the public discussion of issues that have moral and spiritual implications. One indicator of this is the fact that 26 bishops currently sit in the House of Lords. This national ministry is carried out on a territorial basis, through the dioceses and the parochial system. The aim of this approach is to bring the ministry of the word, the administration of the sacraments and the provision of pastoral care within reach of all parishioners. This territorial ministry is complemented by extensive sector ministries (chaplaincies) on an institutional basis. The weakening of local attachments through social and economic mobility makes these sector ministries particularly important at the present time.[21] Other Anglican provinces also are made up of parishes grouped into dioceses, but the sense of territorial identity and responsibility is sometimes less strong and congregations tend to be more eclectic (as indeed they are in some parishes of the Church of England).

The catholic dimension of Anglicanism means that grace and nature are not opposed. There is a strong doctrine of both original and actual sin in the Thirty-nine Articles, but the Calvinist doctrine of total depravity is not part of Anglicanism today, if it ever was. The goodness of God in the natural rhythms of life is affirmed and the stages on life's way can be sanctified liturgically. The 'occasional offices' are particularly important in the Anglican pastoral mission in the community. Baptisms, marriages and funerals, as rites of passage, bring the clergy and those who assist them into contact with many parishioners who are not regular churchgoers. These pastoral contacts are valued by the Church as opportunities for Christian instruction, for leading individuals towards a further stage of Christian initiation, or simply for building up an understanding and trust that may bear fruit in the future.[22]

Confirmation is a rite of passage of a sacramental nature and is understood to be a means of grace within the total process of

Christian initiation and a source of strengthening by the Holy Spirit for Christian discipleship. The minister of confirmation is always the bishop as the 'chief pastor' of all within his diocese and 'their father in God'. However, Anglicans appear to recognize Roman Catholic and Orthodox confirmations (in the case of the Orthodox, chrism) even though the minister of confirmation in these traditions is normally a priest.

Shaped as it is by the rites of passage and by the Christian Year with its liturgical seasons, both festivals and penitential seasons, the ethos of Anglican spirituality is that of pilgrimage. It has an eschatological dimension – moving forward step by step in trustful discipleship into God's future. At the same time, Anglican spirituality is generally world-affirming, though at its best in a prophetically dialectical manner. It is comfortable with marriage, daily work, life in the community, participation in civil society and in political processes. Of course, Anglicans are sometimes slow to see the relevance of their faith to everyday life and, like other Christians, struggle to reconcile spirit and body, the individual and the community, time and eternity. But the incarnational, sacramental spirit of Anglican spirituality is conducive in principle to the integration of these.

ANGLICAN ECUMENISM

The Anglican Communion has contributed some outstanding leaders to the ecumenical movement: Charles Brent, Charles Gore, William Temple, George Bell, Oliver Tomkins, Mary Tanner (all but the first of these being from the Church of England). It has played a leading role in the Faith and Order Movement up to the present. Since 1920, when the Lambeth Conference issued its *Appeal to All Christian People*, the Lambeth Conferences have consistently reaffirmed Anglican commitment to the ecumenical enterprise. For example, Anglicans in the United States, Australia, Central Southern Africa, as well as in Britain and Ireland, have been assiduous, not just in theological dialogue, like the Roman Catholic and Orthodox Churches, but also in developing and implementing agreements with other churches with the intention of building on these in the future. The Ecumenical Canons of the Church of England (B43 and B44) are a signal example of ecumenical good intentions. They set out a breadth of possibilities for local relationships and for Local Ecumenical Partnerships specifically, while remaining 'the ecumenism of exception' that will one day, in God's good time, be overtaken by new relationships of visible unity.

Like other Christian world communions, the Anglican Communion is involved in a wide range of ecumenical dialogues. Some are well established and highly productive (such as the Anglican–Roman Catholic International Commission (ARCIC)). Others are new and rather tentative (such as the international Forum with the Baptist World Alliance). Some global dialogues have resulted in agreed statements. In addition to those of ARCIC, the report of the Anglican–Reformed International Dialogue *God's Reign and Our Unity* (1984) and the Anglican–Lutheran *Niagara Report* (1988) are notable. The status of ARCIC documents is ambiguous since the broad welcome given by the Anglican Communion to the early statements on Ministry and Eucharist was matched by cool diffidence on the part of the Vatican.[23]

One of the most fruitful active partnerships today is that between Anglicans and Lutherans. In many parts of the world – Western Europe, North America, Central Southern Africa, Australia – Anglicans and Lutherans are gravitating together. There are no ecumenical agreements between Anglicans and Lutherans at the universal level, though there are theological statements, forged in global dialogue, that act as midwives to regional or national agreements, notably the *Niagara Report*. There are several relationships between Anglicans and Lutherans at the regional level. These fall into two types: those that represent a stage on the way to visible unity and those that bring about such unity (albeit as a stage on the way to a broader *full* visible unity).

STAGES TO VISIBLE UNITY[24]

The *Meissen Agreement* between the Church of England (not the other British and Irish Anglican churches in this case) and the *Evangelische Kirche im Deutschland* (EKD; this is not purely Lutheran but includes Reformed and United churches also) was signed in 1991. It has become the paradigm of the Church of England's method of seeking unity by stages. It sets out the agreed goal of full visible unity on the basis of a shared faith and a common order. It moves towards the Declaration consisting of mutual acknowledgement of the authenticity of ministries, sacraments and oversight, together with mutual commitment to practical collaboration and further theological work on outstanding issues. Meissen does not bring about the integration or interchangeability of ministries because it does not include full agreement on episcopal oversight, including episcopal ordination.

The *Reuilly Agreement* between the British and Irish Anglican Churches and the French Lutheran and Reformed Churches was signed in 2001 and is modelled on Meissen. The French Protestant churches expressed interest in becoming part of the Meissen Agreement. However, they are already in table and pulpit fellowship with the EKD through the Leuenberg Agreement. The Anglican churches believe that, to have integrity, an agreement must be the result of a theological dialogue in which the issues of faith and order are fully worked through together. The Reuilly Agreement actually refines the theological concepts, such as acknowledgement and commitment, that are involved in this type of agreement.

AGREEMENTS FOR COMMUNION/ FULL COMMUNION[25]

Called to Common Mission (the revised version of the *Concordat*), signed at Epiphany 2001 between the Episcopal Church of the USA (ECUSA) and the Evangelical Lutheran Church in America (ELCA) is the flagship of agreements that bring about 'full communion'. This approach is based on the international Anglican–Lutheran Cold Ash formula of 1983, whereby churches seek to enter into full *communicatio in sacris*, including interchangeable ministries, while retaining their separate identity and structures of oversight. The Cold Ash approach is a classical example of the model of 'unity in reconciled diversity' in ecumenism. *Called to Common Mission* brings this state of affairs about through a mutual commitment to episcopal ordination in historical succession (though the possibility of exceptions for the Lutherans is being explored at the time of writing). The full authenticity of each other's ministries is signalled by immediate interchangeability of presbyters in principle. To make this possible, ECUSA has agreed to suspend for the time being the requirement of the

Preface to the Anglican Ordinal of 1662 for episcopal ordination. For its part, the ELCA has waived the requirement for ministers to subscribe to the Augsburg Confession. The ELCA and ECUSA will remain autonomous churches with a common ministry, linked in fellowship and consultation. The anomaly of parallel structures of oversight, within a common territory, in a relationship of full communion does not appear to be regarded as a serious unresolved issue by the two churches.

The *Waterloo Declaration* between the Anglican Church of Canada and the Evangelical Lutheran Church in Canada was signed in July 2001 and broadly follows the *Concordat/Called to Common Mission* approach. It too implements the Cold Ash formula. Unlike the USA model, however, the Canadians do not appear to have agreed a legal mechanism for integration of ministries, perhaps because they do not need one. There is a strong element of pragmatism, of 'Let's work it out as we go along,' in Waterloo.

The *Porvoo Agreement* (1996) between the British and Irish Anglican Churches and the Nordic and Baltic Lutheran Churches (excluding Denmark and Latvia who so far have not signed Porvoo) is a major regional agreement involving Lutherans and Anglicans. It goes beyond Meissen and Reuilly in being an agreement for communion (the Church of England, at least, tends not to use the expression 'full communion', presumably because it sems to imply that communion cannot become ever more full). Porvoo has a distinctive theology of apostolicity, drawing on the Faith and Order Lima text *Baptism, Eucharist and Ministry* (1982) and the *Niagara Report*. This theology of apostolicity enables the Porvoo Common Statement to recognize that all the participating churches have preserved the historic episcopate, in spite of some presbyteral consecrations of bishops in the sixteenth century. Porvoo recognizes historical and sociological common ground between the participating churches and as such is strongly contextual. The relationship within the communion of Porvoo churches is comparable to that within the Anglican Communion itself: there is interchangeability of ministries (with restrictions), together with various forms of interaction in the conciliar structures of the churches; an increasingly shared life through twinnings of parishes, dioceses and cathedrals and a mutually enriched fellowship. The Porvoo churches exist (with the exception of chaplaincies and ethnic congregations) in geographically separate territories, speaking various different languages, so there is little question of parallel jurisdictions.

ANGLICANS AS DIALOGUE PARTNERS

In spite of these ecumenical successes, Anglican churches tend to fall between two stools when it comes to actually uniting with other churches. In theology and history they have much in common with the churches of the Reformation – who therefore tend to expect unity with Anglicans to be easier than it is. In Church order (for example, the insistence of the Lambeth Quadrilateral on the historic episcopate) they stand close to Roman Catholic and Orthodox churches – who therefore find it hard to understand Anglican doctrinal rapport with the Reformation tradition. The Church of England's own track record shows it to be rather a risky partner in an ecumenical courtship.

The current ecumenical policy of the Church of England, which, needless to say, does not carry any automatic implications for the rest of the Anglican Communion, is realistic about these difficulties. It seeks to progress steadily towards the ultimate goal of full visible unity by a series of agreed steps or stages so that issues can be dealt with sequentially and when, as sometimes happens, this proves difficult, the ground already gained is not lost but rather consolidated for the future. The Church of England has been committed to a policy of all round and every level ecumenism. This ecumenical policy is primarily motivated not by pragmatism or sentiment but by a disciplined theological vision. The vision is shaped and encouraged by the foretaste of full visible unity that is granted to us in our experience of fellowship and collaboration in many areas of ecumenical life. At the end of the day, it is the experience of fellowship – the gift of *koinonia* – that is the driving force of the ecumenical movement.

FURTHER READING

Websites for further information:

The Church of England: http://www.cofe.anglican.org

The Council for Christian Unity: http://www.cofe.anglican.org/ ccu

The Centre for the Study of the Christian Church: http://www.ex.ac.uk/theology/CSCC/

Avis, P. (1996), 'Keeping Faith with Anglicanism' in Hannaford, R., ed., *The Future of Anglicanism*. Gracewing 1996.

Avis, P. (1998a), 'The Distinctiveness of Anglicanism' in Podmore, C., ed., *Community, Unity, Communion: Essays in Honour of Mary Tanner*. Church House Publishing 1998.

Avis, P. (1998b), 'What is Anglicanism?' in Sykes, S., Booty, J. and Knight, J., ed., *The Study of Anglicanism*. 2nd edn, SPCK 1998.

Avis, P. (2000), *The Anglican Understanding of the Church: An Introduction*. SPCK, 2000.

Avis, P. (2001), *Church, State and Establishment*. SPCK 2001.

Avis, P. (2002), *Anglicanism and the Christian Church: Theological Resources in Historical Perspective*. Revised and enlarged edn, T. & T. Clark 2002.

Evans, G. R. and Wright, J. R., ed., *The Anglican Tradition: A Handbook of Sources*. SPCK 1991.

Jacob, W. M., *The Making of the Anglican Church Worldwide*. SPCK 1997.

McGrath, A. E., ed., *The SPCK Handbook of Anglican Theologians*. SPCK 1998.

Sykes, S., *Unashamed Anglicanism*. Darton, Longman & Todd 1995.

Sykes, S., Booty, J. and Knight, J., ed., *The Study of Anglicanism*. 2nd edn, SPCK 1998.

Winfield, F., *Growing Together*. SPCK 2002.

NOTES

1. If I am wrong, Avis (2000) and Avis (2002) take considerable pains to demonstrate the fact!
2. For further discussion of this issue see Sykes (1995) and Avis (1998a).
3. See the classical texts in Evans and Wright, ed. (1991).
4. For the development of the Anglican Communion see Jacob (1997); also Sachs, W., *The Transformation of Anglicanism: From State Church to Global Communion*. Cambridge University Press 1993.

5. See Avis (2001).
6. See Doe, N., *Canon Law in the Anglican Communion*. Clarendon Press 1998.
7. See further on these the several relevant chapters in Sykes, Booty and Knight, ed. (1998).
8. See Avis, 'Anglican Conciliarity and the Lambeth Conference', *Theology* CI:802 (1998), pp. 245–52.
9. See further Avis (1996).
10. *The Meissen Agreement*. Council for Christian Unity 1992. Also *Anglican–Moravian Conversations: The Fetter Lane Common Statement, etc.* Council for Christian Unity 1996. Also *Called to Witness and Service: The Reuilly Common Statement, etc.* Church House Publishing 1999.
11. *An Anglican–Methodist Covenant: The Report of the Formal Conversations between the Methodist Church and the Church of England*. Methodist Publishing House and Church House Publishing 2001.
12. *Together in Mission and Ministry: The Porvoo Common Statement, etc.* Church House Publishing 1993.
13. *Called to Common Mission*. ELCA, Chicago, 1998.
14. See further Avis, P., *Anglican Orders and the Priesting of Women* (Affirming Catholicism series). Darton, Longman & Todd 1999. Also the report of the House of Bishops of the Church of England, *The Eucharist: Sacrament of Unity*. Church House Publishing 2001.
15. See Wright, J. R., 'Sequential or Cumulative Orders vs. Direct Ordination', *Anglican Theological Review* LXXV:2 (1993), pp. 246–51.
16. See *For Such a Time as This: A Renewed Diaconate in the Church of England*. Church House Publishing 2001.
17. *Eucharistic Presidency*. Church House Publishing 1997.
18. See the report of the House of Bishops of the Church of England, *Bishops in Communion*. Church House Publishing 2000.
19. For this way of putting it see Kaye, B., *A Church Without Walls: Being Anglican in Australia*. Victoria, Dove, 1995.
20. See Avis, P. (2001).
21. See LeGood, G., ed., *Chaplaincy: The Church's Sector Ministries*. Cassell 1999. (Includes Avis, P., 'Towards a Theology of Sector Ministry'.)
22. See Carr, W., *Brief Encounters*. SPCK 1985.

23. Anglican–Roman Catholic International Commission, *The Final Report*. CTS/SPCK 1982.
24. See n. 9 above.
25. See nn. 11, 12 above.

7

The Old Catholic Churches of the Union of Utrecht

Urs von Arx

HISTORICAL INTRODUCTION

The Union of Utrecht comprises eight or nine national Churches, i.e. Churches organized on an episcopal-synodal basis within the boundaries of a particular country and being autonomous in their internal administration, but having a central organ in the International Old Catholic Bishops' Conference (IBC) with the first responsibility for its common witness and mission. Listed in the order of their becoming members of the Union they are the Old Catholic Churches in the Netherlands, Germany, Switzerland, Austria, the Czech Republic, the United States of America and Canada, Croatia, Poland and (recently) Slovakia.

We may distinguish three groups as to the historical background of their coming into existence.

The Old Catholic Church in the Netherlands (Oud-Katholieke Kerk van Nederland) may regard itself being in historical continuity with the Church of Utrecht founded in the eighth century by St Willibrord and reorganized as an archdiocese in 1559. The Church, weakened by the Reformation and the Dutch war of independence against the Spanish rule, had to find a new (and often hidden) mode of life in the Calvinist republic. It became a matter of continual debate between Rome and Utrecht whether the Church of Utrecht nominally headed by an Apostolic Vicar was a missionary Church or a continuation of the ancient see in changed political circumstances. A highly complex development involving questions usually connected with the term Jansenism ended up in a breach between Rome and Utrecht when, after a long vacancy in the See, an archbishop (Cornelius van Steenoven) was elected by the local Church in 1723, consecrated by a visiting titular bishop (Dominique Varlet) in 1724, and censured by Benedict XIII in 1725. The Church of Utrecht persevered for a long time in a Tridentine form of Catholicism and showed its reverence to Rome in its (never abolished) name: The Roman Catholic Church of the Old Episcopal Clergy. The sees of Utrecht, Haarlem and Deventer (the titular bishopric has been left vacant since 1982) may claim historical continuity over against the Roman hierarchy established in Holland by Pius IX in 1853. This cannot be said of the rest of the Old Catholic episcopate.

The Old Catholic Churches in Germany (Katholisches Bistum der Alt-Katholiken in Deutschland), Switzerland (Christkatholische Kirche der Schweiz) and Austria (Altkatholische Kirche Österreichs) go back to the refusal of liberal Catholics to accept the conception of the Church as it found its expression in the two decrees of the First Vatican Council in 1870 on the universal jurisdiction of the bishop of Rome and his infallibility as supreme teacher in matters of faith and morals. Being excommunicated they were to organize Churches that were no longer under the obedience of the pope. The protest has been linked from the very beginning with the intention of reform and reunion on the basis of the life and faith of the ancient undivided Church.

While in Germany and Switzerland the organization of the Church (ending in the setting-up of a diocesan synod and the consecration of a bishop elected by the synod) was completed in 1871–4 and 1871–6 respectively, the Old Catholics in the Habsburg Empire were not allowed by the state authorities to have a bishop consecrated; so they had to be content with a diocesan administrator whose seat was in Vienna and (from 1897) at Varnsdorf in Bohemia. After the collapse of the Habsbug Empire two autonomous Churches were established in Czechoslovakia and Austria with bishops being elected and consecrated in 1924 and 1925. The Church in Czechoslovakia was largely of German origin, and those members had to leave Bohemia in 1945. The remaining Czech-speaking Church (now Starokatolická Církev v české Republice) has its roots in an effort at the turn of the century to found a national church claiming to stand in the tradition of Cyril and Methodius and of John Huss.

The Old Catholic Churches of Slav origins do not owe their organization to the controversies over the first Vatican Council, but are the result of a deep wish to live a distinct ethnic identity within the Catholic Church which the Roman authorities were unwilling to concede. Towards the end of the nineteenth century a number of independent-minded communities emerged among Polish emigrants in the USA. A group in Chicago came into contact with the European Old Catholics, and in 1897 a bishop (Antony Kozlowski) elected by a synodal assembly was ordained at Berne and thereby – with his Church – admitted into the Union of Utrecht. In the same year another group at Scranton PA was organized by Francsizek Hodur, who managed to unite other independent Polish communities and who, after the death of Kozlowski, was consecrated a bishop at Utrecht in 1907. Today the Polish National Catholic Church (PNCC) has four dioceses in the USA and one in Canada.

After World War One the PNCC started a mission in Poland then enjoying a new national independence. The missionary diocese established in 1924 became an autonomous church in 1951. Today the Polish National Church (Kościół Polskokatolicki w Rzeczypospolitej Polskiej) comprises three dioceses.

In Yugoslavia an Old Catholic Church was organized among the Croats in 1923, and a bishop (Marko Kalogera) was consecrated at Utrecht a year later. The Old Catholic Bishops, however, terminated communion with him in 1933, upon which a schism occurred, one part siding with the Union of Utrecht. The history of this Church with the two rival groups (1934–74) that had links with other Old Catholic bishops in Slovenia and Serbia (not belonging to the Union) is rather confusing and was a continual source of difficulties for the other bishops of the Union. Today the Croatian Catholic Church (Hravtska Katolicka Crkva) after having suffered severe losses during World War 2 has been without a bishop since 1974 and is limited to a few parishes.

In 2000 a small Old Catholic body in Slovakia (Starokatolícka Cirkev na Slovensku) has been recognized as a new member Church of the Union, although the consecration of the bishop elect has not been taken into consideration so far. As there have never been Old Catholic parishes in the Slovakian part of the Habsburg Empire or of Czechoslovakia, this Church may be reckoned to belong to the third group.

Other Old Catholic groups without synod or bishop in France and Italy, as well as in Sweden and Denmark, do not count as member Churches of the Utrecht Union. They are under the supervision of the IBC.

The Union of Utrecht came into existence on 24 September 1889, when the three Dutch bishops and the bishops of the Old Catholic Churches in Germany and Switzerland declared that 'the Churches headed and represented by them are in full ecclesial communion with each other'. This was the result of a development that started with the consecration of the first German bishop, Joseph Hubert Reinkens, by a Dutch bishop, but was seriously hampered by the further progress of the Old Catholic movement. In the face of rather radical reforms in the Swiss Church – like the abolition of compulsory celibacy or the institution of a diocesan synod with a lay majority and strong democratic elements – the Dutch bishops refused to consecrate the first Swiss bishop Eduard Herzog; it was his German colleague who had to help out. After a certain consolidation of the German and Swiss Old Catholic Churches and a growing understanding of the Dutch theologians for the objectives of the Old Catholic policy as laid down in the fundamental decisions of the first three Old Catholic congresses (Munich 1871, Cologne 1872, Constance 1873) the will to a common witness became prevalent.

In 1890 the administrator of the Austrian diocese joined the Union, as later did the bishops of the third group.

The Union of Utrecht terminated ecclesial communion with two Churches and their bishops repectively: in 1910/13 with Arnold Mathew (consecrated at Utrecht in 1908) and in 1924 with the Polish Mariavite Church (the first bishop having been consecrated at Utrecht in 1909).

The setting up of the Union of Utrecht in 1889 united two of the groups mentioned above. It marked the beginning of a process of reception in which the Dutch Old Catholics gradually adopted the comparatively progressive and ecumenically minded position of Old Catholic theology set out by the first generation of German-speaking Old Catholic divines. It was completed by the mid-1920s and resulted in what I would call the Old Catholic mainstream theology manifesting a marked closeness to Anglican and Orthodox ecclesiology. The leading centres of theological reflection were the Old Catholic Faculty of Theology in the University of Berne and the seminaries at Amersfoort (later Utrecht) and Bonn.

The Old Catholic Churches of Slav origin have hardly participated in the formation of a distinct Old Catholic theology. In the PNCC (the numerically largest Church of the Union of Utrecht) there is a lively literary activity concerning the history of the 'Polonia' and the PNCC in North America (and Poland), occasionally the connection with the (European) Old Catholics in the Union of Utrecht, but virtually nothing like a theological exchange with West European Old Catholicism. This came conspicuously to the fore in the recent debate on the ordination of women to the priesthood: the hermeneutical and systematic considerations of the latter were implausible, if not incomprehensible to the representatives of the PNCC. This is not least due to a language problem: most of the relevant Old Catholic theological literature is still written in German (and to a lesser degree in Dutch). In this respect, the situation is better in Poland, because a considerable number of recent Old Catholic theological contributions have been translated into Polish and there are hopeful signs of a reception of the fundamentals of liturgical reform as elaborated in the framework of Old Catholic mainstream theology.

In the recent past, Old Catholic mainstream theology seemed to lose something of its formative vigour. This may be especially the case wherever clergy and even the younger active generation of entire parishes are recruited from former Roman Catholics (e.g. in Germany): Old Catholicism looks as if it has been redefined along the lines of ideas of Church reform that are deeply influenced by articulate opposition groups within the Roman Catholic Church. On the other hand, signs of flagging can also be discerned in the Swiss Church which has far fewer converts from other denominations.

What follows claims to stand in the line of what I term Old Catholic mainstream theology.

HOW THE OLD CATHOLICS SEE THEMSELVES AND OTHER CHURCHES

The way Old Catholics see themselves is fundamentally marked by the breach within the Catholic Church over the conception of the Church as it was dogmatically fixed in papalistic terms on the one hand and the necessity to organize, live and theologically justify a catholic Church separated from the greater part of the Roman communion on the other hand.[1]

Old Catholic theologians have repeatedly claimed that the Churches that had to be organized as Old Catholic Churches (i.e. all apart from the Church of Utrecht) are not strictly speaking refoundations but communities being in continuity with an ecclesial entity that is somehow the focus and basis of all the Churches. This entity is called the ancient undivided Church of the first millennium, the Church of the recognized ecumenical synods or whatever. In very simple terms, it is the Church not yet marked by the emergence of distinct denominational types and by the rise of a single centre in the West claiming universal authority. Consequently the Old Catholic Church may be seen as representing the ancient Catholic Church in the West.[2] The appeal to the ancient Church replaced another position soon recognized as untenable, i.e. that the Old Catholics represent the Catholic Church of the West as it existed before 18 July 1870, when Pius IX promulgated the papal decrees, and had its doctrinal basis in the confession of faith issued by Pius IV in 1564.[3]

Thus the relation to the Catholic Church of the second millennium is a broken one. Some developments, particularly elements of the Church constitution, are regarded as early stages of a centralized version of the Church that won the day in Ultramontanism, and are rejected as one-sided or wrong. On the other hand certain movements are seen as forerunner phenomena, such as Conciliarism, Gallicanism, Jansenism, Josephinism, Febronianism, the Catholic Enlightenment represented by figures like Johann Michael Sailer or Ignaz Heinrich von Wessenberg. It was the ecclesiological concern of a certain autonomy of the local or the national Church that was perceived as relevant in these 'resistance movements' against papal and curial absolutism and the inherent tendency to uniformity in Church life.[4]

The Old Catholics, however, still have another way to see themselves over against the Catholic Church being in communion with the Pope: they may talk of an 'emergency Church' (*Notkirche*) or they may prefer to speak of the Old Catholic 'Movement' in order to underline the provisional character of the Old Catholic ecclesial organization within the wider Catholic Church.

The task of working for the comprehensive reunion of the Church was an element in the Old Catholic programme from the very beginning. It should be seen as an expression of a deep-rooted Catholic consciousness. However, the Old Catholic appeal to the ancient Church had a selective effect. The clearest response came from two Christian traditions that equally value the ancient Church, though not in an identical way. From 1871/2 there has been a special Old Catholic relationship with the Orthodox and Anglican traditions. The Old Catholics regard themselves as representing the One Church in a particular place, as the Orthodox and Anglican Churches represent the One Church in other places (for this see below).

Relations with the Anglicans, i.e. primarily with the Church of England and the Episcopal Church in the USA, led to the Bonn Agreement in 1931 and consequently to what was then called an 'intercommunion' between the Anglican and the Old Catholic Communions; since 1958/61 the term 'full communion' has been used.[5] It is worth noticing that a consistent theological dialogue has hardly ever been conducted since the Bonn Reunion Conferences of 1874/5. For the Old Catholics the way to ecclesial communion was open once the validity of Anglican orders, and thus the apostolic succession of the Anglican Church, was recognized. German-speaking Old Catholics had no problems in this respect, following their *spiritus rector* Ignaz von Döllinger, but the Dutch Old Catholics came to the same conclusion only in 1925 (after Orthodox precedents). Thus the Old Catholic Bishops' Conference could issue a formal declaration recognizing Anglican orders in the same year.

On the basis of the Bonn Agreement the Old Catholics entered into full communion with the Lusitanian Church of Portugal, the Spanish Reformed Episcopal Church (since 1980 independent dioceses within the Anglican Communion) and the Philippine Independent Church in 1965.

Intense theological dialogues, on the other hand, have repeatedly marked relations between the Orthodox and Old Catholics. Between 1975 and 1987 a dialogue with all the Orthodox Churches was successfully concluded: the joint commission published 26 common texts witnessing to a full consensus of Orthodox and Old Catholic teaching on the classical topics of theology. No progress towards ecclesial communion, the objective of the dialogue, has been made, however.[6]

Now one of the reasons for this is the Old Catholics' full communion with the Anglican Church; the Orthodox feel unable to enter into a similar relationship with the Anglicans. This, however, ought to be possible if there is a common basis of belief on all sides. This is a double problem for Old Catholic theology as well, although at another level. Firstly many Old Catholic theologians have – rightly or wrongly – been assuming a deep convergence of the basic experience and conception of the Church in the three traditions. In Old Catholic perception this was manifest in occasional trilateral efforts at seeking ecclesial communion among the Anglican, Orthodox and Old Catholic Churches (rudimentarily in the 1870s, more distinctly in the 1920s). The existence of a Catholic wing consisting of Orthodox, Anglicans and the numerically insignificant Old Catholics was also discerned in the early decades of the ecumenical movement.[7] Consequently, Old Catholic ecumenists regarded the union among the three Churches of the Catholic type (to include Rome seemed inconceivable at that time) as the first ecumenical commitment of Old Catholicism.[8] Moreover they have tended to take (non-Romanizing) Anglo-Catholicism as being representative of Anglicanism.

In the last decades, the entire constellation has changed, not least because of the full ecumenical engagement of the Roman Catholic Church. This brings me to the second point: parts of the Anglican Communion are involved in manifold dialogues and have entered bilateral commitments with other Churches – commitments that are not followed up by the Old Catholics. Do they or ought they affect the full communion between Anglican and Old Catholic Churches – and in what sense?

These questions are not resolved. Thus the persisting Old Catholic view of the Old Catholic, the Anglican and the Orthodox Churches as representative of the One Catholic Church in their particular places may look rather theoretical because it is not confirmed by visible ecclesial communion.

Relationships with the Churches that emerged from the Reformation, especially with the Lutheran and Reformed Churches, were for a long time marked by a common attitude of defence against 'Rome', which was a source of mutual friendliness. There were many contacts in practical matters, but as the relations were and still are varied in the individual Old Catholic Churches, no general statement is possible. There has never been an all-Old Catholic dialogue, i.e. one conducted by the Union of Utrecht, although such a dialogue with the Lutheran World Federation was suggested in recent times. 'The issues that would have to be cleared in a dialogue concern especially the understanding of the Church, of its unity and its ministry, the sacramental theology, and the understanding of redemption and salvation.'[9] In this perspective the recent Anglican–Lutheran rapprochement as set out in the Porvoo Common Statement of 1992 or the agreement *Called to Common Mission* of 2000 in the USA are followed up with interest in the European Old Catholic Churches.

So, there is ample evidence that the Old Catholic Church recognizes the Eastern Orthodox (and probably the Eastern Oriental) and the Anglican Churches[10] as representations of the *Una Sancta* and thus as true and Catholic Churches – in analogy to the Old Catholic self-understanding of representing the One Church. It is more difficult to make out a coherent evaluation of the Roman Catholic Church, and there is a certain reluctance to render a judgement on the Protestant Churches.

THE SOURCES OF OLD CATHOLIC ECCLESIOLOGY

The sources of Old Catholic ecclesiology are to be found in the Tradition as it has taken shape in the ancient undivided Church. The appeal to the entity 'the ancient Church' needs an explanation. This appeal, which is neither new nor specifically Old Catholic, does not imply an anachronistic restoration of past times. It denotes a basic, yet selective, point of reference for a theological reflection on the nature, mission and structure of the Church.

In contrast to an ecclesiology stressing the jurisdiction and teaching authority of a single primate as the necessary and decisive agent of the universal Church, Old Catholic ecclesiology would stress the theological dignity of the local Church headed by a bishop as well as the fact that the bishop acts in a synodal network with the other bearers of the ordained ministry of the local Church and the laity. As baptized men and women, they all participate in the life of the Church according to their common and individual call and to their gifts discerned and recognized in an act of ecclesial commissioning. This view will determine the necessary elements of the conception of the unity of the Church. Thus the ecclesiological aspect is foremost in the appeal to the ancient Church, as the dominant concern of the Old Catholic movement is the 'struggle for the nature of the Church'.[11]

The entity 'ancient Church' contains all the sources one would expect: Holy Scripture, the ecclesial tradition, the ancient symbols of faith like the Nicene or the Apostles' Creed, the dogmatic decisions of the (seven) Ecumenical Councils, and hence the Trinitarian-Christological dogma. It may well be worth stressing that Old Catholic ecclesiology does not start from Scripture as a somewhat isolated source and principle, but from the 'ancient Church', where these elements are part of an indissoluble community context. Of course Holy Scripture is the fundamental and unique witness of revelation – understood as the self-revelation of the triune God – upon which rests the faith of the Church, however expressed. It is the witness of God's love and salvation destined for all humankind, the whole creation, which has its basis in the mission of Christ and the gift of the Holy Spirit that effect justification and reconcilation by which humans responding in faith find communion with God and in God communion with one another. This communion is the Church, i.e. the manifestation of the reality of reconciliation having its source in God.

It is well known that the New Testament has no single or unified ecclesiology. Its varied approaches seem to converge in the realization that the people touched by the gospel form a communion whose unity, expressed in visible forms, is an essential element. It is incomprehensible for Old Catholic theology to draw the conclusion from the New Testament data that there can be no binding ecclesial structures translating the spiritual experience of unity in God into stable and thus institutionalized forms visibly manifesting this unity. This is what happened in the sub-apostolic time of the ancient Church when it was consolidated and expanded in the *oikumene*. The Eucharist and episcopal ministry serve and manifest unity in the local Church, as do synodal networks.

While our ecclesiology is based on the ancient Church, its outworking depends on theological reflection and on the highly complex sociocultural context we live in, very different from the first millennium. The result will usually show elements of continuity and discontinuity, analogies and transmutations. To take an example: an Old Catholic diocesan synod with clergy and lay delegates from parishes is not an exact restoration of any of the types of synods found in the ancient Church[12] or of Acts 15, but owes much to the parliamentary system in modern states.

Thus the *Declaration of Utrecht*, issued by the five Old Catholic bishops when realizing ecclesial communion of their Churches in the Union of Utrecht in 1889, is not to be seen as a 'confession', like those which established denominational identities in the sixteenth to eighteenth centuries. The document (addressed 'to the Catholic Church' and actually sent to the heads of the Orthodox and the Anglican Churches in 1889) served as a summary of the principles according to which the bishops so far had administered their office. In the beginning they quote the much used rule of faith of St Vincent of Lérins: 'Id teneamus quod ubique, quod semper, quod ab omnibus creditum est; hoc est etenim vere proprieque catholicum' (i.e. that the test of catholicity is what has been held everywhere, always and by all), and they continue: 'Therefore we hold to the faith of the ancient Church, as it is formulated in the ecumenical symbols and in the universally accepted dogmatic decisions of the ecumenical synods held in the undivided Church of the first millennium.' Further the declaration approves of the historic primacy of the pope as *primus inter pares* (first among equals), but rejects the papal decrees of 1870 and other papal statements held to contradict the teaching of the ancient Church. It confirms the belief in the reality and mystery of the Eucharist. It commits the Union of Utrecht to do whatever it can to overcome the divisions of the Churches and to find and establish unity with other Churches on the basis of the faith of the ancient Church.

Gradually the Declaration, which each new bishop has to sign on behalf of his Church, became something like a confession of faith, not least because the Old Catholics were being asked for such a text.

Another text, whose importance has until recently hardly been recognized, is the *Agreement of Utrecht*, also issued in 1889. It is the key to the underlying ecclesiology of the Union of Utrecht. There is a third text (the *Regulations of Utrecht*) which constitutes the standing orders of the International Old Catholic Bishops' Conference (IBC). The *Agreement* and the *Regulations* were revised in 1952, 1974 and 2000. They are now part of the new *Statute of the Old Catholic Bishops United in the Union of Utrecht*, with a preamble outlining the ecclesiological principles of the Union.[13] The *Declaration*, being a historic document, has never been revised.

THE NATURE OF THE CHURCH AND ITS MISSION

The Church has its source and foundation in God who is its future, present and past. It is not possible to expound this fully here; a short sketch must suffice. The Church is the manifestation of the reconciliation initiated by God, for it is in the Church that, as justified sinners, we recognize and accept each other as brothers and sisters. The Church is the communion of humans called to holiness; it is on a pilgrimage to the perfection that will include the entire creation when God is all in all. The Church is participation in the life of God and thus communion of the baptized with God, with other baptized, indeed with all creation. The reconciliation is grounded on God's mission of Jesus, Son and Logos of God, on his death and resurrection, and it is realized and recognized in the gifts of the Holy Spirit enabling humans to act as bearers of the love and knowledge of God and as his responsible partners.

The Church, then, has its foundation in Jesus Christ and in the Holy Spirit, as the life-giving mission of Christ is in the power of the Spirit and as the Spirit makes present this life in time and space, in a continuous process of inculturation. As Son and Spirit have their unity in God, the Church has its foundation in the triune God. 'The reason why the trinitarian foundation of the reality of the Church is important for the Old Catholic understanding of the Church is the fact that it makes it possible for us to understand the human communion in the Church as participation in the life of God being communion.'[14]

Thus this ecclesiological approach starts from soteriological and trinitarian premises, and it presupposes a sort of relational ontology for the understanding of reality as being God's creation. A human being is fundamentally a being in communion, not an isolated one for which to be in communion is a secondary state. This may be expressed by saying that a human being is a person, not an individual, and that the Church is thoroughly constituted by relations of personal beings face to face with others.[15] The participation by grace in a reality that is basically outside the believers and yet becomes their inner reality may in various ways be reflected in ecclesiological metaphors like People of God, Body of Christ, Temple of the Spirit, etc. In this context mention must be made of the popular term *koinonia* or *communio*: it denotes a communion that is constituted through a common participation in an entity that the members of the communion are not themselves.[16] The clearest expression of this fundamental aspect of the Church is the Eucharist, the ecclesiological relevance of which is not sufficiently recognized if it is seen as merely one sacrament among others.

The Church as vanguard and model of the renewed and

redeemed humanity lives in a specific situation between the times: in anamnesis of their foundation in Christ and in the expectation of the perfection of God's love transforming the whole creation. In this tension the Church has to recognize and fulfil its mission. The fundamental aspects of its life may be termed *martyria, doxologia* and *diakonia*. *Martyria* includes the various acts of proclamation of the gospel, catechesis, the accounting for the hope and faith in all its dimensions, statements on social and political issues as far as they are ineluctible consequences of the gospel. *Doxologia* includes worship of God, which manifests in a fundamental epicletic attitude that the Church dares to live on what is promised and given in word and sacrament. In *diakonia* the Church fulfils its mission of healing men and women in material and spiritual distress, resolutely transcending its own institutional borders.

The Church is thus a divine–human communion, but its institutional, structural aspects can be fully descibed in sociological and other terms. It is this communion in radical ambiguity. This is so because the Church is a pilgrim community, and because of the sins of its members which obliterate and compromise its being a creation of God's love,[17] in the last analysis because of the incarnational 'touch' of God's acting in the world. Old Catholic theology takes for granted that human beings, even material elements, may be bearers of God's presence wherever the Holy Spirit – whether invoked in prayer or by its own initiative – makes use of them. Ambiguity affects the perception of the Church in all its utterances. A neutral perception of the God-givenness of the Church apart from faith seems impossible.[18]

UNITY, CATHOLICITY AND APOSTOLICITY OF THE CHURCH

The only truly ecumenical symbol of faith, the so-called Nicene Creed, outlines the reality of the Church in four adjectives (the *notae ecclesiae*) pointing to aspects of its nature. The Church is one, holy, catholic, apostolic. This statement about the Church occurs in the short pneumatological section (that concerning the Holy Spirit), and thus makes the Church an object of belief and confession. The marks of the Church must be somehow – in all ambiguity – manifest and answered for by the members of the Church.

The *unity* of the Church has its source in the triune God. But how and where is this unity to be perceived? Old Catholic theology would give an answer in the framework of an ecclesiology taking as its basic entity the local Church. This ecclesiology is discernible without any systematic explication in some authors writing in the 1870s (e.g. J. H. Reinkens), but a certain consistency has been attained only later, not least because of a theological exchange with voices from the Orthodox and Anglican (also Lutheran) traditions, recently with Roman Catholic advocates of a communion ecclesiology, and generally with the work of the Faith and Order Movement/Commission.

The starting point is the eucharistic community headed by a bishop; in what follows this is called the local Church (i.e. traditionally speaking, a diocese). A few remarks will be appropriate. The Eucharist with all its constitutive elements is the primary representation and realization of the communion of God with humans constituted in the Christ event and opened up for continuous participation in the power of the Holy Spirit. The traditional term 'bishop' designates the person who has the first responsibility for the local Church to preserve its unity, as well as its catholicity and apostolicity (see below). The bishop is, however, fully integrated in a network of distinct levels: on the one hand with the *college* of presbyters (usually called priests) and with the deacons, who together with the bishop assume the tasks of the ordained ministry, on the other hand with the non-ordained baptized, the laity, who share the responsibility for the local Church in various ways.[19] The synodal integration of the bishop into the local Church and the participation of all ordained ministers and the laity in the responsibility for the local Church to remain the Church of God has been one of the principal concerns of Old Catholic reforms after 1870. Old Catholic theology will happily recognize a similar concern in the modern debate on *episkope* (pastoral oversight) and its personal, collegial and communal dimensions. It will interpret the personal dimension in terms of what may be called monepiscopacy (not to be confused with monarchical episcopacy and its modern associations).[20]

A further explanation may be needed: why is it not the parish and its local congregation that serves as the ecclesiological starting point? Historically, bishoprics consisting of a town and its immediate hinterland were soon superseded by bishoprics consisting of a region, in which the presbyters assumed episcopal functions in the eucharistic liturgy of the local congregations. But there are other considerations. The basic unit (called local Church) ought as far as possible to fulfil all its tasks itself. For this a parish is very often too small. On the other hand there should be a limit to the circumscription of a local Church: the bishop ought to know in person those who assume responsibility in a local congregation, e.g. the ordained ministers and leading members of a parish council. If this is the case in Old Catholic dioceses, even though they may cover large areas, it is because they are extreme minority Churches.[21]

Now the local Church is a representation and realization of the One Church confessed in the Nicene Symbol of Faith, and this in a particular place. The extent of the place is dependent on contingent factors (number of baptized, historical developments, etc., see below).

The *catholicity* of the Church is to be determined in the context of the ecclesiological approach just presented. It is the local Church that carries the mark of catholicity inasmuch as it participates in God's reality of salvation and truth encompassing heaven and earth and there finds its unifying centre. The local Church, however, does not possess catholicity in itself, like a monad, but insofar as it is in communion with other local Churches, which are equally representations of the One Church in their respective places.

Thus the local Churches have a soteriological-trinitarian identity – an identity, incidentally, that is to be distinguished from other identities that are marked by manifold sociocultural factors and are and should be diverse. This 'theological' identity points to the real source of the unity of the local Churches, the triune God. This unity is manifest in the form of a communion of local Churches (i.e. dioceses), not in the form of something like a super-diocese in which the dioceses are deficient, somewhat incomplete parts of a larger whole.

There will be communions of local Churches in various geographical extensions, up to the universal communion of local Churches. They are all representations of the One Church, each in their place. From all this follows that the catholicity of the Church is not simply identical with its (geographical) universality.

The *apostolicity* of the Church is also to be seen in the context of the local Church being in communion with other local Churches.

It denotes the continuity of the Church in space and time with the mission of Christ and his apostles performed in the power of the Holy Spirit. This continuity is related to the entire witness of the Church in Word and Sacrament; some constitutive elements can be singled out, but they should not be seen in isolation. The passing on of the ordained ministry by prayer and the laying on of hands is such an element of what is called apostolic succession, but it must be integrated into the ecclesial context of the co-responsibility of the local Church for remaining true to the gospel and in continuity with the ancient Church. The apostolic succession is in the first and last analysis the process of the Church remaining identical with the apostolic foundation in all forms of inculturation and *aggiornamento* (bringing up to date) that will necessarily create varying identities of another order.

The apostolicity of the Church is clearly seen in the consecration of a bishop: he or she is elected by the local Church, ordained by bishops of other local Churches in communion with it. The ordination takes place in the context of the Eucharist: all baptized people who are present share in the commitment of the Church to passing on the faith once and for all revealed and yet laid upon the obedient responsibility of the Church. Two dimensions can be discerned in the event: the horizontal historical continuity within the supralocal communion and the vertical immediacy to God (made clear in the epicletic ordination prayer).

MINISTRY AND LEADERSHIP IN THE OLD CATHOLIC CHURCH

The Old Catholic Church holds to the threefold ordained ministry as it emerged in the second century and was virtually universally maintained up to the Reformation. In view of Protestant criticism levelled against the idea that Holy Scripture considers the three-fold ministry, especially episcopacy, an institution necessary for salvation, Old Catholic authors have sometimes tried to give an exegetical answer to the contrary. But on the whole it is now accepted that this is not really possible, not least because of the divergent ecclesiological approaches in the New Testament mentioned above. As the basic appeal of Old Catholic theology is not so much to Holy Scripture (taken in isolation from the Church of sub-apostolic times) but to the ancient Church, this does not seem to create grave problems.[22] The threefold ministry, the rule of faith, the canon of Scripture are taken as fundamental decisions of the early Church being in legitimate continuity with its apostolic origin.

In terms of systematic theology the following consideration may be worth mentioning. The ministry that is constitutive for the Church and its mission has its origin in the commissioning of the apostles by Christ. It carries on their service in areas that are not limited to the historically unique and foundational aspects of their apostolate: the proclamation of the gospel including its sacramental and pastoral dimension in a comprehensive sense. Now the one ministry is directed to the one local Church (of the earlier urban or the later regional type). This aspect is manifest in the oneness of the minister traditionally called bishop. But the one ministry also has a collegial dimension, and this is manifest in the college of collaborators, traditionally called presbyters (or priests). The aspects of oneness and plurality or collegiality of the ministry are equally necessary, so it makes sense to differentiate the one ministry in episcopacy and presbyterate – it may even be seen as a reflection of the unity and plurality of the triune God.[23]

It is more difficult to give a similar explanation for the diaconate as part of the ordained ministry, or of the apostolic ministry. Incidentally, in some Old Catholic Churches there have been successful efforts to reintroduce a permanent diaconate with a larger pastoral responsibility than is given to the transitory diaconate of candidates for the priesthood.

The threefold apostolic ministry of the Church has to be seen in its connection with the non-ordained baptized. Ministry and laity are being distinguished, but they act in a communion, being a network with different tasks, not with the separation of, say, a teaching and obeying Church. In earlier times the Old Catholic concern for the integration of the laity (and lower clergy) into the responsibility for the local Church and thus in its leadership was given expression with the problematic term democratization. Today the relation of the ministry and the laity is rather seen as analogous to the trinitarian model of the relation of Christ and Spirit. The ministry represents Christ and carries on his and the apostles' mission, though not in an exclusive way; the laity represent the Holy Spirit – again not in an exclusive way – who helps them to recognize whether the ministry remains true to the gospel of Christ (this would be a sort of general lay ministry).

Each has a responsibility for the Church and its proclamation and cannot give it up to or take it over from the other. In the case of conflict over fundamental questions – and this holds good not just for the ministry/laity divide but for bishop/synod, bishop/presbyterate, etc. – discussion must go on until a consensus is reached or a breach of ecclesial communion is unavoidable. In other words, there is no fixed procedure for coming to a decision in the sense that it is the bishop, or the clergy, or the laity, or a mixed majority that has the final vote. This is a consequence of the ecclesiological approach outlined so far, and a lot of encouragement (and instruction) is needed to bring the members of the Church to live this 'high' ecclesiology in terms of shared responsibility. Otherwise many dangers lurk.

There are a number of tasks that are only fulfilled by lay baptized people; in other cases, such as religious education, pastoral and social work, an exclusive connection with the ministry or the laity does not make sense. The administration of sacraments is a responsibility of the ordained ministry.

The leadership in the local Church (or in the nation-wide communions of local Churches, i.e. the national Church) is undertaken by bishop and synod in co-operation, and by a sort of executive, often called a synodal council. Diocesan or General Synods consist of lay delegates from the parishes and all or elected clergy (the majority must always be lay). The way the common episcopal-synodal structure works in detail is rather different in the Old Catholic Churches of the Union of Utrecht. To take an example, the institution called synod in the Dutch Old Catholic Church has – unlike the synods in the other Old Catholic Churches – only an advisory responsibility, decisions being taken by the bishops together with a small steering group of clergy and laity (the Collegiaal Bestuur). Another difference is the frequency with which synods are convened (1–5 years), which affects the allocation of responsibilities to either synod or synodal council.

Issues that concern the faith of the Church and thus its identity and its communion with other local or national Churches require a special awareness of ecclesial responsibility of the local Church and a common consultation beyond the local or national Church. It is here that in the Union of Utrecht the International Bishops' Conference (IBC) comes into play.

SUPRALOCAL AND UNIVERSAL *KOINONIA* OF THE CHURCH

How can we understand the supralocal *koinonia* of the Church in the light of Old Catholic ecclesiology? It is always a communion of local Churches reaching wider and wider up to the universal communion. Following ancient models the first stage could be designated as a Church Province. It may be a communion of local Churches of a particular country or of a part of it. Communions of local Churches for their part may form a communion, which might be called a patriarchate or whatever. The geographical limit will depend on history, culture and tradition. Finally there is the universal communion of communions of local Churches.

Each communion of local Churches, however wide, is a representation and realization of the One Holy Catholic and Apostolic Church being an object of faith and confessed in the Creed. The common element is their soteriological-trinitarian identity as they participate in God. Each type of communion has to manifest the unity of the Church in various ways.

In order to maintain the supralocal communion of Churches there will be appropriate forms of common consultation and decision-making and witnessing to the common faith in the gospel. In this the bishops have a special responsibility, as they are at the interface of local Church and supralocal communion. As individual bishops, they are the personal focus of the unity of each particular local Church; as a group of bishops they are the collegial focus of unity of a particular communion of local Churches. Now the synod of bishops has a common responsibility to manifest the unity and communion of local Churches. One of the bishops, however, is supposed to have the prime responsibility for this. This bishop is a *primus inter pares*; he will not decide for himself nor will the other bishops (the *pares*) cede their co-responsibility to the primate. Consequently there is co-operation between primate and synod within the common responsibility for manifesting the unity of the Church and witnessing to the gospel whenever necessary.

A principal concern of this concept is, on the one hand, to have intermediate elements between the local and the universal dimensions of unity and communion of the Church, which are all representations of the One Church in their places. On the other hand the concept of primacy should be freed from the fixation on the universal primacy (usually seen in the light of the Roman primacy as defined in 1870) and be understood as an important element in the synodal structure of any communion of local Churches.[24]

The above view of the manifestation of unity of the supralocal *koinonia* of the Church arises from taking the local Church as the primary place of the life of the Church in *martyria*, *doxologia* and *diakonia*, and therefore as the primary (though always ambiguous) realization of the One Church confessed in the Creed. Consequently the synods of bishops represent the communion of the local Churches to which they belong in the first place and not an entity called the universal Church (or part of it) of which they would be the college. Measures are taken to ensure that the bishops speak for their local Churches without simply becoming their mouthpieces, for they carry the primary responsibility for the supralocal communion of the *local* Churches and may not cede it to supposedly superior instances. At the local and the first supralocal (and national) levels, regular meeting is desirable, but at geographically more extensive levels the frequency of synods depends on urgency. The Church as a universal communion of local Churches should never become a global bureaucratic machine.

Another element in this kind of ecclesiology is the process of reception. A decision of a synod must be recognized as a true witness of faith and become an element of the belief of baptized members of the local Churches. This process is guided by the Spirit and cannot be steered by canonical machinery. The infallibility of the Church still has its proper place, but the process of reception is a continuing one and we may be more likely to notice when a synodal decision is rejected.

This vision of unity among local Churches may now be compared with the Old Catholic view of the primacy of the Bishop of Rome. A number of official statements acknowledge 'the historic primacy which several ecumenical councils and Fathers of the Ancient Church have attributed to the Bishop of Rome by recognizing him as *primus inter pares*'.[25] What is rejected is a primacy of (universal) jurisdiction that links the Pope in a unique way with the universal Church and moreover implies a form of primacy without *pares* as he is a *unicus* and not a *primus* (*qua* patriarch of the West), i.e. a universal bishop in addition to the bishop of each local Church, to whom as head of the Church all owe obedience.

What is the ecclesiological status of the Union of Utrecht in this scheme? It serves as the primary Old Catholic framework for living and practising unity and communion at a supralocal level, but it was rather late that the ecclesiological implications were made an object of theological investigation, and certain inadequacies were recognized.[26] The Union of Utrecht ought to see itself as a representation of the One Church in its particular place and not simply as a loose association of individual national Churches.[27] However, this view is not undisputed. It seems impossible to see an exact analogy of the Union in a province or in a patriarchate: neither model really fits. There is also a certain Old Catholic temptation to see the autonomy of the national Church as analogous to the sovereignty of the modern state.

UNITY IN DIVERSITY

Each local church has its own theological identity and can be very different from others in sociocultural terms. How can we recognize their unity through this plurality? Let us consider some elements which are often mentioned in ecumenical debate as necessary if separated Churches are to rediscover their lost unity:

- The fundamental faith of the Church as witnessed in the liturgy, in creeds or other common statements and expressed to some extent in the practical life of the baptized.
- The liturgy of the Church, especially the Eucharist structured around the two poles of Word and Sacrament.
- The ministry of the Church, especially the *episkope* (pastoral oversight) as it relates to both the local Church and the communion of local Churches.

All these elements must have enough in common to show the theological identity of the local Churches. To recognize and preserve what is common in all plurality, to make a difference between essentials and other elements, is a constant task of the local Church and the communion of local Churches. Again, it cannot be fulfilled from a neutral point of view, but only by way of a common discernment that verges on a decision of faith. These elements will usually have a greater degree of uniformity within a local Church or a national Church than in a wider communion of Churches.

The Old Catholic belief of the Church is not articulated in a specific document but the Declaration of Utrecht points to the faith of the ancient Church and to certain texts that serve as common elements of reference (like Holy Scripture, the creeds or dogmatic decisions of ecumenical Councils). Formal declarations issued by the IBC (and received by the Church) will enjoy the status of authoritative clarifications in matters of belief. Other important statements showing common opinions in the Union of Utrecht may stem from institutions like the International Old Catholic Congress (beginning in 1890, and now meeting every four years) or the International Old Catholic Theological Conference (beginning in 1950, and usually meeting every year).

Apart from the liturgy of ordination,[28] the liturgical formularies are the concern of individual Churches. The integration in the Western liturgical traditions and the modern liturgical renewal, however, guarantee a considerable degree of homogeneity.[29]

The ministry is perceived as identical in all the member Churches of the Union, although a closer analysis would probably reveal differences in the self-understanding of the clergy and in their social status. However, the ordination of women to the priesthood – performed in the West Eurpoean Old Catholic Churches – has become a divisive factor for the PNCC, whereas for the European Churches their ordination or non-ordination (as in the Czech Republic, Croatia, Poland and Slovakia) seems to belong to the realm of acceptable diversity.[30]

Canon law as another possible common element in the member Churches differs very much in the degree of its elaboration.

So it may be said in conclusion that there is a relatively large scope for diversity in the Churches constituting the Union of Utrecht.

A similar scope for diversity is explicitly provided for in the Anglican–Old Catholic Bonn Agreement of 1931:

> Intercommunion does not require from either communion the acceptance of all doctrinal opinion, sacramental devotion, or liturgical practice characteristic of the other, but implies that each believes the other to hold all the essentials of the Christian faith.

The concluding text of the Orthodox–Old Catholic dialogue (1975–87) says:

The consequence and expression of reciprocally recognized fellowship in the faith is the full liturgical-canonical communion of Churches, the realization of organic unity in the one Body of Christ. The liturgical and canonical consequences, which result from ecclesial fellowship, will be elucidated and regulated by the Church on the basis of the tradition of the undivided Church. This fellowship does not signify uniformity in liturgical order and ecclesial practice, but rather embodies an expression of the fact that the historically legitimated development of the one faith of the ancient and undivided Church is preserved in each of the participating Churches. This fellowship also does not require the subjection of one Church with its tradition to the other Church, for this would contradict the reality of the fellowship.[31]

It would be highly interesting, even ground-breaking, to see this task put into concrete action, but for various reasons this has not been done.

A VISION OF THE ECUMENICAL FUTURE

In Old Catholic theology there are now hardly any detailed expectations of the future united Church transcending the remaining divisions. In earlier decades a somewhat vague two-stage model was held.[32] A constant Old Catholic factor in the vision of the future united Church is the continuity of faith, worship and order with the ancient Church.[33]

Concerning the way to seek the future united Church, mainstream Old Catholic ecclesiology would hold the view that two separated Churches entering into a sacramental, eucharistic communion should have explicitly recognized each other as identical (true, Catholic, etc.) Churches in the sense outlined above, and this on the basis of a degree of unity in faith, worship and order deemed as sufficient on both sides. It sees eucharistic and ecclesial communion in an indissoluble connection. Thus it is cautious about eucharistic hospitality, which two Churches may agree on while yet remaining separated, although it does accept that individual members of other Churches are given communion at the Lord's Supper. There are other tendencies in recent Old Catholicism, however, that advocate the model of growing together in stages, so that a eucharistic sharing is possible even if the identity of the ministry or the catholicity of the Churches involved are not mutually recognized.[34]

The ecclesiology outlined above when dealing with the supra-local and universal communion of local Churches has deliberately not taken account of the actual state of divisions in Christendom. Now, for the vision of the united future Church this situation must be faced. It can be done by asking the question: what is the status of the denominational Churches in their relationships to each other? Could they see themselves as local Churches – or communion of local Churches – which may recognize each other as identical on the basis of the identity markers deemed as a sufficient manifestation of it? Old Catholic theology has done this regarding the Anglican (and Orthodox) Churches. It assumed that the Old Catholic and Anglican (Orthodox) communion of local Churches live in their distinct places, in distinct territories.[35] So these communions, having recognized their theological identity, could more or less continue to live as denominational Churches as before.

It was in this sense that the Anglican–Old Catholic intercommunion or full communion was conceived. It is a consequence of the adopted ecclesiology that there was no organic merger of the two communions which would have resulted in the absorption of the Old Catholics in the much larger Anglican Church.[36] A problem, however, was perhaps an insufficiently developed mode of regular mutual consultation, which may be remedied in the transformation of the former International Anglican–Old Catholic Theological Conferences (since 1957) into the Anglican–Old Catholic International Co-ordinating Council in 1998.[37]

Now the presupposition of distinct places did not apply to North America, where accordingly the Bonn Concordat of 1931 was realized in special agreements between the PNCC and the Episcopal Church in the USA (1940/47) and the Anglican Church of Canada (1955/58) respectively, which were terminated in 1976/ 78 by the PNCC on account of the Anglican ordination of women. But the presupposition was not accurate in the European context either, where there have always been overlapping Old Catholic and Anglican jurisdictions.

This is the normal situation in the relationships of denominational Churches in modern societies marked by an ever increasing mobility and migration: they live their witness in the same place.

How, then, is unity and communion of denominational Churches to be lived and manifested in the horizon of the ecclesiology set out here? Of the well-known conceptual models of the ecumenical movement, 'reconciled diversity' seems to imply a continuation of Churches which remain separated, even though they may recognize each other as true Churches. More appropriate seems a model of 'organic unity', in that the Church in a particular place is a eucharistic community sharing the same personal, collegial and communal *episkope* and where denominational differences no longer divide the Church (which presupposes the mutual recognition of the theological identity as intimated above). But what is the status of these denominational/social/ethnic identities? How can they be expressed as an element of desired diversity in the one local Church? How is the new loyalty to the one local Church and the communion of local Churches to be combined with the ancient loyalty to the denominational family of the Christian world communion?

Questions like these make us realize how much serious ecclesiological work is still ahead of us on the ecumenical agenda.

FURTHER READING

1. General works:

Still indispensable in English is:

Moss, Claude Beaufort, *The Old Catholic Movement, its Origins and History*. SPCK 1948, 2nd edn 1964, 3rd edn 1977 (Episcopal Book Club).

See also:

Huelin, Gordon, ed., *Old Catholics and Anglicans 1931–1981: To Commemorate the Fiftieth Anniversary of Intercommunion*. Oxford University Press 1983.

In German:

Küry, Urs, *Die Altkatholische Kirche: Ihre Geschichte, ihre Lehre, ihr Anliegen*. (Kirchen der Welt 3 (supplemented by Oeyen, Christian), Stuttgart, EVW, 1966; 2nd edn 1978; 3rd edn 1982.

Conzemius, Victor, *Katholizismus ohne Rom: Die altkatholische Kirchengemeinschaft.* Zürich, Benziger, 1969.

Küppers, Werner, 'Alt-Katholische Kirchengemeinschaft der Utrechter Union' in Heyer, Friedrich, ed., *Konfessionskunde* (Berlin, de Gruyter, 1977), pp. 554–74.

Continuous information about the Old Catholic Church and theology is accessible in the quarterly being published in Berne since 1893: *Internationale Kirchliche Zeitschrift (IKZ)*, before 1911: *Revue Internationale de Théologie (RITh)*.

2. A few repeatedly quoted ecclesiological titles:

Aldenhoven, Herwig, 'Das ekklesiologische Selbstverständnis der Altkatholischen Kirchen' in *Österreichisches Archiv für Kirchenrecht* 31 (1980), pp. 401–30.

Stalder, Kurt, *Die Wirklichkeit Christi erfahren: Ekklesiologische Untersuchungen und ihre Bedeutung für die Existenz von Kirche heute.* Zürich, Benziger, 1984. (Collection of previously published articles.)

Koinonia auf altkirchlicher Basis: Deutsche Gesamtausgabe der gemeinsamen Texte des orthodox-altkatholischen Dialogs 1975–1987 mit französischer und englischer Übersetzung, ed. von Arx, Urs. Beiheft zu IKZ 79 (1989), pp. 186–204, 227–9. (The ecclesiological texts in English.)

NOTES

1. For a necessary correction of my strictly ecclesiological approach to the phenomenon of Old Catholicism see e.g. Frei, Walter, 'Die Frage nach der Stellung des Altkatholizismus in der Geistesgeschichte des 19. Jahrhunderts', *IKZ* 71 (1981), pp. 38–55; 'Altkatholisch, einmal abgesehen von den Papstdogmen', *IKZ* 74 (1984), pp. 65–84.

2. Cf. e.g. (the former archbishop) Rinkel, Andreas, 'Die Lehre von der Kirche nach der altkatholischen Auffassung von der Kirche', *IKZ* 39 (1949), pp. 1–15.

3. It was due to the remonstrations of people like Christopher Wordsworth, the eminent Bishop of Lincoln, that the Old Catholics had given up this position by 1872 – a possible exception being when they had to negotiate with state authorities about Church property.

4. Cf. Küry, U. (1978), pp. 21–49.

5. Cf. *Report of the Meeting of the Commission of the Anglican Communion and the Old Catholic Churches Held at Bonn on Thursday, July 2, 1931* (SPCK); reprinted in *Lambeth Occasional Reports 1931-8* (SPCK 1948), pp. 1-38; von Arx, U., 'Zwischen Stabilität und Krise', *IKZ* 81 (1991), pp. 1-40.

6. Cf. *Koinonia* 1989; von Arx, U., 'Der altkatholisch-orthodoxe Dialog. Anmerkungen zu einer schwierigen Rezeption', *IKZ* 87 (1997), pp. 184-224.

7. Cf. e.g. Visser't Hooft, Willem A., *Anglo-Catholicism and Orthodoxy: A Protestant View* (SCM Press 1933), esp. p. 111.

8. E.g. the Resolution of the International Old Catholic Congress 1925 at Berne concerning Old Catholic participation in the Movement of Faith and Order: 'The next goal is intercommunion of the Catholic Churches ... The ultimate goal is the universal Christian Church', *IKZ* 15 (1935), p. 265.

9. Cf. the IBC Statement 'The Relationships of the Union of Utrecht to Other Churches' (1993), *IKZ* 84 (1994), pp. 245-9. Pentecostal Churches and the younger Churches in the Third World obviously do not enter into the Old Catholic horizon.

10. The PNCC, of course, marks an exception (see below).

11. Cf. Gaugler, Ernst, 'Das wesentliche Anliegen der altkatholischen Bewegung', *IKZ* 36 (1946), pp. 8-16.

12. Cf. Sieben, Hermann Josef, *Die Konzilsidee der Alten Kirche.* Schöningh, Paderborn. 1979.

13. The *Statute*, together with (revised versions of) the *Declaration*, has been published in five languages. *Statut der Internationalen Altkatholischen Bischofskonferenz (IBK).* Offizelle Ausgabe in fünf Sprachen, ed. von Arx, U. and Weyermann, Maja. Supplementary issue to *IKZ* 91/2001, Bern: Staempfli, 2001.

14. Aldenhoven, H. (1980), p. 407.

15. Cf. Stalder, K. (1984), p. 111 (he speaks of 'Gegenüber-Verhältnisse'). For a similar approach see Zizioulas, John, *Being As Communion: Studies in Personhood and the Church.* SVSP, Crestwood NY, 1993.

16. Cf. Hainz, Josef, *KOINONIA: 'Kirche' als Gemeinschaft bei Paulus.* Pustet, Regensburg, 1982.

17. Cf. Küry, U., pp. 269-78, distinguishing the Church essential, deficient and coming to fulfilment.

18. This has been stressed by Stalder in a course of lectures posthumously published; cf. Stalder, Kurt, *Sprache und Erkenntnis der Wirklichkeit Gottes: Texte zu einigen wissenschaftstheoretischen und*

systematischen Voraussetzungen für die exegetische und homiletische Arbeit, ed. von Arx, U. (*Ökumenische Beihefte* 38). Freiburg, Universität-sverlag, 2000, pp. 260–431.

19. Cf. Stalder, K. (1984), pp. 110–25.

20. Cf. *Baptism, Eucharist and Ministry* (Faith and Order Paper 111). WCC, Geneva, 1982, para. 26 (without the term *episkope*); *The Nature and Purpose of the Church: A stage on the way to a common statement* (Faith and Order Paper 181) Geneva, WCC, 1998), paras. 89–106. See further Bouteneff, Peter C. and Falconer, Alan D., ed., *Episkopé and Episcopacy and the Quest for Visible Unity: Two Consultations* (Faith and Order Paper 183) Geneva, WCC, 1999.

21. In Germany, Switzerland, Austria, the Czech Republic, Croatia and Slovakia the single diocese covers the whole country.

22. Cf. Küry U., p. 134: developments 'praeter, sed non contra scripturam' are not rejected from the outset.

23. Cf. Aldenhoven, Herwig, 'Einheit und Verschiedenheit von Bischofs- und Priesteramt im Licht eines trinitarischen Kirchenverständnisses', *IKZ* 72 (1982), pp. 145–51.

24. As a consequence of the interrelation of synod and primate the traditional Old Catholic conception of placing the Ecumenical Synod/Council above the Pope is just as untenable as the opposite one to which it is a reaction.

25. So e.g. the Declaration of Utrecht, para. 2. Other statements include the fundamental programme of the Old Catholic movement issued by the Congress of Munich in 1871, the IBC declaration of 1970 'The Primacy in the Church' (both in Küry, U., pp. 450–2; 458–60), and common texts agreed upon by the Joint Orthodox–Old Catholic Theological Commission (in: *Koinonia*, pp. 202–4) and the International Anglican–Old Catholic Theological Conference of 1985 (in *IKZ* 80 (1990), pp. 5–11).

26. Cf. Papandreou, Damaskinos, 'La signification de l'Union d'Utrecht du point de vue orthodoxe', *Episkepsis* 427 (15 October 1989). The Union of Utrecht, its ecclesiological character and possible restructuration were made an object of two International Consultations of Old Catholic Theologians in 1993 (in *IKZ* 84 (1994), pp. 7–61, 92–127) and in 1996 (in *IKZ* 87 (1997), pp. 65–126).

27. See the preamble of the new statute referred to in note 13. There is an irregular situation insofar as the PNCC terminates

ecclesial communion with those member Churches that introduced the ordination of women to the priesthood and, at the same time, insists on belonging to the Union.

28. The first common rite for the ordination of bishops, priests, deacons (and minor orders, now suppressed) was published in 1897/99. The IBC approved of a revised rite in 1985 which was prepared by the International Old Catholic Liturgical Commission (appointed in 1978). It does not seem to be used in all the member Churches.

29. Cf. the Consensus of the International Old Catholic Theological Conference of 1979 on the structure and the theology of the eucharistic prayer, *IKZ* 70 (1980), pp. 226–9.

30. Cf. von Arx, Urs, 'Die Debatte über die Frauenordination in den Altkatholischen Kirchen der Utrechter Union', in Buser, Denise and Loretan, Adrian, ed., *Gleichstellung der Geschlechter und die Kirchen: Ein Beitrag zur menschenrechtlichen und ökumenischen Diskussion* (Freiburger Veröffentlichungen zum Religionsrecht 3). (Freiburg, Universitätsverlag, 1999), pp.165–211; see also idem/Kallis, Anastasios (eds), *Gender and the Image of Christ: Common Considerations and essays of the Orthodox–Old Catholic consultations regarding the role of women in the church and the ordination of women as an ecumenical issue*, 1996, Levadia (Greece) and Konstancin (Poland), tr. Reid, Duncan, *Anglican Theological Review*, Summer issue 2002 (forthcoming).

31. Cf. *Koinonia*, 228.

32. See note 8.

33. Cf. Küry, U. (1978), pp. 361–77, distinguishing various types of ecumenical visions of the One Church according to this criterion.

34. Cf. e.g. the Eucharistic Agreement between the Old Catholic and the Evangelical Church in Germany in 1985. The way this agreement came about was criticized by the IBC and led to an unprecedented major crisis in the Union in the 1990s.

35. Cf. Aldenhoven, H. (1980), pp. 427–8.

36. The full membership offered to a number of Old Catholic bishops in the Lambeth Conference (who, however, refrain from voting) is in my view an ecclesiologically inappropriate solution, but has to be accepted for practical reasons.

37. There were many more issues submitted by Canterbury to the IBC for comment than the other way round!

8

The Lutheran Churches

Michael Root

When Martin Luther posted his Ninety-five Theses against the sale of indulgences on 31 October 1517, he had no intention of creating a Lutheran church. At that time, such a thing was hardly imaginable. His intention was to reform church teaching and practice by the gospel as he and others had come to understand it in the course of intense engagement with the Bible (especially the letters of Paul) and with the texts of certain early church Fathers (especially the anti-Pelagian writings of Augustine). That this reform movement led to the existence of a distinct group of churches called 'Lutheran' was the result of a series of unforeseen historical events, to which the Reformers often reacted with a combination of appeal to fundamental theological principle and pragmatic adaptation to the limits of the possible within the Holy Roman Empire and Scandinavian states of the sixteenth century. Lutheran ecclesiology was not systematically worked out in the abstract and then applied to concrete cases. Rather, it was developed piecemeal within specific historical contexts which often shaped its content more than later generations have been willing to admit. This combination of abstract theological principle and often unconceded concrete historical contextuality has been the hallmark of Lutheran ecclesiology. Thus, any account of the self-understanding of the Lutheran churches will need to take up both history and theology.

FROM REFORM MOVEMENT TO LUTHERAN CHURCHES

For complex reasons still not fully understood, when Luther was summoned to Rome in the autumn of 1518 to answer charges of heresy, he was shielded by his territorial prince, Frederick the Wise, the Elector of Saxony. Frederick had little to gain from Luther's attack; he had himself assembled an outstanding collection of relics, to which significant indulgences were attached. Nevertheless, he not only consistently protected his star university professor and theologian from higher church authorities, but permitted the publication and dissemination of Luther's controversial ideas and the first steps toward a reform of the church in his territory along the lines Luther indicated. Here lay the initial model for the alliance of reform and state that would provide a safe haven for the Lutheran Reformation, but at a price.[1]

Already in 1520, in his 'Address to the German Nobility', Luther had appealed to the princes to intervene and reform the church in their territories if the bishops refused to do so (Luther, LW 44:123–217).[2] Not merely abuses, but the preaching of the gospel itself, the very life blood of the church, was at stake. The princes were to instigate these reforms as the leading lay persons within their churches. In the summer of 1526, the Diet of the Holy Roman Empire, confronted by wars with both France and the Ottoman Empire, implicitly gave the princes permission to carry out such reforms. Each ruler was to act within his church in a way that he could justify before God and the emperor with a good conscience. The roots of the distinct Lutheran churches lie in the reforms the princes then carried out in their churches (Lindberg, 1996:233f).

In Luther's territory of Electoral Saxony, the prince, at the urging of the Reformers, soon began a comprehensive survey of the condition of the church. How to carry out this implicitly episcopal task of oversight was far from clear, as Luther himself noted in the *Instructions* to those who carried out the 'visitation', as it came to be called. The bishops responsible for this task had abandoned their office by abandoning the gospel. The task fell to the prince to organize the inspection and, in its wake, to take whatever measures were needed to restore the church's health (Luther, LW 40:271).

This role of the prince, which Luther had depicted as an emergency measure, became the norm in Lutheran territories. Over time, the role of the prince was institutionalized in Germany in a system of church governance by consistories, essentially state committees, in which administration was divided between appointed clergy and secular officials. Theologically, this arrangement was understood as the embodiment of the role of the prince as 'summus episcopus' of the church in his territory. In Germany, this system continued to evolve, but the basic pattern persisted until 1918. In the Nordic lands, all of which became Lutheran, the preservation of an episcopal order modified this picture, but the power of the king and the integration of the bishops into the structure of the state meant that the picture was modified, not destroyed.[3]

The Lutheran churches thus developed as a group of state or territorial churches, each independent of the others, each governed by varying mixtures of clerical and secular administration. What united the churches and identified them as Lutheran was a common theological confession and a set of basic practices, especially sacramental, laid out in a limited set of authoritative texts, most importantly the Augsburg Confession (1530) and Luther's Small Catechism (1529). In the Peace of Augsburg (1555) that ended the first religious wars in the Holy Roman Empire and that officially recognized Lutheranism, the Lutheran churches were legally defined as the churches that adhered to the Augsburg Confession. Other confessions were formulated in the sixteenth century, but the process of confession-writing ended with the Formula of Concord (1577) and the collection of the confessions in the Book of Concord (1580), which consists of the Apostles', Nicene and Athanasian creeds and seven Reformation texts.[4] The acceptance of some or all of these confessions still today defines the Lutheran churches. The Lutheran churches thus constitute, above all, a confessional communion.

The immigrant and missionary churches that grew up outside the traditional Lutheran homelands of central and northern Europe have no tradition of close attachment to the state, but, like the mother churches, they are usually organized at the national or territorial level and are defined by confessional allegiance.[5] The one new element created in the twentieth century has been an umbrella organization of Lutheran churches worldwide, the Lutheran World Federation (LWF), described in greater detail below.

Especially among English-language Lutherans, the question has been raised whether this development from reform movement to church should be resisted or even reversed. When Lutheranism settles down as a denomination among denominations, has it both claimed too much for itself (a full ecclesial existence) and too little (the reform of only one part of the Western church)? It has thus become common, especially in ecumenically engaged parts of Lutheranism, to refer to Lutheranism ideally as still a reform movement in the greater catholic church, a movement dedicated to the proclamation of the gospel of God's free grace. If there must be distinct Lutheran churches, they exist only despite their own deepest wishes (Jenson, 1991).

THE NATURE OF THE CHURCH

The church as creature of the word

These historical developments were accompanied by the development of a particular theological understanding of the nature of the church. This theological understanding both helped open the door to these developments and affirmed them, once they had occurred.

Decisive for the Lutheran understanding of the church is the insistence that the church is to be understood as *creatura verbi*, a creature or creation of the word, the gospel of God's free grace in Jesus Christ. The theological core of the Lutheran understanding is formed by the attempt to think through the meaning of that assertion.

The nature of the church is stated most clearly for Lutherans in Article 7 of the Augsburg Confession: 'The church is the assembly of saints [or of all believers] in which the gospel is taught purely and the sacraments are administered rightly.'[6] This definition is in itself highly traditional. The phrase 'assembly of saints' appears to be a deliberate echo of the phrase 'communion of saints' in the Apostles' Creed, which the Reformers understood to be an interpretive gloss on the preceding phrase 'holy catholic church' (Ap 7.8). Embedded in this short definition are three central interlocking statements.

- First, the church is an assembly, a group of persons. The Reformers could say that the church was a society (*societas*, Ap 7.5), a people (*populus*, Ap 7.14), or a folk (*Volk*, Luther, LW 41:145).
- Second, this people includes, in the strict sense, all and only those who can be described as saints, as faithful, or as believers.
- Third, this people is constituted as the assembly of saints by the gospel and sacraments preached and administered within it.

In an ultimate, even eschatological sense, this assembly is not a literal gathering, since it includes 'all those who live in true faith, hope, and love. Thus the essence, life, and nature of Christendom [*Christenheit*] is not a physical assembly, but an assembly of hearts in one faith' (Luther, LW 39:65). This body will assemble in the strict sense only eschatologically. It is the universal church of all times and places. As the body of Christ and 'an association of faith and of the Holy Spirit in person's hearts' (Ap 7.5), this assembly, strictly speaking, does not include those who are without faith. 'Those in whom Christ is not active are not members of Christ' (Ap 7.5). If the church is truly 'without spot and wrinkle' (Ephesians 5.27), then it can include only those justified by God's grace.

This highly spiritual and eschatologically oriented understanding of the church is not, however, ahistorical. The church is strictly tied to the concrete proclamation of the word and celebration of the sacraments. Through word and sacrament 'are imparted not bodily but eternal things and gifts, namely, eternal righteousness, the Holy Spirit, and eternal life. These gifts cannot be obtained except through the office of preaching and of administering the holy sacraments, for St Paul says, "The gospel is the power of God for salvation to everyone who has faith"' (CA 28.8f). If Christ and the Spirit, on the one hand, and human faith, on the other, are the poles of the relation which constitutes the church, then the concrete, physical, historical assembly is both the locus where this relation is established and lived (as the place where the word is preached and sacrament celebrated) and the divinely appointed means by which this relation is established and lived (as the community which preaches the word and celebrates the sacraments). The Large Catechism can thus describe the church as 'the mother that begets and bears every Christian through the word of God' (LC II.42).

This close connection between salvation, on the one hand, and word and sacrament, on the other, means that the spiritual community of faith and the heart not only find expression in the historical community, but also exist only in and through the historical community. There is only one community, the historical church which proclaims the gospel, which as this historical church is also the spiritual, eschatological church. This identity explains the ease with which the Reformers can shift back and forth between the heavenly church and the obvious, empirical church. 'Any seven-year-old child knows what the church is, namely, holy believers and sheep who hear the voice of their Shepherd' (SA III.12.2). The Confessions repeatedly refer to the universal Christian church or the catholic church, referring to the same reality to which a historian or sociologist would refer, namely, the historical, concrete people. When the claim is made that 'our churches dissent from the church catholic in no article of faith' (CA Part 1, Summary, 1), nothing esoteric or ambiguous is meant by 'church catholic'. The Reformers can refer to the totality of the historical community extended through space and time as simply 'the church'.

The church is thus not invisible. It is, however, hidden in three distinct senses. First, the eye of unfaith cannot see the Holy Spirit and Christ present in the community, any more than it can see the body and blood of Christ under the elements of bread and wine. For such a view, the church is just another religious community, with no more claim to special attention than the Buddhist Sangha. In this sense Luther says: 'The church is a high, deep, hidden thing which one may neither perceive nor see, but must grasp only by faith, through baptism, sacrament, and word' (Luther, LW 41:211).

Second, this historical community inevitably contains some who hear the word and receive the sacraments, but remain without faith, are not renewed by the Spirit, and thus do not become true members of Christ's body. Because we cannot see into persons' hearts, we cannot know with certainty who does and does not possess faith. The true membership of the church is thus hidden within its apparent membership. There can be no guarantee that such apparent members do not hold positions of leadership.

Third, the church is not removed from the historical battle between Christ and the devil. The triumph of Christ is assured. We have the promise that the gates of hell will not prevail against the church, but the devil both infiltrates and corrupts the church and also uses the mechanisms of the world to slander and persecute the church. In this sense, the church is hidden under the cross of its internal and external oppression (Ap 7.9,18). Since the Reformers generally believed they were living in 'the last times of this transitory world' (Preface to Book of Concord, 2; cp. SD Rule, 5) when the Antichrist had erected his throne within the temple of God (Ap 7.4; 15:19; Tr 39–59), they believed that they were living in a period when this hiddenness under the cross was particularly extreme.

These different senses of the hiddenness of the church's true nature within a world of unfaith, sin and the devil should not hide from us, however, the Reformers' unselfconscious identification of 'the church' with what most people would unreflectively mean by this name. They did not believe that distinguishing the true church from the false church was all that difficult, if one sincerely wished to do so.

The one church and the many churches

The preceding theological description is strikingly abstract. The church is defined without reference to any events in the church's history. The church must be historical, but no particular historical characteristics are essential to the church. Lutheran theologians would not deny that the church was founded at Pentecost when Christ poured out the Spirit on his apostles, but that specific historical event can remain in the background in the discussion of the church's nature. When Lutheran theologians speak of the church being founded on Christ, they are usually referring more to the dependence of the church on the gospel of Christ's saving work than to the event of Pentecost or to a historical connection with the historical Jesus. Similarly, the Reformers tended to define the apostolicity of the church in terms of continuity in the doctrine and preaching of the apostles, rather than in relation to any succession in an alleged apostolic structure. Lutherans, unlike Anglicans, Reformed, Catholics, or Orthodox, have never claimed that any particular polity – congregational, presbyterian, episcopal, patriarchal, papal – was divinely instituted or of the church's essence. The church is defined without reference to such historical arrangements. The typical claim is that this ahistorical definition of the church frees the church to enter into history more fully. The church is free to adapt itself to the opportunities and requirements of every age because it is not tied to the historical contingencies of any age. It is tied only to the gospel of Christ, mediated in word and sacraments, which transcends every age.

More so than in most other traditions, Lutheran ecclesiology has employed a sharp and strict distinction between divine law and human law. Some aspects of the church's life, e.g., baptism as the means by which one enters the church, are matters of divine law. They are instituted by God as unchangeable, permanent elements of the church. For the Reformers, divine law had to be attested as such by the Bible or be clearly implied by the content of the gospel. All that was not divine law was human law. Human law was binding within its legitimate sphere, namely, the regulation of the life of the community for the community's well-being and good order. Obvious examples of human law would be calendar regulations, details of forms of worship, or details of church organization. The church is free to change these and they do not bind consciences (i.e., when an individual violates them for reasons not rooted in contempt for God or neighbour, salvation is not endangered). Violation of such rules is not in itself sin. To make obedience to human regulations a matter on which salvation rests is to combine works of righteousness with idolatry.

For Lutheran theology, very little about the organization of churches is a matter of divine law. Lutheran theology has thus tended to say little about how the one church of all times and places becomes the plural 'churches' of many times and places. The Lutheran Confessions use the plural 'churches' to refer to the churches of the various political units who were the signatories of the Confessions, without any theory of the nature of the local or national church. The Formula of Concord states that 'the community of God in every locality and every age' has the authority to reform ceremonies and usages which are neither commanded nor forbidden in the word of God (Ephesians 10.4). This statement does imply that units smaller than the universal church have a certain authority of self-regulation, but no particular meaning of 'locality' seems to be assumed. The concept of the diocese played no role in the ecclesiology of the Confessions. Lutheran theology soon came to use the term 'particular church' to refer to bodies that were genuine churches but smaller than the universal church, but the term was usually given no more precise definition. This vagueness left the Lutheran churches free to organize themselves in quite various ways. From the beginning, Lutheran churches could be as large as a nation (e.g., the Church of Sweden) or as small as a city (e.g., Hamburg). While a thoroughgoing congregationalism has been rare in Lutheranism, quite varying balances of authority between congregation and larger bodies have been realized.

Common to these various ways of organizing particular churches has been the assumption that such particular churches are churches in the full sense. They are not merely parts of the church. As churches, they bear both the authority and the responsibility to do all that the church does and in situations of emergency can act on their own. This assumption was of great importance when the Lutheran churches faced the need to ordain ministers.

This general understanding of the church as the creature of the gospel, historical but defined by no particular historical ties, permitted the somewhat experimental and ad hoc development of the Lutheran churches described in section I above. Church structures were a matter of human law and could be adapted under the pressure of historical necessity, or even for the sake of mere historical expediency. The point at which this intersection of abstract principle and historical context can be best examined, and the point at which it comes under the most strain, is ordained ministry and episcopacy.

MINISTRY AND CHURCH GOVERNMENT

Ordained ministry

Article 5 of the Augsburg Confession states, according to its German version, that 'To obtain such [saving] faith, God instituted the office of preaching, giving the gospel and the sacraments.' The Latin version states simply that 'So that we may obtain this faith, the ministry of teaching the gospel and administering the sacraments was instituted.' On the one hand, the Confession affirms that there is an 'office' or 'ministry' in the church which is of divine institution. As divinely instituted, it cannot legitimately be removed from the church by human decision. Interpreters debate whether 'office' and 'ministry' here refer directly to ordained ministry. The ministry referred to, however, is certainly realized in the ordained ministry and, in the context of the early sixteenth century, the reader would have understood this article to be discussing ordained ministry.[7]

On the other hand, the article focuses on the concrete functions of that ministry, the proclamation of the word and administration of the sacraments that make possible saving faith, rather than on the person of the ordained minister. Simple distinctions between 'functional' and 'ontological' understandings of ordained ministry are to be avoided, but the consistent Lutheran focus is on the activities that are constitutive of ministry rather than on the person of the minister. What is constitutive of the church is the gospel proclaimed in word and sacrament. Ministerial office may be necessary and divinely instituted, but it is necessary precisely as a ministry that serves the gospel and its proclamation.

Lutheran understandings of ministry were initially developed in connection with a critique of late medieval theory and practice. The medieval association of the power or *potestas* to carry out the tasks of ministry with an indelible character imprinted on the individual and granted only by ordination was criticized by the Reformers as separating the ministry from the larger church. They insisted that the total community bore ultimate responsibility and authority for ministry, not a single caste within the church (Tr 11).

In the context of this argument, Luther developed his notion of the universal priesthood or the priesthood of the baptized.[8] Every Christian participates in the priesthood of Christ by virtue of their baptism. The sheep know the voice of the shepherd (John 10.4) and are empowered to judge whether the shepherds of the community are faithfully carrying out the ministry of the true shepherd (Luther, LW 39:306f). The emphasis did not fall on the possibility of laity carrying out the functions of ordained ministry. (Although Luther rejected the notion that ordination granted a *potestas* required for the valid celebration of the sacraments, it does not appear that he ever authorized or approved actual cases of lay presidency at the Eucharist. See Piepkorn, 1970:117.) Rather, emphasis fell on the role of the larger community as the ultimate subject of the church's ministry. Ordained ministers carry out their ministry for the church, and that community has oversight of such ministry.

A careful balance is necessary here. The ministry of word and sacrament must proclaim the gospel with authority. The Lutheran Confessions regularly cite the words of Christ in Luke 10.16, 'Whoever listens to you, listens to me', in relation to the authority of the ministry. Article 28 of the Augsburg Confession immediately adds: 'However, when they [the clergy] teach or establish anything contrary to the gospel, churches have a command from God that prohibits obedience' (CA 28:23). As will be seen below, this dialectic of authoritative office and Spirit-empowered community lies at the heart of recent Lutheran discussions of church governance.

The precise nature of ordination and the nature of the distinction between clergy and laity have been objects of intense debate among Lutherans over the last two hundred years.[9] Lay presidency at the Eucharist is officially permitted under certain condi-tions by some Lutheran churches. This theoretical uncertainty has usually been combined with great respect for the ordained office and those who exercise it.

EPISCOPACY

The German experience

As noted in Section I, the politically decisive support for the Lutheran Reformation came from selected secular princes, not from the bishops, who, within the structure of the Holy Roman Empire, were themselves princes. The thorough integration of the bishops into the structure of the Empire was itself an object of Reformation critique (the article on episcopacy in the Augsburg Confession deals mostly with the need to distinguish the spiritual and the political powers of the bishops), and it made the issue of episcopacy all the more complicated for the Lutheran Reformation. Few if any of the bishops within the Empire finally sided with the Reformers (or were able to stay in office if they did). When a prince or other political authority introduced Lutheran preaching and practices, it was usually against the will of the bishop.

The Reformers did not wish to eliminate the traditional episcopal polity. 'It is our greatest desire to retain the order of the church and the various ranks in the church' (Ap 14:1). In the course of the sixteenth century, the Reformers worked 'energetically to retain the episcopate in the traditional form. The persistence and the degree of readiness to compromise with which they sought to achieve this end is indeed striking' (Wendebourg, 1997:60). Within the Empire, however, that desire had to remain unfulfilled. The creation of a parallel Lutheran episcopate would have been tantamount to political rebellion. In the few cases in which bishoprics were won for the Reformation, it proved impossible to preserve episcopal authority and independence without the unity with state power and finance represented by the prince-bishop. In the end, the prince-bishops of the medieval and Catholic church were replaced in the Lutheran territories by secular princes who took over the episcopal role, exercising it through various state and state–church organs.[10]

This result, even if not desirable, was theologically acceptable to the Lutheran Reformers. Their desire to preserve episcopal order was rooted in the general conservatism of the Lutheran Reformation, the desire to avoid schism, and the perceived need to provide a counterweight to the authority of the princes in the church. Episcopacy was not a matter of divine law. The argument that the validity of ordained ministry was dependent on an unbroken succession of episcopal consecrations did not enter the Reformation debates until the late 1530s and was then vigorously rejected by the Lutherans (Kretschmar, 1999:300–44). Some system of oversight was needed for the health of the church, but such oversight did not require bishops, not to mention bishops in succession.

Like many medieval theologians, the Reformers saw the difference between priest and bishop as one of dignity and office, not of sacramental order. They saw this understanding confirmed not only in the New Testament, but also in the writings of Jerome. This unity of the office of priest and bishop was theologically underwritten by the focus on the single task of the proclamation of the gospel in word and sacrament. Since this task defines the ministry and this task is carried out by priest and by bishop, their ministries cannot be fundamentally different.

If the distinction between priest and bishop is only one of dignity and office, then in a situation of need, a priest can do whatever a bishop can do, including ordain. While the Lutherans did not, like the Reformed, see the 'parity of ministers' as a rule for the organization of the church, implying a rejection of episcopacy, they did see the unity of the one ordained ministry as permitting, if the situation required, ordination by a priest. The precise form the argument takes in the Confessions, however, should be noted. After stating that 'Jerome, then, teaches that the distinctions of degree between bishop and presbyter are established by human authority,' the conclusion is drawn that 'the distinction between bishop and pastor is not by divine right' and thus 'ordination administered by a pastor in his own church is valid by divine right.' The focus of what follows, however, is not the authority of pastors, but the authority of the church.

Consequently, when the regular bishops become enemies of the Gospel and are unwilling to administer ordination, the churches retain the right to ordain for themselves. For wherever the church exists, the right to administer the Gospel also exists. Wherefore it is necessary for the church to retain the right of calling, electing, and ordaining ministers. (Tr 63–7)

Again, the preference for retaining the traditional practice of ordination by bishops is assumed. But the ultimate authority and power to ordain lies with the church as a body. The church must be capable of doing that which is necessary to its mission of proclamation through word and sacrament. The 'particular church' of a city or territory is truly church and so, in a situation of necessity, it can make use of pastors (i.e., priests or presbyters) to carry out ordinations. The argument turns more on the authority of a particular church to order and maintain its ministry than on the nature of the relation between bishop and presbyter.

The nascent Lutheran churches of the early years of the Reformation in Germany did not start regular ordinations of their own clergy until 1535. When they did, they necessarily turned to priests as the presiding minister at ordinations, sometimes priests who were serving as theological faculty members, sometimes priests exercising quasi-episcopal functions under such titles as superintendent or dean (Lieberg, 1962:181–91).

The Scandinavian experience

The different fate of episcopacy in Scandinavia shows the way theological principle and historical accident have shaped Lutheran ecclesiology.[11] In Denmark (which also ruled Norway and Iceland), the medieval episcopal structure was preserved at the time of the Reformation in the late 1530s. The bishops already in office at the time, however, were dismissed and a new set of bishops consecrated by Johannes Bugenhagen, an associate of Luther's from Wittenberg and himself a priest, not a bishop. Here, unlike Germany, the episcopal office was thus preserved and reformed, but the succession of consecrations by bishops was broken.

In Sweden (which also ruled Finland), the Reformation was less abrupt. Not only was the episcopal office preserved, but a succession of consecrations by bishops was maintained, if only by a thread. Swedish Lutheranism has valued this continuity in episcopal succession, but done so within the Lutheran theological framework described above. The Swedish Church Ordinance of 1571, which has been confirmed repeatedly since then, states that the distinction between priest and bishop was unknown to the earliest church and so the distinction between bishop and priest is within a single office. The Swedish Church has thus consistently recognized the ministry of the other Lutheran churches outside episcopal succession. The 1571 Ordinance also states, however, that this distinction between priest and bishop 'was very useful and without doubt proceeded from God the Holy Ghost (who gives all good gifts) . . . and must remain in the future, so long as the world lasts' (Wordsworth, 1911:232).

CHURCH GOVERNANCE

Just as the Lutheran Reformers saw no particular organization of ministry as divinely instituted, so they considered no particular form of church governance as divinely mandated and so normative. Lutheran churches have thus historically lived with various sorts of governance, although today a certain similarity can be found in the structures of most Lutheran churches.

Luther seems initially to have thought that the ideal church government was through a college of bishops, even if he still accepted some form of papal leadership (Oberman, 1989:254). Such a picture, minus papal leadership, remained his ideal in the Smalcald Articles of 1537:

The church cannot be better governed and maintained than by having all of us live under one head, Christ, and by having all the bishops equal in office (however they may differ in gifts) and diligently joined together in unity of doctrine, faith, sacraments, prayer, works of love, etc. (SA II, 4, 9)

As already described, the integration of episcopacy with state structures made such an episcopal governance impossible in the Holy Roman Empire. In all lands where the Lutheran

Reformation succeeded, it was accompanied by a significant role for the state in the governance of the church. In Germany, this arrangement was known as the *landesherrliches Kirchenregiment*, the governance of the church by the lord of the territory. According to Johann Gerhard, the leading Lutheran theologian of the seventeenth century, the 'internal ecclesiastical authority' (*potestas ecclesiastica interna*) belonged to the pastors, exercised in preaching, the sacraments, and the keys. The 'external ecclesiastical authority' (*potestas ecclesiastica externa*), however, belonged to the prince and was exercised in all matters not related to preaching and sacraments (Lohse, 1970:66). This rule of the churches by the prince continued even when the vagaries of dynastic and territorial history led to a Catholic prince being titular head of a Lutheran church (as in Saxony after the conversion of the Elector to Catholicism at the end of the seventeenth century and in Bavaria after its expansion in the early nineteenth century). The Scandinavian situation was slightly different, but the state was still paramount in church governance (Hope, 1995:78–83).

The integration of church and state in European Lutheranism meant that immigrant Lutheran churches in North America and elsewhere had few useful precedents of church governance to consider. For the most part, the European Lutheran churches did little to aid the immigrant churches. The mass immigration to the US in the second half of the nineteenth century led to the formation of a bewildering array of Lutheran bodies, representing the various ethnic and linguistic groups, as well as varying theological tendencies. These bodies had a wide variety of church governance structures, from the almost congregational to the highly centralized and with varying degrees of lay involvement in decision-making, although the leadership of the clergy was generally affirmed. Until the mid-twentieth century, mission churches in Asia and Africa for the most part remained under the governance of the often semi-independent mission agencies of the European and North American bodies.

While this development was highly conditioned by historical circumstances, a central Reformation theological principle stood behind it. The governance of the church was not given simply to the clergy. The wider community, the laity as a body, also has a legitimate role in judging and participating in church governance. Luther stated that Christ 'takes both the right and the power to judge teaching from the bishops, scholars and councils and gives them to everyone and to all Christians in common when he says, John 10, "My sheep know my voice."' Thus, 'wherever there is a Christian congregation in possession of the gospel, it not only has the right and power but also the duty ... to avoid, to flee, to depose, and to withdraw from the authority that our bishops, abbots, monasteries, religious foundations, and the like are now exercising' (Luther LW 39:306, 308f). Herein lies a principle that has shaped much Lutheran church governance, viz., that the Spirit guides the church through the interaction of, on the one hand, an ordained ministry called by God to proclaim the gospel with authority and, on the other, a larger community whose baptism authorizes and empowers it to judge the exercise of the ordained ministry.

This principle was central for the decisive reshaping of church governance in Lutheran Germany following the end of the German Empire in 1918. The elimination of the princes and the creation of a secular republic meant that the churches were for the first time free to govern themselves as they wished. After some experimentation, all came to refer to the leading office of the church by the title 'bishop' and all developed some kind of synodical body (Schmidt-Clausen, 1970:72–94). This synodical episcopate is typical of most contemporary Lutheran churches, but the ecclesiological theory behind it was most fully developed in Germany. The intent was to relate church governance to the church's essential nature as a creature of the word. Determinative for the governance of the church at both the congregational and broader levels should be the fundamental structure of the proclamation of the gospel in word and sacrament and the relation of pastor or bishop and community within that proclamation. On the one hand, the ordained minister – pastor or bishop – is called to proclaim the gospel in word and sacrament with divine authority. On the other hand, the wider community are authorized and empowered to judge the exercise of that office. This 'over-against-ness' of office and community is the fundamental structure of church governance. 'The tension between office and community, which does not signify opposition, but includes within itself a commonality of hearing, praying, and service, is the fundamental given of evangelical church law' (Maurer, 1955:13). Structures of church governance are thus designed to preserve this relation. At every level, the authority of office and the authority of the wider community are balanced, with neither empowered to dominate the other. The essential independence of the ministerial office is preserved, while the community's duties and authority are realized. Thus, many of the constitutions of the German regional churches give the bishop a veto of varying dimensions over decisions of the synod (Maurer, 1955:55). Recently, this veto power has been exercised in the North Elbian Evangelical-Lutheran Church (encompassing Schleswig-Holstein and Hamburg) in relation to synodical decisions about homosexuality.

While most Lutheran churches now combine some form of synodical government with some form of episcopacy, this pattern is not universal. Some churches have leaders who function as bishop but are called 'synod president', 'ephorus', or some other title. Many of the European Lutheran churches are still linked with the state in diverse ways. The German churches are self-governing, but the church-tax system and a variety of church-state concordats bring church and state into close interaction. A certain 'established church' outlook is unmistakably present.

The most significant contemporary change in Lutheran governance structures has occurred in Scandinavia. On 1 January 2000, a new set of laws governing church–state relations came into effect in Sweden, bringing about a new relationship between the church and the state. Many of the internal governance structures of the church have not changed, but the greater degree of independence from the state puts the Church of Sweden (which still includes more than four out of five Swedes) on a more equal legal footing with other churches (Rasmusson, 2000). Whether the other Nordic churches, all established in varying ways, will follow suit is not clear.

CONTEMPORARY CHALLENGES

The ecclesiological challenges faced by contemporary Lutheranism for the most part arise from external relations among distinct churches rather than from the churches' internal lives. On the one hand, the increasingly close relations among the Lutheran churches have raised questions about the nature of world Lutheranism and its primary embodiment, the LWF. On the other hand, ecumenical relations with other churches, especially Anglicans, have raised questions about ministry and episcopacy. In each case, the Lutheran response is shaped by the interplay of abstract theological principle and concrete historical situation that has been so influential in Lutheran history.

THE LUTHERAN COMMUNION: WHAT IS IT AND WHAT IS ITS AUTHORITY?

For most of its existence, Lutheranism had no world structure within which Lutherans might come together to organize mission, make doctrinal decisions, or simply share worship and fellowship.[12] The integration of the Lutheran churches into their respective states made any such structured international unity of the churches difficult. The primary signs of Lutheran identity and unity, the Lutheran Confessions, had been developed within Germany for the German churches through ad hoc structures: the alliance of Lutheran estates at the 1530 Diet of Augsburg, the Smalcald League of the 1530s, shuttle diplomacy among the major German Lutheran states by theologians in the 1570s. These confessions were later adopted outside Germany by churches that came to accept the Lutheran reform. Lutherans never attempted to convene any international body such as the Roman Catholic Council of Trent or the Reformed Synod of Dort. Even if they had wanted to write a new confession acceptable to international Lutheranism, they had no means to produce such a text.

A movement toward some international Lutheran forum began in the late nineteenth century and reached an initial peak at the 1923 Lutheran World Convention. The convention created an ongoing Continuation Committee, but was only an organization of individuals, not of churches. Only with the creation of the LWF in 1947 were the churches themselves made the constituent members of a world Lutheran body.[13]

The compelling need that led to closer intra-Lutheran relations was the plight of the millions of Lutheran refugees displaced in Eastern and Central Europe by the two world wars. In responding to this need after World War 2, the LWF became a bureaucratically and programmatically much larger institution than its Reformed or Anglican counterparts at the world level. From the time of the Reformation, however, Lutheran unity had been understood as above all doctrinal unity and the Lutheran churches were not sure that such unity truly existed among themselves.

Thus, no Lord's Supper was celebrated at the 1923 Lutheran World Convention and the LWF was defined in its founding constitution as only a 'free association of Lutheran churches'. The LWF was to promote fellowship among the member churches, but the constitution did not assume that the member churches were already in a deeper communion that might include altar and pulpit fellowship, i.e., mutual eucharistic hospitality and the interchange of clergy. In addition, the organization of most Lutheran churches at the national level, originally an unintended accident of history, had become theologically hallowed over time, creating a resistance to any world body. Nevertheless, the developing theological and ecclesial convergence led to the declaration in 1984 that all member churches of the LWF are in altar and pulpit fellowship and to the constitutional redefinition of the LWF as 'a communion of churches' in 1990.[14]

But what is 'a communion of churches'? The discussion has spawned the useful, if slightly odd, phrase 'ecclesial density'. A body such as the LWF has a greater ecclesial density, i.e., a greater density of the elements that constitute a church, than do such parachurch organizations as a mission society or the YWCA, but it is still not a church in the full sense because it does not carry out all the functions appropriate to a church, e.g., the ordination of clergy. The LWF as a communion of churches is thus a church-like body (Root, 1997:236).

Such seemingly arcane issues gain greater relevance when the question is asked: what actions are appropriate to the LWF and with what authority does it carry out such actions? Already in the early 1960s, concern was expressed in world Lutheran circles about the relations between the German-language Lutheran churches of Southern Africa made up of the descendants of European immigrants and the indigenous-language missionary churches drawn from the native populations. Were accommodations being made to apartheid that brought racial division to the Lord's table? In 1977, the LWF Assembly voted that apartheid within the church touched issues of 'confessional integrity' and in 1984, two German-language Southern African churches were suspended from membership. After extended discussion with the affected churches, the suspension was lifted in 1992 (Root, 1997:229–32, 238–9).

The action of suspension was widely supported, but what did it imply about the ecclesial nature of world Lutheranism? The suspension looked like an act of ecclesiastical discipline. By what authority was this act carried out? Discussion of the meaning of this action was a significant element in the 1990 redefinition of the LWF as 'a communion of churches'. The concept of communion indicated the commitment to one another under the gospel that was reflected in the actions in Southern Africa. Nevertheless, the amended constitution still referred to the LWF 'as instrument of its autonomous member churches' (Article IV).

The *Joint Declaration on the Doctrine of Justification* signed by representatives of the Roman Catholic Church and the LWF in 1999 is a good indicator of the sort of action now seen as congruent with the ecclesial status of the LWF. The LWF could not itself authoritatively respond to the claim by various ecumenical dialogues that a consensus existed between the Lutheran and Catholic churches on justification. Such a response would be an action of teaching and the individual Lutheran churches, not the LWF, are the locus of formal teaching authority within Lutheranism. What the LWF could do as the structural embodiment of the Lutheran communion is provide the structure within which the Lutheran churches could come together, reach some consensus, and act as a body. The LWF organized the development of a text in dialogue with representatives of Rome, its revision on the basis of responses by the individual Lutheran churches, and a vote by the individual churches on the final text. The single Lutheran voice that finally spoke was more than the sum of its parts; it could claim to be the voice of the Lutheran communion. For the first time since the Reformation, Lutherans have found an ecclesial structure able to speak doctrinally with some degree of authority for almost all Lutherans in the world.

The linked questions of the ecclesial nature of the LWF and its authority are by no means settled. The 1997 Assembly of the LWF witnessed difficult debates over what the LWF should and should not do to further the ordination of both men and women by its member churches (Lutheran World Federation, 1997:64f). If the LWF should refuse to aid the building of a seminary by a member church because that seminary will not be open to women, has the LWF effectively made a doctrinal decision on the ordination of women, a decision backed with the authority of money?

At the international level, Lutheranism has tended to act and then reflect theologically on the ecclesial meaning of the action.

That theological reflection has played an important role, however, providing a basis for the next action. Such a process of theologically feeling the way forward will probably continue to typify the development of world Lutheranism.

EPISCOPACY, MINISTRY AND UNITY

Despite the leading role of such Lutherans as Nathan Söderblom, the Lutheran churches were often cool to the ecumenical movement in the first half of the twentieth century. The doctrinally oriented bilateral dialogues that came to greater prominence in the century's second half were more congenial to the Lutheran emphasis on doctrinal agreement. In relation to episcopacy and ministry, the dialogues have led to significant internal Lutheran changes.[15]

For most of Lutheran history, only the churches of Sweden and Finland claimed episcopal succession. The churches founded by Swedish and Finnish emigrants to North America did not preserve this feature. Since the presence or absence of episcopacy plays no role in the mutual recognition of ministries among the Lutheran churches, the classical Lutheran affirmation that episcopal succession was a good but not necessary thing remained a paper affirmation.

Anglican–Lutheran ecumenical dialogues, beginning with the Swedish–Anglican Communion dialogue of 1909, made episcopacy a living issue, since the two traditions found they could reach adequate agreement on every question but this one. Anglicans were not willing to recognize ordained ministries outside episcopal succession, and Lutherans were not willing to enter succession if it were seen as essential to an authentic ministry. A breakthrough occurred in the late 1980s and early 1990s. Crucial was the perception that apostolicity is above all a predicate of the church as a whole; it is the church that stands in the succession of the apostles. Episcopacy and episcopal succession serve that larger apostolicity as an embodiment and sign of the church's unity and continuity in the apostolic mission and ministry. As the Faith and Order Commission's 1982 *Baptism, Eucharist and Ministry* statement put it, episcopal succession can be seen as 'a sign, though not a guarantee of the continuity and unity of the church' (Faith and Order Commission, 1982:M38). This larger ecclesiological perspective helped Anglicans see how the essential continuity of church and ministry could be preserved even when a succession of consecrations was broken and helped Lutherans see how episcopacy and episcopal succession could be seen as a significant but not essential sign of the apostolicity of church and ministry.[16]

This perspective formed the background for ecumenical agreements between the Lutheran churches in the Baltic and Nordic region, Canada, and the United States and the neighbouring Anglican churches. While the agreements are not identical, they share a recognition of present Lutheran ministries by the Anglican churches, without any rite that might be interpreted as a supplemental or conditional re-ordination, and a commitment by the Lutheran churches to enter episcopal succession over the next generation. About 40 per cent of the Lutherans in the world now belong to churches within or committed to entering episcopal succession.

These decisions have not been without debate among Lutherans. The American proposal was accepted with difficulty after a first version failed to receive the necessary two-thirds majority in the Churchwide Assembly of the Evangelical Lutheran Church in America. Bitter debate still surrounds the subject there.

More significant is the acceptability of this new perspective on episcopacy to the German Lutherans, who still constitute about one-fifth of the Lutheran world. The German churches lack the long history with episcopacy of all the Nordic churches and, dividing the German Christian population almost evenly with Roman Catholics, they are more suspicious of what might be seen as 'catholicizing' tendencies than North American Lutherans. Initial dialogue results are not encouraging (*Visible Unity and the Ministry of Oversight*, 1997). Lutheranism most likely faces a prolonged future of internal diversity in how it practices and understands the ministry of oversight.

The ecclesial situation is complicated by new relations of full communion established with Reformed churches in Europe (through the Leuenberg Agreement of 1973) and the United States (through the Formula of Agreement of 1997). Lutheran churches are increasingly in communion with both Anglican and Reformed churches not in communion with one another. This admittedly anomalous situation arises from the Lutheran willingness to enter episcopal succession (making full communion with Anglicans possible), but refusal to see such succession as a necessary aspect of church relations (thus making full communion with the Reformed possible). The ecclesial and ecumenical significance of this incomplete overlap of communion requires further discussion, but it may be an anomaly that must be borne as we seek to overcome the greater anomaly of division.

CONCLUSION

'Lutheran ecclesiology' sounds like a contradiction in terms to some people. Lutherans have been notoriously weak in ecclesiology and ecclesiology has often not been very important to Lutherans. Lutheran understandings of justification and the sacraments had ecclesiological implications, but these seemed straightforward and rarely elicited detailed ecclesiological work. The ecclesiastical power wielded by the princes meant that ecclesial questions had been extensively taken out of the hands of the theologians anyway. Again, abstract theological principle and historical circumstance met.

A major question for the future of Lutheran ecclesiology is whether the interaction of theology and context can be forthrightly faced and made productive. All too often, the role historical circumstance has played is repressed; ecclesiastical arrangements are treated as if they were the direct implication of theological principles. As such, they then cannot be altered without a change or compromise of the underlying theology. A contingent historical result becomes set in theological cement. Recent Lutheran debates over the nature of the LWF and over ministry and episcopacy have too often shown just this tendency.

The ecumenical contribution of a Lutheran ecclesiology should be a perspective on the church that stands unshakably on the ground of God's free grace. The church is called to proclaim and mediate that grace and to shape its life in accord with that grace. How fully that contribution can be realized, however, is not clear. Can Lutherans distinguish, on the one hand, those aspects of their ecclesiastical and ecclesiological tradition that are truly the result of theological insights that should be preserved and ecumenically shared from, on the other, those aspects that derive from historical situations that have ceased to be or which have limited relevance for other churches? The fruitfulness of future Lutheran reflection on the Church may depend on that question.

FURTHER READING

1. General:

Bonhoeffer, Dietrich, *Sanctorum Communio*: *A Theological Study of the Sociology of the Church*. (Dietrich Bonhoeffer Works, vol. 1.) Minneapolis, Fortress Press, 1998.

Holze, Heinrich, *The Church as Communion*: *Lutheran Contributions to Ecclesiology*. (LWF Documentation 42.) Geneva, Lutheran World Federation, 1997.

Löhe, Wilhelm, *Three Books about the Church*. Philadelphia, Fortress Press, 1969.

Luther, Martin, *The Babylonian Captivity of the Church*. In *Luther's Works*, vol. 36 (Philadelphia, Fortress Press, 1959), pp. 3–126.

Luther, Martin, *Concerning the Ministry*. In *Luther's Works*, vol. 40 (Philadelphia, Fortress Press, 1958), pp. 3–44.

Luther, Martin, *On the Councils and the Church*. In *Luther's Works*, vol. 41 (Philadelphia, Fortress Press, 1966), pp. 3–178.

Lutheran–Roman Catholic Joint Commission, *The Church and Justification: The Understanding of the Church in Light of the Doctrine of Justification*. Geneva, Lutheran World Federation, 1994.

Meyer, Harding and Schütte, Heinz, 'The Concept of the Church in the Augsburg Confession', in *Confessing One Faith*: *A Joint Commentary on the Augsburg Confession by Lutheran and Catholic Theologians*, ed. George Wolfgang Forell and James F. McCue (Minneapolis, Augsburg, 1982), pp. 173–201.

Nygren, Anders, *This is the Church*. Philadelphia, Muhlenberg Press, 1952.

Pannenberg, Wolfhart, *Systematic Theology*, vol. 3 (Grand Rapids, Eerdmans, 1998), pp. 97–434.

The Unity of the Church: A Symposium. Papers presented to the Commission on Theology and Liturgy of the Lutheran World Federation. Rock Island, Augustana Press, 1957.

Yeago, David S. '"A Christian, Holy People": Martin Luther on Salvation and the Church', *Modern Theology* 13 (1997), pp. 101–20.

2. Works cited in Notes:

Anglican–Lutheran International Continuation Committee, *The Niagara Report: Report of the Anglican–Lutheran Consultation on*

Episcope, Niagara Falls, September 1987. Cincinnati, Forward Movement Publications, 1988.

Asheim, Ivan and Gold, Victor R., ed., *Episcopacy in the Lutheran Church? Studies in the Development and Definition of the Office of Church Leadership.* Philadelphia, Fortress Press, 1970.

Bachmann, E. Theodore and Bachmann, Mercia Brenne, *Lutheran Churches in the World: A Handbook.* Minneapolis, Augsburg, 1989.

Brecht, Martin, *Martin Luther: His Road to Reformation 1483–1521.* Philadelphia, Fortress Press, 1985.

Brecht, Martin, *Martin Luther: Shaping and Defining the Reformation 1521–1532.* Minneapolis, Fortress Press, 1990.

Faith and Order Commission, World Council of Churches, *Baptism, Eucharist and Ministry.* (Faith and Order Papers, 111.) Geneva, World Council of Churches, 1982.

Gassmann, Günther and Hendrix, Scott, *Fortress Introduction to the Lutheran Confessions.* Minneapolis, Fortress Press, 1999.

Hope, Nicholas, *German and Scandinavian Protestantism 1700–1918.* (Oxford History of the Christian Church.) Oxford University Press 1995.

Jenson, Robert W., 'What Ails Lutheranism?', *Dialog* 30 (1991), pp. 3–4.

Kahle, Wilhelm, ed., *Wege zur Einheit der Kirche im Luthertum.* (Die Lutherische Kirche, Geschichte und Gestalten, 1.) Gütersloh, Gerd Mohn, 1976.

Kolb, Robert and Wengert, Timothy J., ed., *The Book of Concord: The Confessions of the Evangelical Lutheran Church.* Minneapolis, Fortress Press, 2000.

Kretschmar, Georg, *Das bischöfliche Amt: Kirchengeschichtliche und ökumenische Studien zur Frage des kirchlichen Amtes.* Göttingen, Vandenhoeck & Ruprecht, 1999.

Lieberg, Hellmut, *Amt und Ordination bei Luther und Melanchthon.* (Forschungen aus Kirchen- und Dogmengeschichte, 11.) Göttingen, Vandenhoeck & Ruprecht, 1962.

Lindberg, Carter, *The European Reformations.* Blackwell 1996.

Lohse, Bernhard, 'The Development of the Offices of Leadership in the German Lutheran Churches: 1517–1918' in *Episcopacy in the Lutheran Church? Studies in the Development and Definition of the Office of Church Leadership,* ed. Ivar Asheim and Victor R. Gold (Philadelphia, Fortress Press, 1970), pp. 51–71.

Lohse, Bernhard, *Martin Luther's Theology: Its Historical and Systematic Development*, ed. Roy A. Harrisville. Minneapolis, Fortress Press, 1999.

Luther, Martin, *Luther's Works*. American edn. Philadelphia, Fortress, 1955–86.

Lutheran World Federation, *In Christ – Called to Witness*. Official Report of the Ninth Assembly of the Lutheran World Federation, Hong Kong, 8–16 July 1997. Geneva, Lutheran World Federation, 1997.

Maurer, Wilhelm, *Das synodale evangelische Bischofsamt seit 1918*. (Fuldaer Hefte.) Berlin, Lutherisches Verlagshaus, 1955.

Meyer, Harding, 'To Serve Christian Unity: Ecumenical Commitment in the LWF' in *From Federation to Communion: The History of the Lutheran World Federation*, ed. Jens Holger Schjørring, Prasanna Kumari and Norman A. Hjelm (Minneapolis, Fortress Press, 1997), pp. 248–83.

Nelson, E. Clifford, *The Rise of World Lutheranism: An American Perspective*. Philadelphia, Fortress Press, 1982.

Oberman, Heiko A., *Luther: Man Between God and the Devil*. New Haven, Yale University Press, 1989.

Piepkorn, Arthur Carl, 'The Sacred Ministry and Holy Ordination in the Symbolical Books of the Lutheran Church' in *Eucharist and Ministry*, ed. Paul C. Empie and T. Austin Murphy (Lutherans and Catholics in Dialogue, no. 4). (Minneapolis, Augsburg Publishing House, 1970), pp. 101–19.

Rasmusson, Arne, 'A New Relationship: Church and State in Sweden', *Christian Century* 117 (3 May 2000), pp. 494–5.

Reumann, John, 'The Ministries of the Ordained and of the Laity in Lutheranism' in *Ministries Examined: Laity, Clergy, Women and Bishops in a Time of Change* (Minneapolis, Augsburg, 1987), pp. 25–77.

Root, Michael, 'Affirming the Communion: Ecclesiological Reflection in the LWF' in *From Federation to Communion: The History of the Lutheran World Federation*, ed. J. H. Schjørring, Prasanna Kumari and Norman A. Hjelm (Minneapolis, Fortress Press, 1997), pp. 216–47.

Schjørring, Jens Holger, Prasanna Kumari and Norman A. Hjelm, ed., *From Federation to Communion: The History of the Lutheran World Federation*. Minneapolis, Fortress Press, 1997.

Schmidt-Clausen, Kurt, 'The Development of Offices of Leadership in the German Lutheran Church: 1918–Present' in *Episcopacy in* the Lutheran Church? Studies in the Development and Definition of the Office of Church Leadership, ed. Ivar Asheim and Victor R. Gold (Philadelphia, Fortress Press, 1970), pp. 72–115.

Together in Mission and Ministry: The Porvoo Common Statement with Essays on Church and Ministry in Northern Europe. Church House Publishing 1993.

Visible Unity and the Ministry of Oversight. The Second Theological Conference held under the Meissen Agreement between the Church of England and the Evangelical Church in Germany. Church House Publishing 1997.

Wendebourg, Dorothea, 'The Reformation in Germany and the Episcopal Office' in *Visible Unity and the Ministry of Oversight: The Second Theological Conference Held Under the Meissen Agreement Between the Church of England and the Evangelical Church in Germany*, pp. 49–78. Church House Publishing 1997.

Wordsworth, John, *The National Church of Sweden.* Mowbray 1911.

NOTES

1. The relation between Luther and the Elector can be traced in the two volumes by Martin Brecht (1985 and 1990).
2. References to LW are to the English translation of Luther in *Luther's Works* (1955–1986), indicating the volume and page numbers.
3. An excellent source on these developments is Asheim and Gold (1970). The integration of church and state in the early modern period is well described in Hope (1995).
4. The most recent English translation of the Lutheran Confessions is Kolb and Wengert (2000). The individual texts of the Confessions are cited by article and paragraph number according to the following abbreviations: Ap (Apology of the Augsburg Confession, 1531), CA (Augsburg Confession, 1530), Ep (Epitome of the Formula of Concord, 1577), LC (Large Catechism, 1529), SA (Smalcald Articles, 1537), SD (Solid Declaration of the Formula of Concord, 1577), Tr (Treatise on the Power and Primacy of the Pope, 1537).
5. A full listing and description of Lutheran churches can be found in Bachmann and Bachmann (1989).

6. The Augsburg Confession exists in slightly varying German and Latin versions. 'Saints' here reflects the Latin *sanctorum*; 'believers' the German *Glaubigen*.
7. On ministry in the Lutheran Confessions, see Gassmann and Hendrix (1999), pp. 124–9 and Piepkorn (1970).
8. The interpretation of Luther on the priesthood of all the baptized (or of all believers) is controversial. For a brief, balanced summary, see Lohse (1999), pp. 289–91.
9. On the history of this debate, see Reumann (1987).
10. This history is surveyed in Wendebourg (1997).
11. The history of episcopacy in the various Nordic countries is well described in *Together in Mission and Ministry: The Porvoo Common Statement with Essays on Church and Ministry in Northern Europe* (1993), pp. 59–108.
12. On the pre-20th century history of Lutheran unity, see Kahle (1976).
13. On Lutheran unity prior to the creation of the LWF, see Nelson (1982).
14. Both the original 1947 and the revised 1990 constitutions may be found in Schjørring, Kumari and Hjelm (1997), pp. 527–34. This volume is a comprehensive history of the LWF.
15. Lutheran ecumenical involvement at the world level is traced in Meyer (1997).
16. The clearest statement of this Anglican–Lutheran perspective can be found in Anglican–Lutheran International Continuation Committee (1988).

Index of Names

Index of Subjects